Not Just
Cricket

The New India Foundation, based in Bengaluru, uniquely matches public-spirited philanthropy with ground-breaking and relevant scholarship. In the seven-and-a-half decades since Independence, there has been a large body of work produced by Indian historians and social scientists. Taken singly, many of these studies are very impressive; viewed cumulatively, they add up to much less than what one might expect. The chief reason for this is the determining influence on the scholarly practice of one single date: 15th August 1947.

Given India's size, its importance, and its interest, and given that this is our country, the lack of good research on its modern history is unfortunate. It is this lack that the New India Foundation seeks to address, by sponsoring high-quality original scholarship on different aspects of independent India. Its activities include the granting of NIF Fellowships for highly researched original work, Translation Fellowships for bringing historical Indian language works to English, the publication of books on the history and culture of independent India, organizing the Girish Karnad Memorial Lecture, and the Kamaladevi Chattopadhyay Book Prize.

Not Just Cricket

A REPORTER'S JOURNEY
THROUGH MODERN INDIA

Pradeep Magazine

First published in India by
HarperCollins *Publishers* 2021
A-75, Sector 57, Noida, Uttar Pradesh 201301, India
www.harpercollins.co.in

2 4 6 8 10 9 7 5 3 1

Copyright © Pradeep Magazine 2021

P-ISBN: 978-93-5489-211-0
E-ISBN: 978-93-5489-117-5

The views and opinions expressed in this book are the author's own.
The facts are as reported by him and the publishers
are not in any way liable for the same.

Pradeep Magazine asserts the moral right
to be identified as the author of this work.

Supported by the New India Foundation

All rights reserved. No part of this publication may be reproduced,
stored in a retrieval system, or transmitted, in any form or by any means,
electronic, mechanical, photocopying, recording or otherwise,
without the prior permission of the publishers.

Cover design: Saurav Das
Cover photograph: Sajad Rafeeq
Author photograph: Sunil Ghosh

Typeset in 11.5/15.2 Dante MT Std at
Manipal Technologies Limited, Manipal

Printed and bound at
Thomson Press (India) Ltd

HarperCollinsIn

To my mother, Raj Dulari, who gave me my first lessons in loving-kindness, and father, Kishen Lal, who taught me the value of inclusiveness.

Contents

1. Past in the Present — 1
2. Learning the Game — 48
3. Chandigarh 1978–1994 — 69
4. Money Games — 92
5. Capital Times — 112
6. Fixers and Fixing — 130
7. A World of Uncertainties — 152
8. Enter Sourav Chandidas Ganguly — 171
9. The 2003 World Cup and After — 195
10. More Discord — 217
11. Great Comeback, Great Fall — 237
12. Life as a Columnist, Television Journalism and the IPL — 260
13. A Board in Need of Fixing — 279
14. Pakistan Visits and the Kashmir Issue — 303
15. Cricket as a 'Unifier'? — 331

Acknowledgements — 349
Notes — 353
Index — 355
About the Author — 371

1
Past in the Present

The house in Karan Nagar had crumbled from neglect, having been uninhabited for nearly two decades. The roof of the three-storey building had caved in at many places and the stairs inside were on the verge of collapse. I still attempted to climb to the small room on the third floor where I had spent most of my early childhood. The armed policeman escorting me was too scared to follow me up those stairs. For him, the climb was not worth risking his life.

For me, the place held multiple layers of tangible and intangible memories as it was there, around fifty years ago, that I had been haunted by imaginary ghosts while preparing to sleep, waiting for the reassuring presence of my mother, who would be busy in the kitchen on the ground floor till late in the night.

Only two of my cousins were still living in Srinagar in 1990 when violent militancy swept through Kashmir. They had to abandon the house. People were protesting in the streets of Srinagar and violence and killing became widespread in the region. Anyone suspected to be 'an Indian agent' was on the hit list of the militants. While those from the majority Muslim community were also being killed, Hindus in particular feared for their lives. Slogans laced with Islamic sentiments in support of freeing Kashmir from India were getting louder by the day. Most Pandit families had begun migrating to Jammu and beyond in the stealth of the night, hoping that normalcy would soon be restored and they could return to their homes.

My parents had migrated from Srinagar in far more peaceful and harmonious conditions in 1964, when my father, a customs official, was transferred to a small township in Haryana (then still Punjab). I visited my grandparents in Srinagar once a year, reviving ties with my relatives and basking in the nostalgia of a childhood that was fast becoming a speck in my memory. By the late eighties, our visits to Srinagar became more infrequent as most of my relatives left their hometown due to a lack of jobs in the Valley. They sought greener pastures in cities far away that may have been formidable and alien but offered economic security and a bright future for them and their children.

My profession as a cricket writer and journalist offered me many opportunities to revive my ties with my lost roots. Working for the *Hindustan Times* from 2001, I would look for any excuse to do a story in the Valley and let the pangs of the past course through my veins, causing me immense anguish and simultaneously great joy. Migration, city life and job compulsions can make one insensitive and robotic but a whiff of the past lived in innocence and even ignorance of harsh realities makes one human again.

Be it the story of Parvez Rasool, the first Kashmiri Muslim cricketer selected to play for India in 2013, or the separatist politician Sajjad Lone's pathbreaking decision to fight the 2009 Lok Sabha elections, I would visit the Valley to gather material on them. These stories held a touch of poignancy tinged with irony for readers, as a Kashmiri Pandit in 'exile' was writing about prominent Muslim figures of the Valley without rancour and even celebrating their successes.

It was on one such sojourn in 2006 that I forced my way into the Karan Nagar locality. The area where we lived was like a ghost town, dotted with rows of dilapidated, empty houses, ravaged by time and utter neglect. For me, it was like visiting a tomb, trying to connect with a past buried in the ruins of those houses, yet alive in my memory.

I had to literally force my way in, as the stretch where the Pandits used to live was, and still is, occupied by the security forces. The Rashtriya Rifles and other units had made the area their headquarters. Permission from them was necessary to make a visit, which I was denied initially. However, when I threatened the officer that I would write about this treatment in the papers, he relented.

On the main road, just before the turn towards the lane leading to our house, I saw the *goor* (milkman) sitting in his shop. I immediately recognized the old man as the one who would deliver milk to our home every morning. I became emotional and told him who I was. I don't know whether he could really remember me as the child with whom he had once enjoyed playful exchanges. But when he said, 'Why did you do this to us?', pointing towards the barbed wires and the armed security men, I was left unnerved.

My wife, Mukta, and daughter, Aakshi, were with me. Seeing the red bindi on my wife's forehead, the security men realized we were Hindus. One of them asked me with hissing venom, 'Why are you talking to these bhan...choo...' I could not agree with his language and did not share his sentiment, but I did understand where his anger came from. Being in an alien land where the majority consider you an occupying enemy force that kills before it talks must take its toll on one's psyche. I would witness a similar outpouring of rancour from a young Rashtriya Rifles jawan I met at the Delhi airport in 2015.

I was on my way to Jammu and the jawan, possibly in his twenties, was sitting next to me in the plane. We started to converse and that was when I heard his story. He felt envious of the fact that I was living with my family and could air my views without any fear. His own life, he felt, was nothing but miserable. He had recently become a father and was returning to work from his village in Rajasthan.

He told me that his life in the camp in Srinagar, though comfortable in material terms, was not worth living. 'We are in an enemy territory. The locals are not with us, and no matter what we do, kill or love, they are not going to be with us. We are told that we should do this for our *tiranga* (national flag), so I do it, but at what cost? I am away from my wife, my parents and child, trying to hold on to a place which we all know is not with us. I don't understand politics. I am doing this job for a living and wish all this could be solved so that I can be closer to home.'

Home

Even today, 200 Magazine House, Karan Nagar, Srinagar, is not a mere memory to be recreated through words or seen in dreams. It is a place where I formed my first impressions of the world, cocooned as I was in the care of my parents. Life then was like drawing lines on a blank sheet of paper.

It was a house inhabited by around two dozen people, all relatives. We were a joint family that shared a single kitchen, where the women would be busy from early morning to late in the night cooking and serving their husbands and children. There were servants, both Hindus and Muslims, mainly helpers from the Public Works Department where most of the adults in our family worked. However, for a servant to enter the kitchen, he had to be a Hindu.

The Saraswat Kashmiri Brahmins did socialize with Muslims, but only in their offices. Very rarely were they invited home. God forbid, if one of their tribe touched a utensil, it had to be washed and scrubbed many times over. A Muslim touching a vessel in which we ate was considered similar to that of the 'untouchable' castes in Hinduism, a pollutant which could lead to catastrophic consequences in the life hereafter.

It was in this environment that I took my first steps in a world that I could make little sense of. My mind was overwhelmed by images, some pleasant, some frightening, that it was seeing for the first time. Father, mother, grandparents, uncles, aunts, cousins: their interactions with one another and the outside world were laden with so many meanings that I could not decipher at that time, and probably can't even now.

I am still trying to make sense of those epochal moments of my life that have shaped me and are still shaping me. When you progress in life and add years you also add layers and layers of experiences that condition your worldview. Adding these layers seems like a natural process; unpeeling them, as I am trying to do now, feels extremely difficult. Human beings do not have a skin that they can shed, like some animals do, without going through extreme pain and agony. And each time you shed a layer, you have already acquired a new one without even realizing it.

My parents wanted to send my elder brother, Lalit, and me to a missionary school. They believed that to do well in life, learning the English language and manners was a must. However, my father, who worked as a sub-inspector in the central government's excise and customs department, could not afford the exorbitant fees of Srinagar's elite Burn Hall School. Our grandfather became our benefactor.

During classes, school was torture. The piercing voice of one of the teachers, pulling me up for my low marks and admonishing me with the words 'You will grow up to become a tonga driver' haunted me for a long time. Outside the classroom, the memories that always flash through my mind have the shimmering red of the cricket ball, students running around the field in whites, the sound of the ball hitting the bat and my brother being hailed as a player to watch out for. It was a Catholic school run by the Parish. The vice principal was Father Farrow. His teeth were smeared with tar from smoking cigars. At school, we were told that cricket was a way of life, that it taught the values of discipline and fair play, among many other virtues.

Even today, after having played the game till I finished university, and having watched and reported on it all over the world and interacted intimately with some of the best players the sport has ever known, the memory of my first sight of the game played in whites stands out almost as a spiritual experience. There still are moments, though they become rarer with each passing year, when a cricket field, players in whites and the glistening red ball create an image in my mind of a world that can be experienced only in a blissful dream.

Playing cricket became a passion. Being too young to get an opportunity at school, it was at home and in the lanes of Karan Nagar where my friends and I played. A *daubin* (a broad wooden stick used to beat clothes while washing them) became our bat, and a *beera* (a wooden sphere) the ball.

Weaved in with these pleasant reminiscences are many childhood pranks and aberrations, such as never paying for aloo tikki or gol gappa. We believed that the seller could not spot us stealing his ware among the melee of people who would throng his stall in the evenings. That the reality of the world is not what we choose to believe was brought home to us the day the owner of the shop came to our house to complain.

The act of stealing, so thrilling and even exhilarating when not caught, became a cause of shame and painful guilt the moment the world came to know about it. It has never ceased to amaze and trouble me that the same act can lead to contrasting emotions if the circumstances change.

My childhood years in Srinagar had a pulsating rhythm, with school, teachers, exams, cricket and pranks. One of the lasting images of the period for me is spending a lot of comforting time with Souna, a Muslim employee in my grandfather's office, who would do a lot of our household work that did not need him to be in the kitchen. Though I was becoming slowly aware of the fissures between the clan I was born in and the majority community of Muslims around us, the bond with this Muslim domestic help, who indulged a child's outlandish demands and fancies, has stayed with me as a symbol of love and genuine human ties.

The world outside of home appeared both friendly and hostile: friendly in its indulgence towards children and hostile in its acerbic remarks often directed against us. It slowly and imperceptibly seeped into my subconscious that we lived in a divided society. Home was like a temple that should not be desecrated by the 'Mussalman'. Not that they were not allowed in—the vegetable seller, the milkman and the scavenger were all Muslims—but the kitchen was strictly off limits to them.

Another major difference between the two religious communities was the level of literacy. Education was more a 'preserve' of the Hindus, and as a result most of them would secure the white-collar jobs in administration, banks, schools and hospitals. Kashmiri Hindus in the Valley are all Brahmins as it is believed that the other castes converted to Islam, either through the influence of Sufism, the lure of equality or the threat of the sword. These are questions for historical research and debate and I am not qualified to elaborate upon them. All I know for sure is that even though we were a minority, we still enjoyed a privileged status that perhaps very few minorities enjoyed anywhere else. A minority of approximately 5 per cent (figures vary) of the population had the influential jobs that ensured protection from any kind of resentment that may have prevailed among the rest.

It was not uncommon to hear Muslims refer to Hindus as 'Daali Bhatta'. It was a derisive term labelling Hindus as eaters of lentils and rice, inferring meekness. However, the majority of Kashmiri Hindus are meat eaters. Meat and fish were a must during Shivratri, the major Kashmiri Brahmin festival, and meat was part of our prayer offerings too.

On the surface, the tension was muted, never visible. The only instance I remember of the simmering tension spilling over was the time Hindus protested on the streets when one of their women had married a Muslim man. Almost six decades later, the words of my uncle still echo in my ears: 'Our community has woken up and we are not going to take this lying down.' There was palpable anger and hatred for the 'other' in the voice, which left me shaken and disturbed even as a young child.

The Hindu girl, I was to discover later, had most probably eloped with the Muslim boy. The Hindus claimed she was abducted, and the Muslims insisted that she had acted of her own will, having fallen in love with the boy. Whatever the truth, the incident sparked a very rare Hindu–Muslim skirmish out in the open. Such fights were unheard of in those times.

It was around this time my father got transferred to what we in Kashmir used to call 'India'. Any place outside of the Valley was India for us, a world far removed from our culture, heritage and language.

My father, Kishen Lal, was a Nehruvian at heart. He was a huge admirer of Sheikh Mohammad Abdullah, the first elected Prime Minister of J&K after it acceded with India in 1947, and a symbol of Hindu–Sikh–Muslim unity in the state. My father would never tire of narrating the incident when Kabalis (tribals)—a euphemism for what probably was the Pakistani Army—had attacked Kashmir in 1947. The incident had led to bloodshed and killing deep inside the Valley. The major role in keeping the local communities united was played by Sheikh Mohammad Abdullah, the National Conference leader. His followers coined a slogan that spread the message of communal peace and harmony: '*Shere Kashmir ka kya irshad, Hindu, Muslim, Sikh, ithad* (What does Sheikh sahib want? Unity among Hindus, Sikhs and Muslims).' His call did have a salutary effect and Kashmir was saved from any communal riots that would have caused widespread death and destruction, especially among the minorities.

I considered my father to be a recluse as he barely interacted with us, but in rare moments of conviviality he would always tell us that Gandhi and Nehru were leaders with great vision who believed in religious harmony and peace, and fought for social justice and equality. I still wonder where he and many others around him had acquired this deeply pluralistic worldview, living as they were in an orthodox and conservative environment where suspicion of the other was cloaked in civility and the fear of the unknown lurked in the shadows.

An Alien World

At the age of eight, almost without warning I was uprooted from the very secure and comforting environment surrounded by family and transplanted to a world that seemed aloof, even menacing, and lacking the warmth of the home I had lived in. My brother remained in Srinagar, being too attached to his grandparents, while I moved alone with my parents to my father's posting in Yamunanagar, a small town in Punjab (in 1966 it would become part of the new state of Haryana).

Everything there was different: the food people ate, the language they conversed in and the looks of suspicion they had for outsiders. Our landlord told us that we were not allowed to cook meat at home, but we surreptitiously defied him. The lure of old eating habits was stronger than the fear of eviction.

It was 1965, and war had broken out against Pakistan. My memories of the time are of the forced blackouts in the night, the sirens signalling air attacks and the rush to grab a spot in the trenches dug out in the vacant spaces outside the houses. The English-medium school I studied in was run by an old Christian lady and her three daughters. Playing cricket was out of the question and gilli-danda was the most common sport that we played whenever we could.

A few years later, my father was transferred to Panipat, another town in Haryana. It was here that my love for cricket blossomed. Among my classmates in the new town was Shekhar Gupta, who was later to play a major role in my getting into journalism.

The school I attended in Panipat was the opposite of what I had been used to. It was a Hindi-medium higher secondary school called the Sanatan Dharam School, where teachers would brutally beat children with sticks if they 'misbehaved', were disrespectful towards their teachers or did not complete their homework. A Hindi teacher called Shastriji would remind us time and again of the differences between high and low castes and the virtues of being from an upper caste. For him, the act of eating meat was sinful and eating eggs meant actually consuming sperms of the rooster.

Unable to adjust to the new medium of instruction, and never a keen student, I always struggled with my studies and hated going to school. Cricket came to my rescue. The school team was looking for new players and our English teacher was in charge of the team. I went for the trials and was selected. I was only in the seventh grade, but my off-spin bowling helped the school to win the inter-school tournament for the first time. From a backbencher in the classroom dreading the violence of the teachers, I had suddenly become a hero at school for my match-winning performances. Yet, it was still difficult to get encouragement for sports from the teachers, and my memories of that time in the district school team are less about cricket and more about filthy toilets, dirty dormitories and awful food when we travelled to play.

The school in Panipat was rooted in the realities of our times with obvious class and caste divisions in society, though its import was to sink in much later in life. I had a friend in school called Suraj. Like many at school, he would always be dressed in kurta–pyjama. He once saved me from classroom bullies who would tease and torment me for being *chikna* (having a smooth, fair skin). But one day he stopped coming to the school and his name was struck off the rolls.

I wondered where he had disappeared, till I saw him one evening on the street. He was playing the trumpet in a wedding band as it marched by. I recognized the tune as the hit song from the new Rajesh Khanna film *Aradhana*. Suraj's hairstyle was modelled on Rajesh Khanna. Excited at seeing him, I shouted his name, but he refused to recognize me. He looked through me as if I did not exist. This is an image I have carried all through my life, and it has traumatized me and somehow made me feel guilty, as if I was in some way responsible for his plight.

Amidst all these adventures, I entered my teens. I was still being praised at school for my cricket skills, and I dreamt, like millions of kids do, of becoming famous like the cricket stars of the time: Polly Umrigar, B.S. Chandrasekhar, Tiger Pataudi, Chandu Borde, Salim Durani and Jasu Patel, among others. They were household names, with All India Radio broadcasting live commentary whenever India played a Test series at home.

Shekhar Gupta, the classmate who by then had become a very close friend, was also a passionate follower of the game, encouraged by his father who was an inveterate listener of the radio commentary. Together, we followed India's fortunes ball by ball and swung from joy to anger, depending upon how well or poorly India performed. It was an era where the real action had to be visualized in our minds through the words the commentators used to describe what was happening on the ground.

My first introduction to the world of commentary was in 1959 at my maternal grandfather's house in Amritsar, where we went every winter. He would be glued to his transistor set whenever a cricket match was on. 'Jasu Patel has taken another wicket,' the excited scream of the commentator boomed. Even though I was only four, I knew something special was happening, but was too young to grasp the real meaning of it. It was India's first-ever victory over Australia. The significance of the game sank in much later in life, and I consider the off-spinner Patel a hero even today.

But I also remember the dejected adult faces around the radio, when yet another poor performance from the Indians led to defeat.

During these years, my brother had developed a reputation for himself back in Srinagar, in the local inter-school cricket tournaments. On our family visits to Srinagar during the summer holidays, I would look forward to not only discussing with him the intricacies of the game but also to reading the sports magazines being published during those times: *Sport and Pastime* and later the *Sportsweek* I always looked forward to its centrespread, which usually had full-page photographs of cricket stars.

The pictures that would fascinate the most were those of White players. Besides their outstanding performances, this could also have something to do with our subconsciously admiring their white skin. Even today, I remember the names of the Australian Paul Sheahan, the Englishman M.J.K. Smith or the New Zealander Graham Dowling—not because I remember any of their feats, but because they were fair, blue-eyed, handsome, debonair young men in whites adorning the cover or the centrespread of the magazine.

Battling these giants of the game were our puny Indians. Ajit Wadekar became an instant hero to me, as much for his Bradman-esque batting records in domestic cricket as for his ability as a slip catcher. When the Australians led by Bill Lawry came to India in 1969, they easily won the first Test in Bombay and drew the second in Kanpur. Lawry predicted an early end to the Delhi Test and said he would have enough time to play some golf too. But Erapalli Prasanna and Bishan Singh Bedi, the magicians with the spinning ball, ran through their side, and it was a great moment of pride as an Indian when India won the Delhi Test within four days. Lawry was indeed left with enough time to play golf. Even today, the names of Doug Walters, who used to score runs at a rapid rate, or Ian Redpath, who could tame our spinners with his nimble feet, are etched in my memory.

Apart from the polio-stricken Chandrasekhar's mesmerizing achievements and the emergence of Sunil Gavaskar on the 1971 tour of the West Indies, it was the pint-sized Gundappa Viswanath's century at Kanpur on his debut that stands out in my memory. It was against the Australians in the 1969 series. When Anant Setalvad, the most eloquent and objective of all Indian radio commentators, would describe his counterattacking, we would swell with pride, as if we had something to do with his skill-filled strokes.

The popularity of the radio commentators was such that it was difficult to choose between your favourite cricketer and the commentator. Vijay Merchant, whose batting exploits had made him a legend, was the expert on radio whose ratification of players was what most fans accepted as correct, regardless of how the players were evaluated by others or what their performances suggested.

My enthusiastic and successful forays on the cricket field were interrupted when we moved from Panipat to Amritsar, also in Punjab. This move again caused uncertainty, tension and disturbance in an impressionable mind.

Amritsar is a sprawling city, a spiritual and religious centre for the Sikhs, famous for the Harmandir Sahib (popularly known as the Golden Temple). The city is also known for the Durgiana Temple, which is modelled on the Golden Temple but can't match it in majesty and opulence.

My mother's closest friend in Yamunanagar was a Sikh lady, whom we fondly addressed as 'Sardarni'. She had been a tremendous source of strength to us, especially at a time when we had barely adjusted to our new surroundings. But never before had I encountered Sikhs in such large numbers as I did in Amritsar.

In Kashmir, the Brahmins had the derisive nickname of 'Daali Bhatta', and in Amritsar it had become 'Oey Brahmina'—a derogatory term that referred to one who exploited others. Though they hated the nickname, the Brahmins didn't react. Yet, unlike in Kashmir, the relationship between the two communities, Sikhs and Hindus, was more harmonious in Amritsar, both in business and personal ties. This ensured a peaceful coexistence. The Sikhs were marginally in the majority, with about 60 per cent of the overall population of the state. However, urban Punjab was majority Hindu with the rural areas predominantly Sikh.

For me, the change from Hindi-speaking and ultra-conservative surroundings to a more aggressive Punjabi-speaking environment was dramatic. Punjabis were given to expressing themselves expansively, be it through language, eating habits or wearing trendy clothes. Here, it seemed that life was to be celebrated and not lived in a sulk. Everything appeared so formidable that I lost my confidence.

I may have been a cricket star in the school in Panipat, but here I was too scared to appear for the trials and compete with the other boys for selection to the school team. I made a couple of attempts but my nerves failed me. Watching the boys being trained in the nets by a screaming, burly sardarji, I felt inadequate. I gave up my desire and dream to become a cricket player.

Yet when I played in my colony with the same boys who were making an impact in Amritsar's inter-school tournaments and even at a higher level, I would stand out, whether at bowling, batting or fielding. It was too late by then to be selected for the school team, but my success in mohalla cricket restored my confidence. In college, the first thing I did was to sign up for the cricket team trials.

I was inspired further after watching the West Indies–North Zone match at Jalandhar in 1974. It was only the second professional match I had ever watched. It created a lasting impact on my own game and further deepened my interest in cricket. Since then, I have watched a lot of international cricket but that day at the Burlton Park—as the stadium in Jalandhar was known then—holds a special place in my memories.

What a thrilling experience it was to watch Clive Lloyd, a giant of a man, butcher the North Zone bowling. I had never seen a man as tall and as strong as Lloyd. His merciless pounding of two of the greatest left-arm spin bowlers of all time—Rajinder Goel and Bishan Singh Bedi—is imprinted in my memory. I also recall vividly Amritsar boy Madan Lal, an outstanding athlete and fielder, not attempt to stop a straight drive from Gordon Greenidge that had passed just beneath his hands in his bowling follow-through. Had he tried to, he would have gone off with an injury, such was the ferocity with which the stroke was hit.

I remember that Ashok, a friend from school, was with me at the ground watching the match. We were simultaneously listening to the radio commentary, which was a common practice those days as without the commentary it was difficult to keep track of the match scores and identify the players. Listening to the accomplished Tony Cozier on air was an education. He made me almost feel as if he could describe the game first and the action would follow, such was his mastery over his craft and knowledge of the game.

A lasting influence the match had on me was in learning the art of fielding. I watched in awe at how the West Indian fielders, through the movement of the batsman's feet and the length of the ball, anticipated the direction in which the ball would go even before the shot was made. It gave them ample time to move quickly and stop the ball from going towards the boundary. The lessons I learnt that day improved my game to the extent that I started believing I could field as well as any first-class fielder in India.

It was not easy to get into the college team. The competition was strong and some of the guys were either playing in the Punjab First-Class (Ranji Trophy) team or were in the running to be selected for that team. I was selected on the strength of my brutal hitting in the nets. But just as I was hoping to make a mark, a back injury while fielding ended my dreams. I was forced to quit playing on medical advice.

Cricket Highs and Lows

The romance of cricket and the addictive excitement of rooting for the country's team were deepened for me in 1971, when India toured the West Indies. To the bitter disappointment of many, Tiger Pataudi was removed as Indian skipper by the chairman of the selection committee, Vijay Merchant. I was indifferent to the raging controversy and instead was happy that my favourite, Ajit Wadekar, was made the captain.

The huge time difference between the two regions meant that millions of Indians, including my brother and I, would remain awake for the entire night listening to the radio commentary. Sunil Gavaskar, an understudy of Wadekar's in Bombay and a prolific run-maker in inter-varsity cricket, had from nowhere emerged as an Indian Bradman, an opener whose phenomenal scoring in his debut series surpassed every expectation we had.

It was around 3 a.m. when the commentator Ravi Chaturvedi broke down on the radio at the moment of India's win in Trinidad, the country's first-ever Test victory in the West Indies. Sobbing, Chaturvedi likened the moment to the greatest events in Indian history, even comparing it to gaining independence from the British. His words '*Ye Gandhi ka desh, Nehru ka desh* (this nation of Mahatma Gandhi and Jawaharlal Nehru)' were a reminder to all of us that we were a great nation, and with this victory we had taken another great step. Both my brother and I had tears in our eyes.

Today, many of us might squirm at how a cricket win could evoke such comparisons and dismiss it as a crass manifestation of the kind of jingoism that we abhor, but times were different then. That night the spirit of the nation resonated with each word Chaturvedi uttered on the radio while sobbing like a child.

Then, in the same year, when India beat its colonial masters at the Oval, another first, it seemed as if this '*Gandhi ka desh, Nehru ka desh*' was unstoppable in its victory march. The freakish yet spectacular bowling of leggie Chandrasekhar and some breathtaking catching from Eknath Solkar close to the bat had made that victory possible. Chandrasekhar's 6 for 38 in that innings is stuck in the memory like a favourite record that one never gets tired of listening to. Again, it was the radio, this time BBC's *Test Match Special*, that brought the action live to us at home. The lyrical quality of John Arlott's flowing commentary and the tongue-in-cheek humour of Brian Johnston paired with the measured perfection of their experts, Jim Swanton and Trevor Bailey, added a new dimension to live broadcasting for us. The vividness with which they captured the game—never losing sight that not one but two teams were competing, and never talking down to the listener—enhanced the enjoyment of that victory. For the first time I realized that words could be very powerful even without indulging in sentimentality. From that time onwards, Arlott, Johnston, Henry Blofeld and Chris Martin Jenkins became heroes for us, comparable to the cricketers themselves.

Years later, in the late eighties, I happened to hear a familiar voice at a dinner in Chandigarh hosted by the Punjab Cricket Association. The voice evoked memories from a cherished past. It was Trevor Bailey, the former England all-rounder and BBC expert. I was starstruck.

It was the era of Vivian Richards, whose maverick skills were, for many, the ultimate in batsmanship. But Bailey, with the typical Englishman's belief that being orthodox is a virtue greater than breaking new ground, did not agree. Speaking at that dinner, he said that technical correctness and patience to build an innings were far greater qualities. Hence, he felt Gavaskar was the greater player. I could have never imagined I would one day disagree with a pundit whose views I had revered when I was young, but I did that day.

In the seventies, inter-college cricket tournaments were contested with ferocity and competitiveness, and witnessed massive crowds that could put to shame Ranji Trophy matches of the current era. Like the St Stephen's College–Hindu College rivalry in Delhi, in Amritsar, thousands would turn up to watch DAV College play Hindu College. The games would be close.

DAV's star players were the Amarnath brothers—Mohinder and Surinder. But Hindu had Madan Lal. The son of a grocery shop owner from Amritsar's Lawrence Road, Madan was a larger-than-life figure in the city. He could bowl and field with energy and alacrity all day and then mount a rescue operation with the bat against all odds to keep his team afloat. For us, Mohinder—who was later acknowledged as a much superior batsman and, like Madan, played with distinction for the country—was no match for Madan's guts and spirit.

In 1972, at the same stadium where the Hindu–DAV matches would be held each year, I had the opportunity to watch the English team play against India's North Zone team. We were fascinated by the idea of watching some of the greats of the game live. The sight of Bishan Singh Bedi leisurely tip-toeing towards the bowling crease left us enthralled. He seemed to move almost in slow-motion, as if to let the beauty of the sight sink in for the watchers.

Bedi would toss the ball high and we would fail to understand why the batsmen were unable to play him confidently. In between these seemingly innocuous deliveries, he would suddenly bowl one that moved in sharply and defeat the batsman's attempt to cut it, rattling his stumps. I still remember the magic of the moments when the bowler, after having teased the batsman with his lazily tossed-up deliveries and lulled him into a false sense of security, left him stunned with his unplayable magic ball.

If 1971 was a watershed year for Indian cricket, the 1974 tour of England left a deep wound that refused to heal for a long time. The Lord's disaster—where India was bowled out for 42 following on in the second innings—left a whole nation shocked and in dismay. It was the first match we watched on TV, albeit just the highlights and that too on a Pakistani TV station. In fact, it was on Pakistani television, which our antennas in Amritsar could pick up, that most of us first watched international sports. As Amritsar was only fifty kilometres from Lahore, the reception was crystal clear. Doordarshan was still an amateurish operation, and television in Pakistan was of a higher quality at the time, with their family soap operas attracting massive numbers. They showed a lot of sports footage and telecast many of Muhammad Ali's boxing bouts live. This led to Indians living near the Pakistan border buying TV sets.

Wadekar, under whose leadership India had its first-ever wins in the West Indies and England in 1971, was now the target of the choicest abuses from the fans. Whatever may have changed in Indian cricket, this aspect of Indian cricket fans has remained constant—they can't digest defeat.

In the early nineties, when I was reporting on the Ranji season for *The Indian Express*, I heard insider accounts of the infighting in the team at the time. There had been a resentment against Wadekar among the spinners, and bowlers like Prasanna and Bedi had thought that Wadekar was not fit to lead India. Some of these stories were narrated to me by Bedi himself, who had been a key member of the Indian team in 1974. By the nineties, he had become the coach of the Punjab Ranji team. I spent many long hours in spirited conversation with him, during which he revealed the ego battles in the team back in the seventies.

Spinners like Bedi and Prasanna had been nurtured by Tiger Pataudi, who was revered by the duo. The seeds of discord were sown in 1971 when Tiger was removed as captain for the West Indies tour. For many in the Indian team, it was a sign of the Bombay lobby at work. Many saw in the move a trace of vendetta on the part of Vijay Merchant, who had been made deputy to the senior Nawab of Pataudi, Tiger's father, on the tour of England in 1946. Merchant rightly believed he should have been the captain, had the decision been taken on cricketing skills alone. The conspiracy theory was that when the right opportunity came, Merchant exacted his revenge. As soon as the junior Pataudi struggled with form, Merchant acted to ensure he was axed.

It is difficult to say if this is true, though my later interactions with Tiger would suggest that he too may have believed in these conspiracy theories. It was in 2004, when I was working on a biography of Tiger. We spent a lot of time at his home at Delhi's Vasant Vihar working on the book and recording his accounts of his playing days. These recorded tapes have almost twenty-four hours of Tiger's stories. He was reticent in the beginning but eventually shared many insights about an era we knew only from newspaper accounts or radio commentary.

Tiger did not dwell too much on that 1946 tour where his father—who had played for England—was made the Indian captain despite being out of touch with the game by then. If Tiger is to be believed, it was Pandit Jawaharlal Nehru who pushed for the senior Pataudi to lead India; with India on the cusp of independence, making a Muslim the captain of an Indian team would create a positive image of the kind of secular India he envisaged. The senior Pataudi, as expected, failed miserably with the bat, with the likes of Merchant resenting playing under him.

Merchant, many believed started to 'strike back' when he became the chairman of the selection committee in 1967. The first evidence of this were to be found in his whimsical selections when New Zealand toured India. The tour followed India's historic win at Dunedin, the first on foreign soil. It was a victory in which Prasanna had played a major role and it was there that Tiger had first successfully tested his theory of spin being India's main weapon. The formidable combination of Bedi and Prasanna was at the forefront of this strategy.

Yet, when India played at home, Merchant started fiddling with the team selection, much to Pataudi's bemusement. 'I told him not to disturb the team as I had, with great effort, forged a combination that believed in themselves, and we had just won a historic series on foreign soil,' Pataudi told me. 'But he wouldn't listen. People tell me that he was a great batsman and an astute captain. But all I found was an obdurate man, in love with listening to his own voice and shutting out voices of sanity that pleaded with him.'

Pataudi told me that Merchant was obsessed with his own preferences, and that once in the nets he introduced a bowler with: '*Mil gaya, mil gaya, Amar Singh* (We have discovered Amar Singh).' Amar Singh was the legendary fast bowler who played for India on its first tour of England in 1932. However, the bowler introduced by Merchant not only did not bowl very fast, but he was also blatantly chucking the ball.

It was, therefore, no surprise to Pataudi when Merchant used his casting vote to remove him as captain for the 1971 tour of the West Indies. In fact, Pataudi had made himself unavailable for the tour much before the selection took place, a fact that Merchant hid from the world. Many thought that the decision reflected the democratization of Indian cricket, as a commoner had replaced a nawab as Indian captain.

There were other controversial selections in the team bound for the West Indies, which have rarely been talked about because of the subsequent success the team enjoyed. Merchant selected five players from Hyderabad—Syed Abid Ali, M.L. Jaisimha, Kenia Jayantilal, D. Govindraj and wicketkeeper Pochiah Krishnamurthy. Jaisimha was well past his prime and medium pacer Govindraj never played a Test. Jayantilal played in one Test and Krishnamurthy played all four Tests, but both were forgotten after that tour.

If one believes that Merchant was gunning for Pataudi, it is not hard to imagine that he may have tried his best, by including five players from Pataudi's state team, to appease the selector from the South Zone, C.D. Gopinath. Gopinath, however, did not support Merchant's decision to remove Pataudi in the selection committee meeting. I did not find Pataudi bitter when he talked about the whole episode, but there was no doubt that he felt Merchant's actions reeked of bias. It could be assumed that this was based on his dislike of the Pataudis for having been denied the captaincy on that tour in 1946.

Tiger, by all accounts, was a very popular captain, particularly among the spinners. The simmering resentment among Pataudi loyalists and India's pathetic performance aside, the 1974 England tour was mired in other controversies, such as when the Indian team arrived a couple of hours late for a reception hosted by the Indian ambassador in London. This was seen as an insult by the Indian consulate and the team was publicly rebuked.

It was no surprise that the Indian team was hammered on that tour. Bedi and Prasanna considered it a blot on their cricketing careers. I still remember Johnston saying during one of the Test matches of that series, 'I have not seen captain Wadekar communicating with his spinners, Bedi and Pras. If he is, it must be through telepathy.' It illustrated the breakdown of the relationship between the skipper and his main bowlers.

At that time, I was not aware of the politics behind the scenes, and those defeats were heartbreaking experiences. The Indian team's poor performance in England and the fury with which Wadekar was attacked by the fans and the press led to his premature exit. Thus, the man who had been cast out of the Indian team in 1971 was brought back to lead India again. When the West Indies toured India after that, it was time for redemption.

A Reluctant Cricketer

While working with Pataudi on his biography, I had the opportunity not only to interact with my childhood hero but also to have an insider's view on an era of Indian cricket that I had closely followed as an adolescent fan.

It is a fascinating story of a man whose elite background and cricketing exploits—despite having lost sight in one eye—had made him a larger-than-life figure in the public imagination. His aura and glamour spread wide, winning him respect and admiration from not only his peers but from cricket fans across all caste and religious divides.

His father, Iftikhar Ali, was the titular head of Pataudi, a small principality near Delhi. He had played for England in 1932 and 1934, and was chosen to lead India in 1946.

An outsider who had spent most of his youth in England, the younger Pataudi made his Test debut in 1961. His rise was swift, and he was appointed vice-captain for the West Indies tour in March 1962. He was catapulted to the captaincy in tragic circumstances on that tour. The regular skipper, Nari Contractor, was struck on the head by a bouncer during a tour match at Barbados. Contractor had to be rushed to the hospital in a critical condition. His life was saved through emergency surgery and his recovery was considered to be a miracle by many, including the doctors who operated upon him. Contractor was flown back home and never played international cricket again.

Pataudi was just twenty-one when he was appointed captain. He led India for almost a decade, during which time the team recorded many firsts, including its first overseas victory against New Zealand in 1968. Despite his own modest Test batting record, he occupies a place in Indian cricket history on par with the greatest Indian players for his contribution towards shaping, forging and moulding a diverse group of players with disparate regional loyalties into a unified team.

Many believe the sobriquet 'Tiger' had to do with his outstanding fielding, a rare skill for an Indian cricketer to possess in those days. But it probably originated with his having shot a tiger on his eleventh birthday. His father had died that day, and the hunt had been arranged by his maternal grandfather to distract the young boy from the tragedy at home.

Pataudi's career is a compelling one, much like his personality. Though a man of few words, many anecdotes reveal that he could be the heart and soul of a gathering if he wanted to. Contractor, the man he replaced as Indian captain, described to me an incident that took place during that 1962 tour of the West Indies. The story reflects both the lighter side of Pataudi's persona as well as the resentment Contractor harboured against him.

Pataudi did not play the first two Tests, declaring himself unfit with a pulled thigh muscle. Contractor believes that the truth was simply that Pataudi was too scared to face the battery of lethal West Indian fast bowlers, which included Wes Hall. His suspicions were reinforced by what he witnessed during the first Test. 'All of sudden we saw a commotion,' Contractor recalled of that evening. 'Tiger was being chased by a couple of friends. I have never seen a man run as fast as he did, and he even climbed a tree with unbelievable speed to avoid being caught. Is this a man suffering from a pulled muscle that had forced him to miss a Test? I knew he was feigning injury as he was too scared to face the West Indian quicks.'

When I told Pataudi about this anecdote, he laughed—a rare occurrence during my meetings with him. This suggested to me that Pataudi was aware of Contractor's suspicions that Pataudi's privileged background had influenced his appointment as vice-captain on that tour despite the presence of senior players. Contractor could also have been bitter about not getting another chance to play for India despite having recovered from his near-fatal injury.

Contractor may have had his reasons to dislike the man who replaced him, but there are hardly any stories that indicate any resentment or protest among the players—some of whom were very senior cricketers—at a rookie being thrust upon them as their captain. In fact, Pataudi said he got the full support and cooperation from every team member on that tour—including the likes of Vijay

Manjrekar, Chandu Borde and Polly Umrigar, each of whom may have felt that they deserved the captaincy.

Umrigar was not just the best batsman on that tour but is considered among the finest Indian batsmen ever. The young Pataudi found him to be a very astute strategist, and began to value his advice. 'Umrigar was very happy in his role as an advisor, which included no responsibility,' said Pataudi. 'I doubt he would have wanted to lead and burden himself with decision-making.' Though Pataudi had the support of his seniors, the Indian team could not deal with the challenge of facing the West Indian fast bowlers and safeguarding not only their wickets but also their bodies.

Salim Durani was a maverick genius who is remembered for the two dream balls he bowled at Port of Spain in India's historic win in 1971. He was part of the squad on the 1962 tour as well. Pataudi remembered him as a man who never did justice to his immense talent, wasting his time on pursuits inimical to a sportsman's career. Durani was also a chain-smoker, leaving Pataudi exasperated by the man's indifference to his vast potential.

Many blame Pataudi for not nurturing a rare talent like Durani with care and sensitivity. Pataudi agreed in hindsight, but did not think any captain could have tolerated Durani's whims and tantrums without losing his cool. He narrated an instance of Durani's 'weird' behaviour. 'He walks upto me and tells me that his teammates are conspiring to kill him,' recalled Pataudi, who was stunned and asked what made Durani think that. The answer he received was: 'I am a Muslim and all the others are Hindus. They don't like me and are planning to kill me.'

Pataudi lost his cool. He told Durani, 'Look, I don't know what the players would do to you, but let me tell you that if you continue like this, the two Muslims in the team will kill you first—the captain, and the manager.' (Ghulam Ahmed was the manager on that tour.)

When I met him, Pataudi was already in his sixties, and was reserved when it came to talking about himself. One would expect stories about his grand vision for the team or how heroically he navigated Indian cricket in its nascent phase. Bishan Singh Bedi, one of his many protégés, never tires of saying that 'he taught us what it means to represent the country'. However, he always steered the conversation to the larger issues of what ailed Indian cricket during his captaincy.

Pataudi gave me the impression of being a reluctant player and a reluctant captain. From the long conversations I had with him it became obvious to me that he rarely enjoyed his cricket, especially after the loss of one eye in a car accident in England. Whatever he did after that injury required more effort, physical as well as mental, than before and he seemed very hesitant to speak about the hard work he had to go through to play cricket again.

Batting became extremely difficult after the accident, as he could never be sure of the line of the ball. 'I could never relax at the crease,' he recalled. 'I had to play outside the line of the ball to actually be behind it. Concentration was the key and even when the ball was not in play, I could not afford to relax as that would affect my concentration. If I failed, people would say things like "What else can you expect from a man who is blind in one eye" and when I succeeded, people would say, "he must be lying about his lack of vision in one eye".' Pataudi's frustration at how unfairly people spoke of him was clear.

As captain, he had to regularly deal with the ineptitude, indifference and callousness of the cricket administrators in India. He had seen a more efficient system operating in England, where he had played in school, college, university and county cricket. He was an outstanding sportsman at his school in England, an elite boarding school in Winchester. It had been chosen for him as it never pampered its students. 'It was a school meant to teach the elite class an ordinary, austere life and the value of discipline,' stated Pataudi, recalling that when he had challenged and beaten his senior at squash, he had been thrashed and, though a son of a nawab, had been made to polish the shoes of his seniors. But it was cricket at which he excelled.

Before he lost his right eye, experts believed that he was destined for greatness. That he still managed to play Test cricket and even lead a national team says a lot about his grit, resilience, leadership skills and hard work. His elevation to captaincy was an anomaly in the hierarchal system in India that usually rated age and experience over talent when it came to leadership.

Though Pataudi did not undervalue the honour of playing for and captaining the country, the unending problems he faced made him wonder if it was worth doing. 'Many times, I asked myself why I was playing,' he said. 'It was not easy for me to bat with my disability, and on top of it I had to deal with people who were obsessed only with themselves!'

In the course of our many conversations, Pataudi referred to several incidents that left him disgusted and wanting to quit. One of the most disturbing of them was the scene at the 1966–67 Test against the West Indies at Calcutta, where the players were in physical danger from an agitated crowd. There are many versions of that incident, and Pataudi's is how it was seen from the players' point of view.

'I don't remember the exact details of what went wrong but the stadium was overflowing with people and I think there was some sort of political uncertainty plaguing the state,' recalls Pataudi. 'Some local political leader jumped in front of the crowd and got them very excited. He may have even started giving a speech. This prompted policemen to arrive and start beating this leader in front of 70,000 people. At that the crowd just erupted and went berserk.

We were rushed to our dressing rooms while the police had to resort to lathi charges. They even used tear gas. I went to the bathroom to wash my eyes because the doctor said it could be damaging to the eyes. I then spotted Amarendra Nath Ghosh, then president of the Cricket Association of Bengal (CAB), clutching a briefcase full of unsold tickets and repeating *"Mar gaya, mar gaya* (I am dead, I am dead)" to himself. We had to hide him inside our coffin (a box where players keep their equipment) and bundle him out through the gate in our coach once the pavilion was set ablaze.

'I don't think the crowd was against us. So they let us pass. But when the next day Gary (Sobers, the West Indian captain) stated that his team would not play, the officials asked me to persuade him to play. I said, "Why should I do that, we would lose the match anyway." Then the senior board members sent me the same request, saying, *"Hamari izzat ka sawal hain* (It is a question of our reputation)."

'So I went and told Gary, "I think you should play", explained the bit about our "izzat". He started laughing and said, "We are not going to play. We are going to get killed if we play in front of this mad crowd." I said, "Don't worry, I know Bengalis and I know the Indian crowd well. The tension is gone, they are all relaxed now and you can't lose the match." Eventually he played and his team won.

'You know what happened the next day? One bloody *chamcha* (bootlicker) from CAB knocks at my door and gives me Rs 100. He said it was a token of appreciation from the CAB. I told him to give that same amount to every member of the team.'

Pataudi was in good nick on the 1967 tour of England, and scored the only century for his team in the first Test at Headingley. But India was routed 3–0 in the series. Pataudi remembered that tour for reasons other than cricketing. The daily tour allowance of a measly 1 pound was forcing his players to search for cheap food, and the pair of white flannels and the socks provided were of such poor quality that in just one wash they would shrink and it would become difficult to wear them again. Then there was the case of the player in his squad who had taken a fancy for the telephone operator in the hotel. He would knock on her door almost every night. 'The lady complained and I had to use my best skills to assuage her feelings and prevent the situation from going out of control,' remembered Pataudi.

By the end of that long tour, he had had enough. Home and family were where he found the most comfort, and he decided that he would no longer lead India nor go on tours as they 'bored him to death'. On his return, he wrote a letter to the selectors telling them of his decision. 'Knowing that they would try to persuade me to change my mind,' he said, 'I retreated from public life and went to a place where only Sharmila Tagore could reach me.' The two were to get married two years later. The administrators appealed to Sharmila who eventually prevailed upon Pataudi to change his mind.

1971 was the year when Prime Minister Indira Gandhi was planning to abolish the privy purses, money that the government was paying to all the former maharajas and nawabs in India for having signed the instrument of accession to the Indian state in 1947. It was an extremely emotive issue of that time, lending heft to Mrs Gandhi's slogan of '*Garibi hatao* (remove poverty)' and catapulting her to the centre stage of Indian politics and the faction-ridden Congress Party.

The decision itself may not have upset the Pataudis as much as it did some other princely families; however, the sudden politically motivated announcement found them unprepared to face the new reality. 'We were not against the move if it helped remove poverty or helped in creating an egalitarian society,' said Pataudi. 'We just felt that it was a cynical move to hoodwink the masses and gain votes. We felt betrayed by a state that had promised us some rights we believed we were legally entitled to.'

Pataudi had jumped into a different arena, where he would be occupied with legal consultations and even taking on the battle politically. 'I had no time for cricket and could not even imagine going on a long tour. I had even filed my nomination papers to fight in the elections and that was the reason why I wrote to the Board making myself unavailable for the tour.'

The Board of Control for Cricket in India (BCCI) and the selection committee went about their task of selecting the captain and the team for the tour without making public the fact that Pataudi had opted out. This led to the inevitable headlines in the next day's papers: 'Nawab becomes a commoner', 'Tiger casted out', 'The vote that sealed Tiger's fate', among others. Nowhere was there even a hint that Pataudi had declared himself unavailable for the tour in advance.

'Those were tumultuous times for us and I thought there was no point in giving my side of the story,' said Pataudi. 'Though it still intrigued me as to why did the Board and Merchant not make my letter public.' Pataudi seemed neither angry nor upset at what had transpired four decades before, though at the time it must have been nothing short of humiliating.

The Tiger Roars Again

Indian cricket experienced some momentous triumphs in Pataudi's absence, and it seemed that the Nawab's era was well and truly over. However, life has a way of springing surprises. Pataudi's return as captain was as dramatic as his exit. It came about in circumstances that had left Indian cricket completely demoralized and groping for answers.

Raj Singh Dungarpur—whom I came to know later as a raconteur par excellence because of the relish, feeling and detail with which he would narrate past incidents in Indian cricket—was the chief selector at that time and knew Pataudi and his strengths well. He believed that only the Nawab could put Indian cricket back on track. Even the players felt the same, and they had conveyed to the Board that the only person who could reunite the players was Pataudi.

But Pataudi, when requested to take on the responsibility to lead India against the touring West Indies team in 1974, had hardly played any cricket since his axing. 'I think I told Raj Singh that I hadn't played cricket for a while and had not even kept in touch with what was going on in international cricket,' said Pataudi. 'I didn't even know who the West Indies players were. I told him it wouldn't be practical for me to make a comeback to international cricket. In any case, given my handicap, I would be even more inconsistent in my batting than ever before, therefore it did not make any sense for me to play again.'

To his complete surprise, Raj Singh told him not to worry about his batting. This was not about his batting but about helping to rebuild a team in ruins. He was the only person the Board thought capable of doing so, and was needed as a captain.

After much persuasion Pataudi agreed, only to find out that he was being made captain for only the first three Tests of the five-match Test series. This shocked him and he told them he was not interested. He said he was given a week's time to make up his mind and finally he did agree as he realized from a personal point of view it was a great compliment to him and all that he stood for. Yet, he was also aware that it was 'going to be a huge headache'.

Headache or not, sport had rarely if ever seen such a comeback. More than his batting skills, his return was an acknowledgement of his leadership and charisma in keeping individuals of disparate temperaments and regional affiliations united and well-knit. That historic series, whose results and individual performances are well documented, enthralled the cricketing public.

From 0–2 down, India came back to level the series 2–2, a superhuman effort against a team that was being led by Clive Lloyd. That series also saw the debuts of the fearsome Andy Roberts, who rattled the Indian batsmen with his sharp pace and steeply climbing short balls, and perhaps the greatest batsman of our times—Vivian Richards. No matter what the stats say today, it is not Sachin Tendulkar or Brian Lara who qualifies to be called the greatest. In the minds of those who have seen Richards, be they the players or the fans, there are no comparisons when it comes to who is the best and the most destructive batsman of our generation. In his second-ever Test at the Kotla, Richards gave us the first glimpses of his matchless abilities. The magical Indian spinners were brutally hit for sixes, some of which landed outside the stadium in the adjacent football ground.

Pataudi the batsman may have failed miserably—as he himself had foreseen—but as a leader he had successfully united the team and despite the loss of the final Test at Bombay's Wankhede that gave West Indies the series 3–2, his team had against all odds played on equal terms against formidable opponents.

Pataudi wasn't always able to remember scores and match statistics, but he had clearer memories of the chicanery of the officials and how the selectors had played regressive politics with the team. This time the bone of contention had been the choice of vice-captain. When the team for the first Test against the West Indies was being selected, Pataudi recalled that 'the selectors made a huge effort to make Venkat (Venkataraghavan) the vice-captain. I told them that I don't mind his selection but the problem is that there is huge competition between Venkat and Prasanna and there are times when a choice has to be made between the two for the final eleven. Therefore, I can't guarantee Venkat will be in the playing eleven.' Pataudi's choice for the role was Sunil Gavaskar.

The selectors finally agreed, but strangely, Pataudi was told that no one should know who the vice-captain was. Pataudi agreed, but he quietly informed Gavaskar that he was the deputy and that this knowledge should remain a secret. Maybe the selectors didn't foresee a situation where Pataudi wouldn't be available and someone else would be needed to lead the side. However, that eventuality did arise during the first Test.

Pataudi injured his finger while fielding and had to retire to the dressing room. No one knew who the vice-captain was, and an ugly situation developed on the field. Pataudi was not sure what exactly transpired, though he did remember that Gavaskar, having been told that he was the deputy, believed he should lead, but Venkat insisted it should be him. 'I think an argument ensued on the field while I was searching for a selector,' Pataudi said. 'I couldn't find anyone to sort out the problem.'

Providence struck again, this time to sort out this embarrassing problem. Gavaskar too injured his finger and the Indian team arrived in Delhi for the second Test still unclear about who would lead them in Pataudi's absence. Pataudi remembered that one of the selectors gave a hilarious speech which included the line, 'Anyone among you can lead, even Farokh (Engineer) can lead.' Eventually, it was Venkat who was given the responsibility.

For Pataudi all this came as no surprise; he had seen petty squabbles and ego battles too often in the past. This was one of the main reasons why he always felt that he was wasting his time playing for and leading the country. He had realized right at the beginning of his career that he would be a misfit in a system where personal egos, jostling for power and fighting for non-issues were more important than addressing issues that could help India build a good team. He recalled that in one of the selection committee meetings in his early days as captain of the team, he had seen selectors 'screaming, shouting and creating a ruckus over something as trivial as a shortage of pakodas while the team was being picked'.

Pataudi never doubted the integrity of his players while he was leading them, but touching upon the topic of match-fixing—which has bedevilled world cricket since the nineties—he recalled a shocking incident he was witness to.

It was the 1979–80 India–Pakistan series played in India, a six-match series that India was leading 2–0 after five Tests. The last Test was to be played at Eden Gardens, and Sunil Gavaskar, the captain, had opted out of the final Test. Viswanath, the vice-captain, took over leadership duties.

Pataudi happened to be staying in the same hotel as the Indian team in Calcutta. On the eve of the Test a distraught Viswanath knocked on his door. He was there to confide in his former captain and mentor an incident that had not only shaken him but had serious implications for the game itself.

'He told me that Asif Iqbal had approached him and suggested that regardless of who wins the toss tomorrow, he will declare that India has won the toss,' recalled Pataudi. 'This offer of toss-fixing had naturally shaken Viswanath, who was now trying to make sense of what was going on and probably thought that I was the most trustworthy person at that moment to confide in.'

What was baffling was Asif's brazenness in making this offer to Viswanath, who was the Indian captain only for that Test. How could Asif take the chance that his offer would not be revealed and his career ruined? Pataudi would not say if Viswanath told him anything else or gave any explanation for Asif's lack of caution. It was unusual enough for the Nawab to have even mentioned this incident after so many years, and to me that was strong enough reason to believe that Pataudi felt this incident had never been probed with the seriousness it deserved. Maybe if the authorities had taken corrective measures at the time, cricket would not have had to take such a massive blow to its credibility in later years.

During our long conversations, Pataudi talked about many other issues—including his identity as a Muslim that for the first time made him feel insecure as an Indian when the Babri Masjid was demolished in 1992. For a man who never betrayed emotion, presenting a stoic face and always appearing very distant, it was unnerving to watch him fight tears while narrating what it had meant to be a Muslim during that sordid period of India's contemporary history.

There were many suggestions from my friends to locate Pataudi in the larger framework of the Hindu-Muslim issue, especially in the present political context. I have refrained from doing that for the simple reason that I, like most Indians, thought of him not as a Muslim but as a talented sportsman, one who had used his inclusive vision and leadership qualities to give a new direction to the Indian cricket team in the sixties and early seventies.

Icons of College Days

While I was growing up in Amritsar in the early seventies, cricket and Hindi cinema were the leitmotifs of my life, as for many Indians even today. From the world of cinema, it was Dilip Kumar and his brooding, expressive face that fascinated me, and in the sporting world it was Vivian Richards who caught the imagination with his relaxed yet intimidating presence. What contrasting images these two superstars presented: the understated hero, who could convey a sea of emotions through just a twitch of a muscle, proving that silence can be more eloquent than a thousand words; and the player with burning eyes and the ability to destroy the best of bowlers with strokes of palpable violence.

A third name, an unlikely hero for a teenager involved with the mundane activities of life, got added to the list. In my teenage years, I was spurned in love. I found it hard to bear the rejection, feeling worthless and unwanted. That was also a period when there were a lot of heated discussions about which political ideology was right for the country. As hot-headed youngsters we would outright reject Gandhian pacifism and non-violence. To us, this philosophy seemed to be the root cause for India remaining poor and powerless. We would even try to find legitimate reasons for Nathuram Godse killing Gandhi. I desperately tried to look for *Why I Killed Gandhi*, the book based on his testimony in court. The book was banned, and to us that seemed to indicate that the government did not want the public to know and discuss another side to the story.

In the confusion of our half-baked knowledge that stemmed from the lack of any proper study of history, we would debate for hours on end without reaching any conclusion. We were more focused on defending our beliefs than on arriving at a reasoned conclusion. For us, men like Gandhi represented the image of a weak and sterile nation, whereas India's first nuclear test at Pokhran in Rajasthan in 1974 under the authoritarian Indira Gandhi was an achievement to celebrate and be proud of.

I am not sure whether I really believed this in my heart or all this aggressive talk was just an outpouring of my own insecurities and frustrations as a middle-class youth aspiring to a life of comfort and security as led by some of my friends who belonged to well-off business families. While it was possible that this insecurity could have influenced my ideas, it was also true that my wealthier friends had even more militant, aggressive and xenophobic mindsets than I did.

In this state of confusion, curiosity, restlessness and feelings of rejection, I started reading the Gita. There were two authentic English versions available at the time—one by P. Lal, which was called a 'transcreation' and not a translation, and the one by Gandhi, which included a more detailed interpretation of the verses. Finding P. Lal's version a bit difficult to understand, I immersed myself in Gandhi's text, seeking refuge from a world that appeared cruel and unjust because the girl of my dreams had decided to reject me.

I suddenly discovered a new world. It was a world where good and evil were engaged in a battle that Gandhi describes as eternal, one that also rages in the souls of mankind. The greedy Kauravas and the righteous Pandavas represented these two sides of human nature. For Gandhi, the brutal war and bloodshed between the two groups of the same clan was imaginary, not real, and the essence of its meaning lay in its emphasis on the ultimate victory of good over evil. For me, the meaning that emerged was that sufferings are a part of life and one should never work for reward but do one's duty regardless of the consequences. Much later in life, I read historian A.L. Basham's widely appreciated book, *The Wonder That Was India*. In it, Basham writes: 'No one so ungrudgingly admitted his debt to its doctrine of tireless and unselfish service as Mahatma Gandhi, who strongly opposed the two features of ancient Indian society which the Gita itself was in part written to defend—militarism and class system.'[1] It was then that I saw the contradiction in Gandhi's interpretation.

The chapters that preached stoicism in adversity and adoption of a detached view of the world were a balm for my restlessness and anxiety.

What reading Gandhi's interpretation of Gita also did was to instil in me a tremendous curiosity about the man whom I had been so critical of. I started reading more about Gandhi. Did he really live his life in the way of the Gita? I thought it was not possible. But reading *My Experiments with Truth*, in which Gandhi never hesitates to talk about his worst deeds with total candour and honesty, I was mesmerized.

The Gita may not have sorted out my inner turmoil. But what it did was to convert me into a tremendous admirer of Mahatma Gandhi, the man who had the courage to fight the British empire with non-violent means, and his immense spiritual strength to become one in action and thought.

Chandigarh and Kapil Dev

My completing graduation coincided with my father getting transferred to Chandigarh. It was a big change from the vibrant, throbbing and chaotic life of Amritsar to the more orderly, almost geometrical structures of Chandigarh where everything was so planned. The city was envisioned as the symbol of a modern India by Jawaharlal Nehru and designed by Le Corbusier. Numbers had replaced street names, and our first modest one-bedroom house was in Sector 22. Everything appeared sanitized and so similar that there was always the danger that one could lose one's way and mistakenly knock on the door of a house in some other sector.

Panjab University wasn't too far from where we lived and I decided to enrol in a master's degree programme in English literature there. This move was life-changing in more ways than one. My first encounter in the department was with a very lean, tall, turban-wearing Sikh student, Randhir Singh Dhindsa, who couldn't understand my terrible English accent, and thought I was speaking Russian!

Randhir belonged to a land-owning class, the Jats. His father was a retired Indian Army colonel. He had studied in elite public schools and graduated from North Point College in Darjeeling. He appeared bored with studies, not unlike many of the other Jat Sikh students from rich families.

Randhir became my first Sikh friend and introduced me to a new world whose social norms were very different from what I had known till then. I immediately understood that Randhir had money to squander and his dream was to settle in America, a country he considered to be the ultimate place to live in.

Randhir had been caught up between two cultures, poles apart, and it had bred an identity crisis in him. The traditional milieu at home, especially when he visited his village, contrasted sharply with the life he led away from home in his school and college hostels. He was docile and almost timid by nature but would be transformed into an aggressive person who cared little for what others thought once he hit the bottle, and that was very often.

There was nothing in common between us, because I was rooted in a middle-class ethos, unsure of what I would do in life, taking every new step with caution—a result of the inbuilt insecurities of my class. Yet we became friends almost instantaneously, developing a link that still remains intact. For me he became a window into a different culture and outlook that I had never known intimately. Bored with the repetitive routine of my own life, I started spending a lot of time with Randhir both at university and at his huge house, where he lived with his parents.

In Chandigarh I was reintroduced to cricket by another classmate, Chander Vijay. He played for Haryana as a wicketkeeper–batsman in the Ranji Trophy and, needless to say, was a star for us. I soon became part of the campus cricket team, and once again began to fancy myself as an all-rounder with the potential to at least be selected for the Panjab University team.

The captain of our campus team was Ashwani Minna, who was playing for Punjab in First-Class cricket. He was once even in contention for a place in the national team, having represented Rest of India in the Irani Trophy against the 1975 Ranji champions Bombay. Dilip Vengsarkar made his First-Class debut in that match, scoring a whirlwind century for Bombay.

Minna, a garrulous character who would regale us with crude Punjabi jokes, was a wizard with the ball. I have never seen a man turn the ball as much as he did. He had all the varieties that make a leg-spinner the most dangerous bowler to play. He could finish off a batting side in an inter-college match within the span of a few overs.

Minna had a mischievous twinkle in his eyes and an earthy sense of humour so typical of Punjabis who know how to also have a laugh at their own expense. He would take immense delight in telling us how he mocked the two legendary Indian spinners Bedi and Prasanna on their hammering at the hands of the young Vengsarkar in that Irani Trophy match. According to him, he told Bedi: '*Paaji, tanu taan edan kut pe rahi hain, jinda thuse mohalle de bowler honde ho* (Elder brother, you people are being hammered by this kid as if you are bowlers from some mohalla team).' When he repeated his comments to us, he shook with mirth, thrilled at having embarrassed the two greatest spinners the world has seen.

For us, Minna was a source of inspiration, as he had rubbed shoulders with the best. Playing cricket became a passion again (though my own performances were very modest) and my interest in studies, that was already lacking, dwindled further.

While on the university cricket circuit, we heard of two players whom everyone admired but dreaded to play against: Kapil Dev and Yograj Singh. Both were tall and well-built, and could hurl the ball at dangerous speeds. Yograj was the more aristocratic of the two. He was a Jat Sikh and owned a petrol pump and a large independent house in Chandigarh's posh Sector 10. He was considered to be a better batsman than Kapil.

Kapil's family were Punjabi migrants from Multan in Pakistan, and had settled in Chandigarh to do business in timber. So he was, relatively speaking, from a more modest background than Yograj. Kapil's family home was in Sector 16, a much smaller house than the one Yograj lived in.

My first and only encounter with Kapil in a cricket match was a painful experience. First, I was struck on my gloves while trying to avoid a short, lifting ball. It injured my finger. As if this was not enough, my pride in being an off-spinner of some merit suffered a worse blow when Kapil stepped down the pitch and struck one of my deliveries so hard that I again received an injury to my finger. The ball raced towards the boundary and I was left with a fractured finger. My cricketing aspirations came even worse off, as I realized that a weekend cricketer like myself could not compete with those who might one day be international cricketers.

The mercurial Yograj, who later did play one Test match for India, was the more flamboyant of the two. More of an extrovert, he had an aggressive persona but his exploits in the nets overshadowed his performance on the field. Many in those days believed he was more talented than Kapil, but he could not fulfil the potential he had as a cricketer. Today, he is better known as the father of the explosive Yuvraj Singh, one of the best One-Day cricketers India has ever had.

Chance Meetings

I accepted that playing professional cricket was not in my destiny, and wondered what future lay ahead for me. One day, while heading towards the university bus stop on my way home, I suddenly found myself looking at a face from the past. We both stared at each other for a brief moment before recognition dawned and we embraced warmly. It was Shekhar Gupta, my close friend from my school days in Panipat.

Shekhar had completed his mass communications course from Panjab University and was now enrolled in the master's degree programme in economics. He was also freelancing for *The Times of India*, writing for them on whatever little bit of sports action of national interest was taking place in Chandigarh. Shekhar was from the hinterlands of Haryana and had a passionate interest in sports, especially cricket. It was his burning desire to make a name for himself in journalism and backed his ambition with tremendous self-belief.

I now had two friends of contrasting natures and backgrounds, who had charted different courses in life for themselves. Shekhar was from a modest middle-class background but sure of his abilities and goals; Randhir was the opposite—directionless, feeding on the bounties of his land-owning forefathers, yet sensitive to the sufferings of others, dreaming of someday becoming an American citizen and hurtling towards alcoholism.

As for me, I had no special skills and was unable to focus on any one thing. I would have possibly ended up in a clerical job either in a bank or some government office had I not met Shekhar on the streets of Chandigarh that day.

Shekhar had a very good memory: he could remember faces, names and passages from a book, even their page numbers. This was a quality that is still one of his prime assets, one that has helped him become one of the best-known journalists in India. It was he who introduced me to journalism. It was a world I was completely unaware of, even though I used to read the sports pages of the newspapers diligently.

Those were the years of the Emergency, and the students in our university had strong and varying views on it. But my most vivid memories of the Emergency are not of what transpired during those days nor of the contentious debates we had on the subject. What stands out in my memory is the newspaper coverage of that tumultuous period in Indian history.

When elections were announced by Indira Gandhi in 1977, most newspapers predicted a Congress victory. There was no hint of the suppression and atrocities committed by the government nor the resentment of the public. The day after Congress was swept out of power, the most moving and powerful coverage appeared in *The Times of India*, which spoke of the courage shown by the people of India in throwing off the yoke of oppression imposed by a dictatorial government. Most of the newspapers proclaimed the dawn of a new freedom.

There was a celebratory tone, with flowing prose that talked about restoring of civil liberties and India being a great nation that valued freedom over oppression. It was in sharp contrast to the sycophantic writings in support of the state that we had been forced to read during the entire period of the Emergency. As a student, raw to the ways of the world, it was a shock to see some of the best-known names in journalism change their views overnight from servility to flag-bearers of freedom. I realized that courage in adversity is possibly the rarest human trait. The pouring of strong emotions into words does not necessarily make them true, and one may not always practice what one believes in.

Around that time, Chandigarh organized a tennis tournament to which some of the best-known Indian players were invited. Among them were Ramanathan Krishnan—arguably the greatest tennis player India has ever produced—and also Premjit Lall, Jaidip Mukerjea and a teenage prodigy Ramesh Krishnan, Ramanathan's son. Ramesh was barely fifteen.

The matches were to be played on the grass courts of Panjab University, and much to Shekhar's excitement, he was assigned to cover the event for *The Times of India*. During the tournament, Ramesh and his father kept winning, beating the rest of the field with ease despite Ramanathan having had retired from active tennis by then. Ramesh's sensational play and maturity beyond his age created a sensation. When the father–son duo reached the finals, the national press were suddenly interested.

For Shekhar, a rookie freelance reporter trying to make a mark, this was a great opportunity. With the clash of two generations in the final, a lead story on the sports page was guaranteed. On the day of the final, Shekhar was flushed with excitement.

Right towards the end of the match, with Ramesh on the verge of beating his father, Shekhar was shocked to see R. Sriman, the sports editor for *The Times of India* and the best-known name in sports journalism of the time, walk in. Anyone following sports through *The Times of India* would have been in awe of Sriman. He had covered a range of sports, and his writings reflected both his deep knowledge of sporting history and his biting sarcasm. At any other time Shekhar would have welcomed Sriman with great delight, but that day his face fell as he realized that his opportunity to write on the finals was gone.

Sriman had read the news of the father–son clash early morning in his paper, and since he had reported on Ramanathan playing a match against his father, he now wanted to witness him playing against his son. However, despite having caught the first flight from Delhi to Chandigarh, Sriman had missed the entire match. But that did not deter him. He immediately took charge, enquiring how far the *Times* office was and directions to get there. I borrowed Randhir's Lambretta scooter and took Sriman to the office.

Once settled, Sriman sought details of the match from me, wanting to know when the service breaks were made and what kind of shots were played during crucial passages of the game. He was impatient at my inability to remember every detail he wanted to know, castigating me for my ignorance. However, once he started to type his tale of how lucky he was to have witnessed two father–son duels in the same family, Sriman created through words a picture of the match as if he had himself witnessed it. By the time Shekhar reached the office, Sriman was through with his 'masterpiece', little realizing that he had left the real witness to that piece of history smarting in frustration and disappointment.

That was my first introduction to the real world of journalism. Shekhar may have been crestfallen, but I was thrilled at having met the man whom I had read so often in print. For a while, Shekhar continued to write for the paper, often frustrated at the lack of big-time sports activities in Chandigarh. Eventually, he could get a full-time position with the Chandigarh edition of *The Indian Express*. But to my surprise, Shekhar did not opt for sports journalism—he chose city reporting. His explanation for this decision reflected his pragmatism as well as his foresight: he said that there were limits to what a journalist can achieve in reporting only on sports.

My life went on as usual with my major worry being what to do after I finished my studies. A moment of great celebration came when Kapil Dev, our one-time rival from DAV College, got selected to play for India and flew to the 'enemy' territory of Pakistan for a three-match Test series. It was the Pakistani television broadcast of that cricket series that paved my way to journalism.

The Indian Express office was in Chandigarh's industrial area. The person in charge of the printing press, addressed fondly as Kancha, used to live in the office premises. He had a television set that could clearly receive the Pakistani broadcasts. Shekhar took me to watch the Tests there. The resident editor of the *Express* at that time was Prabhash Joshi, a doyen of Hindi journalism and a cricket fanatic. It was at Kancha's house where I met Joshi for the first time.

From 10 a.m. to 5 p.m., we would sit in front of the television set watching India get a hammering from Pakistan. The wristy Zaheer Abbas scored at will while Imran Khan's swing and pace did great damage to our batting. As we watched a match live on TV for the first time, cricket forged a bond between Joshi and me, a bond which put me on the path to becoming a cricket writer. When Joshi understood that I played cricket myself and had even played with Kapil, his fondness for me grew.

Those purely academic discussions on the game with *The Indian Express* editor in Kancha's room became something more when Joshi told Shekhar to ask me whether I would be interested in joining his two-member sportswriter team. It was a dream come true. I was asked to meet Joshi in his office, which I did with trepidation and a fluttering heart, not knowing whether it was an interview or a test of my abilities and aptitude for the job. But he simply asked me whether I would like to become a sports journalist.

When I said yes, Joshi pressed the bell in front of him. An attendant promptly walked in. He was told to ask the man in charge of the sports desk to come to the room. A few minutes later, a man in his forties walked in. Joshi introduced him as Krishan Kashyap. 'He is going to work with you from today,' Joshi told him. 'Take him to your desk.' In one swift, informal stroke, without any serious preparation or training, I was transformed from a post-graduate student into a professional journalist.

I walked out of the editor's room and entered a huge hall. Before me were desks, chairs, rattling typewriters and agency tickers on which news with blue ink was getting printed. I am not sure what emotions I had felt in that moment, but I remember wondering if I was good enough for the job.

It was the end of one phase of a life that had been conditioned until then to see the world through a prism of idealism. The real world, as we all get to discover, is very different from the one we visualize while reading textbooks and getting lessons on morality and ethics from our parents and teachers.

2
Learning the Game

My introduction to the world of sports journalism was initially limited to learning how to edit copy by hand. I was taught how to mark the page with symbols that would convey to the linotype machine operator where to delete text, where to insert commas and full stops and what other corrections were needed.

Until the eighties, publications used metal typesetting. The operator, or typesetter, keyed in the stories from the journalists' typed copy with editing marks. The linotype machine created a mould of each line of type using lead, and these were assembled into the various pages of the newspaper by a page-maker, a specialized job, under the supervision of the sub-editor or the chief sub-editor. It was a difficult job but it was made to look easy by their skill. From today's perspective, where technology has made the job so easy that the same person can write, edit and make the page, the work those guys were doing seems impossibly hard.

The monotony of editing a piece, giving it a headline, then proofreading the manually typeset copy and finally supervising the page-making would take about eight to ten hours. The deskmen and the reporters were usually antagonistic to each other, given the different nature of their jobs and the perks. The deskman lived a life of anonymity, polishing the language of the reporter, embellishing it with a good headline and then deciding how to display it. But it was the reporter's name that appeared next to the article. Jealousies and disputes over display were bound to create friction between these two groups.

However, in the sports section, the deskman and the reporter were the same person. It is a practice followed by most newspapers even today, perhaps because sports is a specialized subject and its jargon requires the same person to report as well as edit and make pages.

We were a department of three people, with Krishan Kashyap being the senior-most. There was also a reporter called Balbir Singh, and I was the third. I soon discovered that even between the other two, the relationship was not always warm. Discord often arose over who got a plum assignment, such as reporting on an important match that had wider public interest. However, since I had played cricket myself and the editor had hired me directly, I got cricket assignments rather quickly.

Being a reporter also meant being invited to press conferences where the organizers would give information that could have been communicated through a press release. However, grand cocktail and dinner parties were thrown to make these announcements. These were not so subtle ways to please the reporters to ensure good coverage in the paper. It really did work: the grander the party, the better the coverage.

I soon was part of this system, enjoying a drink or two and in the process getting addicted to the 'good life'. I believed I was doing no wrong: that as a reporter I would be judged not by the number of parties I attended but by the 'objective' reporting I did. Being pampered by the influential elite of society and interacting with the best sportspersons in your city can lead one to have an exaggerated idea of one's own importance.

I wanted to believe, like most of us do, that it did not affect me, but on days when there were no press conferences, the evenings would be boring. I soon discovered that Kashyap kept a bottle of rum under the seat of his scooter. After the first edition was finished, usually around 8 p.m., he would vanish from his desk for an hour or so. When he came back, he would be in high spirits. Soon, I too was initiated into this practice of drinking rum after signing off the first edition.

Kashyap and I were not alone in hurrying to the nearest vacant spot outside the office once the first edition was completed. A few others on the general desk would do the same. After the break, we would have to return to our tedious work that continued well into the night. The last edition deadline was around 2 a.m.

Our salaries were a pittance. A beginner like me in the late 1970s was on a salary of Rs 500 per month. Back then, it was enough if one lived a decent frugal life, but too little if one wanted to indulge. It wasn't possible to afford meals in restaurants and drink Old Monk on that salary. Thus, it was not uncommon to see reporters—especially outstation stringers (part-time reporters whose emoluments were linked to the number of stories the paper carried)—take advantage of this weakness by treating deskmen to gifts of sundry useful items, especially liquor, in order to push their articles into the paper. It was a good way to have one's evening's entertainment taken care of. No one cared if in the process a few brief, 'harmless' news stories appeared in the paper.

Most of us were night owls, our brains ticking sharply once the sun set. The mornings were spent dozing in bed or trying our best to shake off the hangovers and petty jealousies that were part of office life.

Chilling Facts

Among the memories of my early professional life is a chilling incident that keeps returning like a nightmare. It played a significant role in shaping my responses to the work I was doing. It happened during one of my early important assignments, when I went to cover a Delhi–Punjab Ranji Trophy match in Patiala in 1979.

As usual the organizers, the Patiala District Cricket Association, were taking good care of us. One of the dinners thrown by them ran late and some of us got a bit too drunk, so one of the public relations officers (PRO) of the Punjab government was given the responsibility of seeing us to our hotels safely. He was a burly man with a big turban. I was asked to sit in a jeep in a parking lot. I probably dozed off in the front seat, and when I woke up I realized there were two people in the back. I gathered that one was the public relations man, and the other was a professional photographer who was assigned to cover these kinds of events for a fee.

What startled me was the desperate tone in which he was pleading with the PRO not to stop giving him work, as it would affect his earnings. The PRO was stern and rude, saying, 'How can you refuse our demand? Fulfil that first and your assignments won't stop.' The photographer continued pleading, 'Please understand, she is my daughter, how can you ask me to do this? Ask for anyone else, I will do it, but *please* not this …' He was begging, his voice choked.

The burly Sikh wouldn't budge. Like the debauched maharajas of old, he said, 'No one can refuse us. Fulfil the wish and it will be business as usual. Otherwise …' By then I was wide awake. Was this for real? Was this conversation really taking place? A wave of emotions—fear, disbelief, disgust and even a feeling of humiliation—overwhelmed me.

That conversation haunts me even today.

That PRO went on to become a very influential man in Punjab's political set-up when he was appointed as one of the key advisors of Punjab police chief K.P.S. Gill, the controversial officer who is credited with finishing off the Khalistani terror movement through brutal use of force. He would hobnob with top journalists of the country, especially during the years of extremism that plagued Punjab in the eighties.

I was a regular visitor to Chandigarh's Sector 16 stadium, where the coach was Desh Prem Azad. He had coached cricketers such as Kapil Dev, Yograj Singh, Ashok Malhotra and Chetan Sharma. The captain of the Haryana Ranji Trophy team was Dr Ravinder Chadha, whom I had watched play for the North Zone against England during my school days in Amritsar. For a while, he was my morning jogging partner in the Sector 16 stadium. The stadium, part of the city's Leisure Valley, had the Rose Garden adjacent to it, and each morning we would jog for a few kilometres. Once we had finished, Chadha would start his more vigorous routine while I would listen to his gossip. Though guarded and careful with what he said, the following story he told me said a lot about the horrendous way in which Haryana cricket was administered.

Left-arm spinner Rajinder Goel has a stupendous First-Class record and is the highest wicket-taker in the Ranji Trophy. Many consider him to be unlucky to have played his best cricket when Bishan Singh Bedi was playing for India, which made it harder for him to get an India cap. But this incident is not about Goel's achievements as a player. Rather, it is from the time he was Haryana's junior selector.

In one of the selection committee meetings, Goel insisted on selecting a particular boy, though reluctant to explain why he was so keen on him. On being pressed, he finally revealed his reason. The boy's father was the postman who was tasked with deliveries to Goel's neighbourhood, and each time his son was not selected, he would deliberately misplace Goel's letters, not delivering them at his address. This harassment was causing the great spinner so much inconvenience that he thought it more prudent to appease the postman rather than suffer being denied communication from his friends and family living in far-off cities.

You can laugh this off as a joke, but this is for real. That is how team selections for Haryana took place in those days. Children of far more influential people than a postman used to get selected for the Haryana team before being weeded out after playing one match. That secured for them the credential of having played First-Class cricket, that in turn helped them to either get jobs or admission to colleges on the basis of sporting achievements. This is a practice prevalent in many state teams in India even now, Delhi being the most notorious example.

Being in a city where no international sport was played, covering international cricket was still a distant dream for me, but I did get to report on a few Ranji games played in our region. Many of my stories would expose malpractices, much to the annoyance of the officials. One of the stories I had done was on the son of a judge who got selected to play for Haryana while more deserving players were left out. This story acquired greater meaning four decades later during a hearing at the Supreme Court, which had passed an order to implement the reforms in Indian cricket as recommended by a panel headed by former Chief Justice of India, R.M. Lodha.

Various state associations were arguing against the recommendations. I heard a lawyer argue on behalf of the Haryana Cricket Association. He was articulate and forceful, and gave his own example as an ordinary person who could play for the state because of its good infrastructure and fair selection policies. A long-forgotten memory flashed in my mind as I realized the lawyer was the player, whose selection I had criticized many years back.

Decades ago, he had been selected ahead of more talented players. He had played in a couple of matches and failed to do anything of note and was now proudly flaunting his own credentials as well as that of his state association.

Immediately after the imposition of the Emergency in 1975, the Haryana Cricket Association was usurped overnight by the then Haryana chief minister Bansi Lal's son Ranbir Singh Mahendra. It became a one-man show with Mahendra as a virtual dictator. He later became secretary and president of the BCCI, and is best remembered for calling Sourav Ganguly an ill-mannered, pampered cricketer on India's tour of Australia in 1991–92.

Chadha was removed as captain, a decision that the players—including Kapil and Ashok Malhotra—resented. In protest, they decided to withdraw from the team and even signed a letter expressing their intent to do so. But to their utter shock, Chadha agreed to play under the new captain, Rajinder Goel. This was a betrayal that the players did not forget or forgive, and Chadha became very unpopular.

Kapil, by now a major star of the Indian cricket team, would visit Chandigarh whenever he had time off from his national duties. Local journalists would often seek quotes from him whenever he was in the city. Having known him from my days of playing inter-college cricket, I had greater access than most of my tribe of hacks. Most of the information I got from him was of the informal kind, something which fell in between the realms of truth and gossip. It was all mainly off the record and not for publication. It made me wiser to what was happening in Indian cricket, a sort of insider's account that the public was not supposed to know.

On one of Kapil's visits to the town, he and other senior players told me various stories about the autocratic functioning of the Haryana Cricket Association. They said that Chadha would himself travel by air or in first-class train berths and stay in luxurious hotels, while the rest of his teammates had ordinary arrangements. Kapil, Malhotra and the rest of the Haryana players chided me for not having the guts to write against the officials, and in this case against Chadha, who they assumed was my friend. Since my integrity was being questioned, I wrote a story critical of Chadha and the neglect of the players by the state association.

The next day I met a shocked and hurt Chadha on my morning exercise routine. He could not understand how a 'friend' could do such a story without seeking his version. How could I have believed what his teammates had to say against him? I could sense that he not only felt betrayed but also believed that I had been used by my sources to malign him.

For me, these were the early lessons in how sportspeople are not always united, but instead succumb to various jealousies and rivalries even while they are playing for the same team.

Superstars Are Human

Over the years, I have had several interesting experiences of players' rivalries, which I now realize were a result of a number of factors—high-tension situations, public pressure, the insecurities of the players themselves, clashing commercial interests and exploitation by the administrators, who used them as pawns to settle their own scores. If I highlight a few such incidents, the purpose is not to show any of them in poor light or to pit one against the other, but to show that players are as human as any of us, vulnerable to the pressures they face.

Kapil had become a larger-than-life figure after leading India to an unexpected World Cup victory in 1983. While his cricketing story is well known and documented, what is shrouded in mystery and controversy is the relationship he shared with another icon of Indian cricket, Sunil Gavaskar. To complicate the relationship further was the game of musical chairs that the BCCI orchestrated between the two when it came to captaincy, replacing one with the other twice within a span of just four years. This must have scarred both, leaving each probably mistrusting the other even if there was no substantial ground for suspicion.

A lot of it found mention in news reports of those days, which both the players always dismissed as the figment of a sensation-seeking reporter's imagination. Each of them maintains that their relationship has always been one of cordiality and mutual respect. Yet there are some jarring notes that paint a picture of an uneasy disquiet. It was the result of an insensitive system that over the years has cared little to understand what it means to be young and playing for the nation, trying to compete at the international level. The stakes are high and the competition is tough.

When Kapil replaced Gavaskar as captain for the 1983 tour of the West Indies, before they played the World Cup in England, Gavaskar did not travel with the team but joined them later. There was much speculation whether he had a genuine reason for his late arrival in the West Indies or whether he was being troublesome. He had also expressed a desire to not open the batting, which Kapil overruled. Though his record against the West Indies is phenomenal, Gavaskar was an utter failure on that tour. Many believe the seeds of suspicion in Kapil's mind were sown at that time. From Gavaskar's point of view, he probably saw injustice in Kapil's surprising elevation to captain at such a young age.

Gavaskar had become the Indian captain in 1978, replacing Bishan Singh Bedi, who had a history of run-ins with the cricket establishment as a player, captain and even post-retirement. Gavaskar's captaincy came at the time when the major exodus of top players to Kerry Packer's revolutionary World Series Cricket weakened cricketing teams across nations. India was one of the only countries not to see a player defecting from its team.

A West Indies team shorn of its stars visited India for a six-Test series, Gavaskar's first assignment as captain. He performed exceptionally well, scoring 732 runs at an amazing average of 91 while leading his team to a 1–0 series win. Yet he was removed as captain for the next series in England, with S. Venkataraghavan becoming the new leader. This bizarre change was justified by the Board on the grounds that Venkat had more experience of English conditions. However, unofficially it was being said that Gavaskar was being punished because he was secretly negotiating with Packer's World Series Cricket to play for them.

In England, Gavaskar averaged 77 in the four-match Test series, and in another bizarre twist, was reinstated to captaincy after the tour. He remained India's captain during 1982–83, before a 3–0 series loss to Pakistan cost him his captaincy. Gavaskar, despite his team's failure, was in good form, averaging just under 50 against the home side, whose bowling attack included Imran Khan, Sarfaraz Nawaz and Abdul Qadir. Though Gavaskar had been synonymous with Indian cricket in the seventies, Kapil was now slowly becoming the superstar, and he took over the captaincy for the West Indies tour.

Kapil has never talked to me about that tour, nor have I ever got an opportunity to know Gavaskar's side of the story and his relationship with Kapil. My impressions of that tour come from players who were part of the team, which leads me to believe that Kapil may have felt that Gavaskar had undermined his captaincy. At the camp held in India before the team embarked on the tour, Gavaskar had expressed his desire to bat in the middle order.

Kapil had turned down the request, insisting that if Gavaskar was to play then it had to be as an opener. The new captain did not budge even after intervention by the then Board joint secretary, Ranbir Singh Mahendra. Kapil of course knew Mahendra through their Haryana connection, and it was the first of many run-ins that continued after Kapil's retirement as well. The West Indies were a strong side, and the heavy defeat India suffered would have left any player shattered, leave alone a young man who was on his first assignment as captain.

To understand Kapil Dev better, it is worth taking a close look at his cricketing origins. In his quest for excellence he worked hard with a strong will and resolve to accomplish his aim of playing for India. Anyone who watched him grow as a player and person from his early days would testify that rarely has one individual been bestowed with such a combination of abundant all-round skill, aggression, self-belief, discipline and the motivation to succeed. What is even more amazing is that he perfected his skills almost in a vacuum, without any support system or any past cricket tradition to motivate him. He was one of a kind, different in his approach to the game from anything India had seen before.

Kapil's close friend and teammate from his school days in Chandigarh, former Test cricketer Ashok Malhotra, remembers Kapil telling him while they were still in school: 'I will surely play Test cricket for India, even if it is just one or two Test matches.' Ashok says he laughed and told him to first try to get selected for the state junior team before dreaming of playing for the country.

When Kapil was selected to play for India in the 1978 tour of Pakistan, the larger-than-life figure in Indian cricket was Sunil Gavaskar, whose batting skills, technique and patient resolve had led to staggering feats. Kapil was the antithesis of Gavaskar, molten lava compared to the rock-like solidity of Gavaskar. He was a genuine fast bowler in a land of slow trundlers with an aggressive, impetuous streak that complemented his daredevil attitude, be it in bowling, fielding or batting. India fell in love with him.

Even the great Gavaskar was now overshadowed. His teammates, in awe of Kapil's talent, started calling Kapil 'Sensi' (short for sensation). Suddenly Gavaskar and the great conservative cricket tradition he represented were being challenged by a Punjabi-speaking boy who had not been forged in the traditional crucible of cricket. This was a titanic change that came with its own set of problems.

When captaincy came to him within four years of his international debut, Kapil assumed it as a matter of right, given his talent, knowledge of the game's intricate technicalities and stupendous all-round performances. Even today, he resents being called an 'instinctive' captain, which implies that he was not a thinking captain. To prove his point that he did not rely on talent and instincts alone, Kapil once said, 'Without looking at their face, I can recognize all the batsmen to whom I have bowled—by only seeing their stance, how they hold their bat and how they stand at the crease.' He meant to say that he had minutely studied a batsman's grip and feet position to figure out his strengths and weaknesses. He does not like his achievements being put down to his being naturally 'gifted' and his leadership skills being labelled as mere intuition and luck.

Always his own man, driven by ambition and self-esteem, Kapil was never insecure about his astounding ability. But after he become captain at a very young age, he had to deal with many seniors in the team. That was when he began to fear that extraneous influences might derail his quest for solid team performances. Notwithstanding his immense respect for Gavaskar, Kapil may have felt that the world's finest batsman was undermining his leadership by refusing to open the batting. The mistrust that may have developed between the two had its fallout during the 1983 World Cup as well, where Gavaskar was dropped for a couple of matches. Although, he did return to the side for the final against the West Indies.

However, after the World Cup the West Indies toured India and walloped the home team in the Test series. In the fifth Test of the series, played in Calcutta, the Indians lost by a huge margin of an innings and 46 runs. It was their third loss of the series and a section of the crowd pelted the Indian team with eggs, tomatoes and even stones. Gavaskar was singled out for special attention.

When I met Kapil in Chandigarh a few days later, he was still recovering from the psychological wounds of that humiliation. Like any reporter, I was after a few quotes, and I got them simply by mentioning the defeat and the Calcutta crowd's behaviour. Kapil fired off some serious charges against his teammates during the interview, which appeared across all editions of *The Indian Express* the next day, some of them even carrying it on page one. The message was clear: Kapil thought his teammates were 'more interested in money than playing the game'.

Of course, it did not go down well with either the players or the establishment. What had prompted Kapil to make such an accusation? Did Kapil feel that the team's focus had shifted after the World Cup win to the money that the sponsors were keen to shower on them? Was the target of his ire the entire team or a few individuals?

I met Kapil again the morning after the interview appeared. By then he had realized the import of what he had said and the adverse repercussions he would have to deal with. He had not read the interview but had got many phone calls from his friends and other players and it had left him worried. He was unhappy at the use of the word 'money', and felt that I should not have been so direct. I reminded him that I had not misquoted him, and in fact had cautioned him at the time of the interview that what he was saying could cause problems. He responded in his typical manner, saying that now the damage had been done, he would deal with it in his own way.

A few days later, I was horrified when an agency news item appeared on the ticker saying that the Indian captain had denied the words attributed to him in the interview he gave in Chandigarh.

Learning the Game

I was badly shaken, not having expected Kapil to retract. His retraction had an impact on my credibility as a journalist.

The reason for that terse denial is detailed in Gavaskar's book *Runs 'n Ruins*, an account of that 1983 season, in which he describes what went through his and his teammates' minds when they read the accusation made in that interview. He seriously considered withdrawing from the team for the final Test, which was to be played in Madras, because despite the denial he was not convinced that Kapil had not made those remarks.

Gavaskar felt the accusations were directed against him and the other senior Bombay players. I quote verbatim from the book:[2]

After the Calcutta Test there were reports in the press about an interview Kapil gave when he returned to Chandigarh. In the interview, Kapil was reported to have said that some senior Indian players were only interested in money and not in the game. This was a very strong statement from the skipper and it implied motives which were suspect. I waited for a couple of days for a clarification to come through from Kapil that he had been misquoted and when that did not appear I rang Mr Salve [N.K.P. Salve, the Board president at that time] up and said that if the skipper thought his players were not giving their 100 per cent and he lacked confidence in them then I was not going to play the last Test at Madras. Mr Salve responded by saying that he had already sent a cable across to me to meet him in New Delhi. So I went over to New Delhi and met Mr Salve in the morning. It turned out that the reason he had called me to New Delhi was not entirely a cricketing one, however I took the opportunity to apprise him of the feelings of the Bombay players who were very upset by Kapil's latest statement. Mr Salve said that since Kapil also happened to be in Delhi he would check with him about the statement over lunch at his house where both Kapil and I were invited. Now Mrs Salve is an absolutely brilliant cook and a super hostess. She fed us so well that when the three of us went out to sit in the lawn I was feeling distinctly drowsy.

Mr Salve asked Kapil about the statement and Kaps immediately denied that he had used the word money and said he had been misquoted. Mr Salve then drafted out a statement to the press on Kapil's behalf denying that he had ever made a statement like that and though not completely satisfactory, as far as I was concerned, that was the end of the matter. We then discussed our prospects at Madras and the feasibility of me batting lower down the order. That was all. It was therefore amusing to read in the papers subsequently that Mr Salve had called both of us over to give us a talking to, to come together and play together. Never once during that meeting did Mr Salve do any such thing. He knows the admiration and respect that Kapil and I have for each other and the love of cricket which we share, and so there was no question of giving us a pep talk. But for the media it was not so. They wanted to believe that Kapil and Sunil were not getting on and their reports made that out. I was in no frame of mind to even deny, because after my failure in the last four innings all I wanted to do was to think to improving and doing well in the last Test.

And yet, as the subsequent paragraphs show, Gavaskar was still contemplating withdrawing from the Madras Test, despite Kapil's retraction.[3]

I returned to Bombay not quite happy with Kapil's denial and the statement and when I came home I told my father and wife that I still felt I should not play the last Test. They very wisely did not say a word. My uncle, Madhav Mantri, who also happened to be home that day, suggested that if I did not want to play, then I should make some other excuse like injury and pull out from the team. Now right through my career this is something I have never done. If I have an injury and feel that playing might aggravate it then I may not play but to fake an injury is not my scene.

It was, as I was shaving, that it struck me that by not playing I was quitting and that is another thing I have never done, in spite of obstacles, and so with shaving foam on my face, I rushed to tell my father and Pammi, my wife, that I would indeed go and play. They were relieved and said I was doing the wise thing. However I must add that if they had argued earlier with me when I told them of my decision not to play perhaps I would not have played. Their silence and lack of argument made me pause and think and stopped me from being a quitter. I was reminded also of a photo frame on the office wall of a friend, Pravinbhai Kamdar, which says, 'A winner never quits; a quitter never wins.' So it was off to Madras for me.

He scored a double hundred in the Chennai Test. It was his thirtieth Test hundred, taking him past Donald Bradman's tally.

Gavaskar mentions his failures in that series, but he had also scored a hundred in the second Test, played at Feroz Shah Kotla in Delhi.

I was fortunate to be present at the ground that day, watching what my memory says is the best batting exhibition I have seen, a daring display of aggression and skill that puts Gavaskar easily among the best the game has ever seen. The West Indians were out to get revenge for the defeat in the 1983 World Cup final, and were at their aggressive best. In the first Test at Kanpur, a lifting Malcolm Marshall delivery had Gavaskar fending the ball so awkwardly that the bat slipped from his grip. He was caught by the wicketkeeper, Dujon, out for a duck. The manner of his dismissal became a talking point, with a certain section of the media, especially from Delhi, taking delight in highlighting his slow reflexes as a sign of his declining powers.

Gavaskar responded in the most telling fashion, taking the bull by the horns. I still get goosebumps whenever I recall his innings in the next Test. The fearsome duo of Marshall and Holding were given a hiding as Gavaskar unleashed his majestic strokes—even the hook, which he had avoided most of his playing career. He appeared a man possessed, swatting any ball pitched short in front of his helmet-less face repeatedly to the leg-side fence. Those who have watched Gavaskar will swear to the perfect balance of his stance and the majesty of his straight drives. That day he added a third element to his batting—the hook—to be appreciated with similar awe. Gavaskar, the epitome of technical perfection and the master of playing the waiting game, was a transformed man. It was a stunning display of batting that, given the difficult personal as well as team circumstances under which it was played, has to be among his greatest innings, at par with some of his other great knocks—the Oval double hundred in 1979 or his farewell Test innings of 96 on the treacherous turner in the 1987 Bangalore Test against Pakistan.

The fallout of the 0–3 drubbing in that series was that the two superstars of Indian cricket were made to swap captaincy once again. Kapil was stripped of the captaincy for England's tour of India in 1984, with Gavaskar back at the helm. More drama was to follow.

India lost to an average England side on the final day of the Delhi Test in a match that had seemed to be heading for a draw. India needed to bat out the final two sessions with six wickets in hand. However, in a dramatic collapse, they rapidly lost those six wickets, adding a mere 28 runs to their score. Kapil was batting down the order and was expected to bat with maturity to see out the game. Instead, he played some airy-fairy shots. He hit a six and then was out caught in another attempt to repeat the stroke. The lower order showed no resistance and England wrapped up an unlikely win.

The blame for this unexpected defeat fell on Kapil and Sandip Patil, who too fell while playing his natural aggressive game. The selectors decided to axe Kapil and Patil. It would be the only time in his long career that Kapil had to miss a Test. Gavaskar maintains that he had no role to play in Kapil's sacking, as it was the selection committee and not the captain that had the authority to drop a player. Hanumant Singh, who was the chief selector at the time, later went on record to claim responsibility for the decision, stating that the captain had no role to play in the matter.

Kapil's sacking not only shook the Indian public but also played havoc with the former captain's mind. A few days after the event, I visited his new home in Chandigarh's Sector 9. I could sense that he was still furious. When we talked, his whole body shook with anger as he expressed his despair in very harsh words.

In the next Test, a Kapil-less Indian side batted for two days to score 437 in 200 overs. So slow was the pace of the innings that the crowd again became incensed, showering abuses on Gavaskar and attacking the team with slogans and even stones. The match ended in a draw and Gavaskar was so piqued by the crowd's behaviour that he decided never to play in Calcutta again. He skipped the next Test match held there, two years later. The series, which India had been expected to win, especially after their comprehensive win in the first Test at Bombay, ended in a 2–1 victory for England.

There was further drama during the One-Day series that followed, in particular during the match played in Chandigarh. The day was a very significant one for me, as it was the first international match I covered. My excitement was almost washed away by a downpour the previous night, which had made the ground so wet that eventually the match got reduced to a 15-overs-a-side game. India lost again. I was so excited at finally covering an international match that I missed the dramatic events that unfolded after the match.

Gavaskar reveals them in detail in his book *One-Day Wonders*.[4] He writes that the selectors had asked Ravi Shastri to be present in Chandigarh, an indication that he too was in contention for the captaincy. Since India had lost the Tests as well as the One-Day series, Gavaskar was not sure he would be retained as captain. After more than three hours' wait, Gavaskar, who was sitting in Shastri's room, was asked by his wife Pammi to return to their room. There, she told him that he had been reappointed as Indian captain. However, what put him off were the strange instructions he was given.

> Pammi then told me that I had to go to a car parked across the road from the hotel where the Board joint secretary, Ranbir Singh Mahendra, was waiting to drive me to where the selection committee was meeting. She said that I should not go by the main entrance as the press was waiting there. But scale the wall that ran alongside the lawn and thus escape the eyes of the press.
>
> This did not make any sense to me, because if I was the captain, why play hide and seek with the press? I argued but she said, 'just go and don't waste time discussing this with me because I am only conveying what Ranbir said to me when he came here with the news.'
>
> It was in the act of scaling the wall and dropping to the road on the other side, that my mind was made up that I would quit the job after the Australian tour.

Gavaskar led India to one of its most emphatic One-Day tournament victories in Australia, which people today remember more for Ravi Shastri's drive around the Melbourne Cricket Ground in the Audi that he won as Man of the Tournament.

After the tour, Gavaskar stuck to his guns and relinquished the captaincy. Shastri was one of the contenders to replace him. However, the selectors decided to reappoint Kapil as captain. The relationship between the new captain and the man he replaced may have even worsened following this appointment, as the happenings during India's tour of Sri Lanka in August–September 1985 suggest.

In that series, Gavaskar's wish not to play as an opener had been granted and he batted at five, five, six and five in the first two Tests and at six and seven in the final Test. India lost the series 1–0. Interestingly, in the three One-Day matches, Gavaskar batted at six, five and seven. The media was intrigued and soon came up with stories about the rift between the two. Kapil, obviously unhappy with Gavaskar not opening, may or may not have had cricketing reasons for this reshuffling of the batting order.

Kapil was in Chandigarh to visit his ailing mother after the tour had ended. When I visited him, he told me that before one of the One-Day matches, he announced the batting order in the dressing room by naming the first five or six batsmen. Gavaskar was not among them. 'I paused after that,' he said, 'and looked at my players before saying, "The rest we will decide, depending upon the match situation."'

India Today carried a detailed story written by the late Raghunath Rao, in which he mentioned how the atmosphere in the dressing room was vitiated on the tour due to the differences between India's two leading players. Yet, one of the magazine's later issues carried a letter written jointly by Kapil and Gavaskar that rubbished the rift story and blamed the writer for presenting unfounded information and playing with the truth. These denials may have been necessitated to keep harmony in the team or perhaps forced by the Board to avoid smearing the image of Indian cricket. Whatever the reasons, this chapter in Indian cricket reflects the complexities of relationships in an extremely competitive environment that can bring out the worst in human beings, especially those who are young and driven.

Today, Kapil and Gavaskar have a warm and friendly relationship, and perhaps both look back at those events with regret. However, neither publicly accepts that there was any problem in the first place. Kapil, though, does admit that he was not mature enough to lead the Indian side the first time he was appointed in 1983, and that Gavaskar should have continued in the role.

Two decades later, during the Chappell–Ganguly rift in 2005 and the appointment of Rahul Dravid as captain, I had a better insight into the events that transpired, most of which were not very pleasant. At the time, Kapil said in an interview that the Board needed to handle this issue with care, as such matters could destabilize the team; he then referred to the captaincy musical chairs played by the Board with Gavaskar and him.

Sunil Gavaskar and Kapil Dev were not just among the greats of cricket, but they were also ahead of their time in understanding the commercial value of the game and the possible benefits for the players.

3
Chandigarh 1978–1994

In my formative years as a journalist in Chandigarh, I was a reporter covering local leagues and Ranji Trophy matches in the backdrop of political turmoil and sectarian violence in Punjab. In the eighties and early nineties, we lived in an atmosphere of terror. Punjab was akin to a killing field where thousands of innocents perished. Yet, we continued to cover cricket matches across the state, travelling in public buses while fearing for our lives. Even at home, we never really felt safe.

The strongest memory embedded in my consciousness from the time is, however, not any tale of heroic batting or bowling nor of the horrors of violence. It is an episode that shows the resilience of the human spirit.

One of my first articles for *The Indian Express* was on Narendra Sharma, who was among the highest wicket-takers in the local league. He had two thumbs on his right hand, so was popularly known as 'Changa' (six). A few years later, Changa was diagnosed with blood cancer, and not given much longer to live. Shaken and distraught, I went to see him in hospital with my friend Jatinder Chadha, who had played a lot of cricket with him. It was an unnerving prospect to be meeting a man who faced imminent death. Many thoughts crossed our minds, the uppermost being how we would face him and what he must be going through.

Instead of the crestfallen, hopeless figure we expected to see in the hospital room, we found Changa busy installing a TV set that he had borrowed from his friend. He was keen to watch India play a One-Day match in which his mentor, Kapil Dev, was playing. Changa was determined not to miss his idol's performance. He dismissed our concern for his health, as if that was the least of his worries. Instead, he talked about cricket and the greatness of Kapil.

When we came out of his room, we felt ashamed and even sorry for ourselves. The man whom we had feared to face was full of life, not thinking beyond his present delight of watching his favourite sport and sportsman. He was full of hope, living in the moment. It was a life lesson that I have not forgotten.

Booze and the Written Word

This was a period when Ranji Trophy matches still drew crowds and their coverage in the papers would compete for space with international matches. Today, it may be hard to find even a brief report of a Ranji Trophy match, as international cricket dominates the sports pages. In those days, there were fewer international matches so almost all the top stars would play domestic cricket and the grounds would be swarming with people.

I would often travel to Faridabad to cover Haryana's Ranji Trophy matches. The ground in Faridabad would later became a full-fledged stadium and host One-Day internationals, but at that time it was a bare patch of land with no boundary walls. The match could be viewed from a hillock adjacent to the ground.

The hillock had a special attraction for us scribes. It housed a Haryana Tourism–run restaurant that had a bar. Lunch would be arranged for us in the restaurant, and the bar came in handy to lift our spirits. Few activities were more appealing to us than sipping a drink in the winter sun while watching cricket.

The cocktail in demand back then was Bloody Mary. On popular request from our fraternity, this drink was served at lunchtime during any important match that the Punjab Cricket Association hosted. The association's president was Inderjit Singh Bindra, an IAS officer who later became a very powerful BCCI official and one of the key persons credited with changing the financial state of Indian cricket. Bindra loved to indulge journalists, whether at a press conference or during a cricket match. This generosity was reciprocated the next day, with Bindra's photo and quotes prominently appearing in newspapers.

One of our colleagues was an unknowing victim to the kindness of our host during a cricket match. I knew my colleague to be a teetotaller, but found him in a convivial mood, a glass of Bloody Mary in his hand. He told me he was on his fourth or fifth glass of this 'fantastic tomato juice'. On being informed about the true nature of his drink, his mood changed, and he suddenly felt giddy. 'I am finding it difficult to stand, I will rush home and sleep. Please take one extra copy of the scorecard for me, I will take it from you later, once I reach the office,' he said before rushing out of the press box.

With most of the journalists having several drinks, one would think that the next day's reports would have had factual inaccuracies. But this was rarely the case, or at least we believed so. Most of us had become experts at decoding match details from the scorecard. With live television coverage not reaching every home, and in any case absent from the games we covered, the facts were what we wrote in the paper, even if on occasion they may have been at variance with reality.

One of the idols of the sports writing fraternity those days was Ron Hendricks, the Bombay-based sports editor of *The Indian Express*, whose prose, pithy and yet vivid, had made him a much-admired journalist. He was a legendary drinker as well, and those who have worked with him say that unless he got drunk, he could not write copy. There are stories of how his colleagues would have to literally seat him in a chair and put a typewriter in front of him. He would then come to life, his fingers moving furiously over the keys as he typed out his match report. Incredibly, it would be free of errors, factual and grammatical and very readable. Even the players about whom he wrote were his fans. Ron's accomplishments only encouraged us to justify our drinking bouts even while we were covering matches.

Though I had played a bit of cricket, it was not easy to judge players far superior in skills and achievement. Yet, we cricket reporters did that regularly. There were some among us who did not know even the basics of the game. I remember having to explain to a fellow reporter the difference between cover and midwicket. We quickly learnt to write scathing remarks about those who failed and to gush over those who succeeded. In that era, articles in the newspapers mattered a lot, and young, aspiring cricketers would be scared of reporters, fearing a critical word from them could cost them selection in the state team.

In India, people are sometimes hired without checking their aptitude, abilities and suitability for the job. Like in most fields in the country, so too in journalism, people are frequently hired because of who they know. In my own case, I doubt I would have been anywhere near journalism had Shekhar not been my schoolmate and had fate not led us to meet again. Employment in India often has more to do with connections and less with merit.

Interlude with Radio

One of my early exposures to the big names of Indian cricket came in 1980 when Haryana qualified for the semi-finals of the Ranji Trophy. On a treacherous turner in Rohtak, I watched in awe as Dilip Vengsarkar displayed his masterly skills in countering the spin of Rajinder Goel with his pads even as his other star colleagues—the likes of Sunil Gavaskar, Ravi Shastri and Sandeep Patil—struggled to score.

That match holds personal significance for me as it was then that I had my first chance to appear for a radio commentary selection trial. I recorded five minutes of live ball-by-ball commentary. However, it was only six years later that I received the results of that trial, when a telegram arrived asking me to go to Jodhpur to be part of the All India Radio's commentary team for the Irani Cup match.

After that, I started getting radio commentary assignments regularly. The crowning moment came when I was assigned to do the commentary for a One-Day match between India and Pakistan in Nagpur. I will always remember the date, 24 March 1987, for reasons other than cricket.

It is a memory of great personal sorrow and loss. While sitting in the commentary box, I heard an announcement on the public address system calling me immediately to the pavilion as someone wanted to convey an important message to me. When I went to the pavilion, I was told that my father was no more. He had passed away suddenly the previous night.

There was no flight to Delhi until that night. Having no choice, I decided to carry on with the commentary as if nothing had happened. I must have been numb with shock, but somehow saw the day through. I eventually reached home at night to join the mourners. In the sorrow that had engulfed us I still remember my seven-month-old daughter breaking into innocent gurgles at the enjoyment of seeing so many people around.

My amateurish career as a radio commentator seemed to hold greater promise for me than my work as newspaper reporter. Later the same year I covered my first Test match for radio when India took on the West Indies at the Kotla in Delhi. I enjoyed my stints on air and began believing myself good enough to make a career out of it. But my dreams were dashed when I was told by my bosses that my knowledge of the game was poor.

This disappointment came in 1993, when I was commentating on India's One-Day match against England in Jaipur. England won despite Vinod Kambli scoring a magnificent hundred. During one of the breaks, the director of the Jaipur radio station complimented me for describing the game accurately and swiftly. I was still savouring his appreciation when I got a call from the head of the sports division in Delhi. On that call, I was told that my technical knowledge of the game seemed very poor and that I was not describing the game properly. I didn't know what to make of it.

Whatever the reasons, from then onwards my radio assignments started to dry up. I still believe I was not that bad, especially in comparison with others doing regular radio commentary those days. Yet, I was eased out of the sycophantic world of All India Radio.

Guns and Legends

I worked for *The Indian Express* in Chandigarh for fifteen years. The later years of this period would be spent drinking in the Press Club in Sector 27 and having loud, boisterous arguments with friends while indulging in inane gossip or debates on cricket. Around us was emerging the spectre of Punjab terrorism and strained Sikh–Hindu relationships, the Mandal commission that exposed the hierarchical fault lines in Hindu society and the Hindu right wing symbolized by their Ram Temple movement and the demolition of the Babri Mosque. What amazes me today, when I recall that period, is how we managed to focus on the game despite the killings, the fear and the sectarian and caste divides that were devastating lives.

The eighties and early nineties in Chandigarh may have been professionally exciting times for a rookie cricket reporter like me, but those were also dark days. Amidst a growing demand for an independent state of Khalistan, terrorism had reared its ugly head in Punjab and people were regularly dying in bomb blasts and gun attacks. The hitherto unknown Jarnail Singh Bhindranwale was becoming a figure of fear for many and of admiration for others.

It became clear to me that Sikhs and Hindus shared a different worldview. Newspaper headlines would daily announce murders of people, killed simply for being either Hindu or Sikh. The world was becoming a difficult place to understand. I still shiver when I recall travelling in buses to cover cricket matches in different parts of Punjab—Patiala, Jalandhar, Amritsar—and dying a thousand deaths whenever the bus stopped to pick up a passenger. I would scrutinize each face, praying that my life would be spared if an assault took place. The air was laden with the stench of death, and reaching one's destination safely appeared nothing short of a miracle.

In April 1983, the top Punjab police officer, DIG A.S. Atwal, was gunned down by terrorists at the Golden Temple in Amritsar. This began a wave of terror, and finally President's rule was imposed in Punjab on 6 October. It was just ten days before the West Indies match against North Zone in Amritsar. Today, I wonder why that match was held in the midst of these tragic events. And also how it drew almost a full house.

I was back at the same Gandhi ground where as a college student I had played cricket and watched some intense inter-college rivalries.

It was during this match that I discovered that Viv Richards was idolized even by rival players. On the eve of the match, Richards was mobbed by the North Zone players, including Yashpal Sharma, Ashok Malhotra and Gursharan Singh. Among them were two young and extremely talented cricketers who would go on to play for India—Chetan Sharma and Navjot Singh Sidhu. The players made an arc around Richards, sitting on the ground while he sat on a chair. It was a scene straight out of a fanboys' club.

Both Sidhu and Sharma made an impact during the match. Sidhu scored a scintillating century and among Sharma's wickets was Richards, who until his dismissal had combined the grace of a nimble dancer with the ferocity of a German Shepherd. His walk to the wicket had been so relaxed, as if he was sauntering in a park on a Sunday evening. The bat had been like a toy in his big hands. That day in Amritsar, nearly anything bowled by medium-pacer Sunil Valson—who had been in India's 1983 World Cup squad but didn't play a match—was hit mercilessly to the fence. What added to the spectacle was the disdainful manner in which Richards would show his back to the bowler immediately after completing the stroke, neither looking in the direction of the ball nor of the bowler. This arrogance had become a symbol of Richards' imperious play.

There are some stories about how certain players, even after binge-drinking the night before the match, had gone on to score blazing hundreds. It is said that Gary Sobers was one such character who would pull off such feats very often. He would drink the whole night, and would then fall asleep in the dressing room. He asked to be woken up only when his time to bat came. There is a story that in one of the matches, he was snoring loudly until woken up just before he had to walk in to bat. Sobers, the story goes, got up, walked straight to the crease and proceeded to hit a century. After being dismissed, he headed to the dressing room and went back to sleep. Such incidents are not likely to occur in the modern era, where discipline, hard work and a rigorous fitness regimen are basic requirements for a cricketer.

I was witness to something similar in 1987 when the West Indies team were playing the Indian Colts in Chandigarh. On the eve of the match the host association had thrown a dinner, at Punjab Cricket Association president Bindra's house.

Booze was flowing and we all were excited to find that even some of the West Indian players were taking rum, the staple drink of us journalists, and not Scotch. Late into the night, very few guests were still boozing and one of them was Richards, who now wanted to leave for his hotel. Mr Bindra, like a good host, insisted he could not leave without having one more drink. Richards agreed, filled in the glass with as large a peg as possible, mixed it with coke and gulped it down, ready to say goodbye again. Mr Bindra had not expected such a swift end to his offer for Richards to stay on longer and again insisted he have one more. Richards repeated the same act, maybe this time pouring an even larger drink, gulped it down and sought leave from Mr Bindra.

The next day, at the Sector 16 ground among the first few balls Richards faced was a sharp bouncer from medium pacer Jaspal Singh. To everyone's surprise, Richards did the most un-Richards-like thing: he almost fell on the ground while avoiding that short ball.

The next ball from Jaspal was hit so mercilessly and hard, that it went miles into the air and landed way beyond the stadium, in the Rose Garden adjacent to the ground. It was as stunning a shot as I have ever seen, once again reinforcing the belief that some players are so special, they are unaffected by what they have done the previous night.

Prejudice and Hatred

The magic of cricket and being able to watch some of my sporting heroes up close was not enough to ease worries about the increasingly tense political situation around us. The most disquieting feeling was the suspicion with which we Hindus started looking at our Sikh friends. For my family and among Hindu friends, it seemed like the Sikhs were negating the teachings of Guru Nanak and were on a suicide mission for reasons difficult to fathom.

Among my close friends at that time was Jatinder Chadha, a banker by profession. He was also an amateur cricketer who played for the State Bank of India team with the likes of Rajinder Goel. A proud upper-caste Khatri Hindu, Jatinder sympathized with the RSS view of the world. During our evening drinking sessions, as booze would stimulate the senses, the talk would become more and more intense as we tried to make sense of what was happening around us. From his perspective, the pristine Indian culture had suffered at the hands of invaders, the Muslims being the major culprits but the British no less culpable. This belief was apparent in an incident that has stayed in my mind.

Jatinder and I were driving in his car late at night. We spotted a young White man on an empty road, signalling us to stop. He had lost his way and wanted directions to the hotel he was staying in. To my surprise and horror, Jatinder started yelling at him, telling him to leave our country. The poor man fled from our sight. Jatinder started explaining to me that these White men were the cause of India's ruin and should be treated with contempt. He had failed to respond to a person in need of help because of what he believed were the 'collective misdeeds' of that person's ancestors.

Jatinder's grandparents had migrated from Pakistan and settled in Jalandhar. That the perceived slights of history have a deep-rooted effect on the psyche is chillingly clear: Jatinder's father, in a deep coma for some months after a road accident, showed signs of awareness when his son told him on 6 December 1992, that the Babri Mosque had finally been demolished.

I somehow came from more neutral territory: in Kashmir the chasm between Hindus and Muslims had remained muted till the late eighties and my childhood conditioning had not instilled in me hatred against the Muslims or the 'other'.

In Punjab of the '80s I was witnessing Hindus pitted against Sikhs. Randhir and most Sikhs would tell me that the Hindu Baniya (mercantile class) had looted Sikh villagers by charging them huge interest on loans they had given them and the peasantry was in huge debt as farming was no longer viable for them. They refuted the simplistic theory that Pakistan was exploiting their imaginary grievances to urge on the separatist Khalistan movement. In the office, reporters from each community would have their own interpretations of the unfolding events. The Sikh reporters were never in agreement with their Hindu counterparts on the historic and immediate reasons for these brutal killings. For the Sikhs, the Indian state with its bias towards the majority Hindus was one of the major reasons for this fratricide. However, there was agreement on the point that violence was not the solution and that it had no place in a civilized society.

Very often the debate would be about whether Bhindranwale, who was heading this pro-Khalistani and anti-India/Hindu movement, was in fact a creation of Indira Gandhi's own power games. The Indian state and the Congress had protected him till he turned against them. Then came Operation Blue Star in 1984, in which the Indian Army raided the Golden Temple in an attempt to flush out terrorists from the temple complex. Among the hundreds killed was Bhindranwale. In its aftermath, Indira Gandhi was assassinated by her Sikh guards, and the retaliatory massacre of innocent Sikhs in Delhi and many other places across India threatened to tear apart the social fabric of the state.

During Operation Blue Star, newspapers were prohibited from publishing any news regarding the operation. At the time, Rahul Singh, a Sikh, and son of the famous writer and editor Khushwant Singh, was the resident editor of *The Indian Express* in Chandigarh. He was an uncomplicated man who handled deftly a difficult situation where the Sikhs on the staff were getting agitated and feeling victimized, whereas the Hindu reporters were happy that some strong action was finally being taken. There was a high possibility of clashes taking place even among friends and colleagues.

As news of the operation started pouring in, there was panic all around. There were also reports of desertions from the army by Sikhs across the country, and also retaliatory action by some of them, in which fellow soldiers were killed. A sense of doom engulfed us all.

Among the many Sikh colleagues I had was Kamal Dhaliwal, holding views very similar to what Randhir and many others believed. I still remember him riding pillion with me on a scooter in the dead of night, both of us drunk and Dhaliwal shouting provocative slogans while armymen were patrolling the city in the days of curfew post Operation Blue Star. I still wonder how we escaped getting shot or arrested.

At the time, the Indian cricket team was touring Pakistan. The kind of cricket played in that Test series was a reflection of the insecure mindset of the two teams, each loath to lose and face the ire of their public. The first two Test matches ended in boring draws and the third was cancelled after the Indian Prime Minister Indira Gandhi's assassination by her Sikh security guards. The umpiring generated more talking points than the cricket. The

Indians complained that they were done in by some atrocious and biased umpiring, and the clamour for neutral umpires grew. Thinking about it now, it was a wonder that an Indian team was touring Pakistan at a time when India was accusing Pakistan of sponsoring terrorism in Punjab.

Television beamed live pictures of people paying their respects to Indira Gandhi and laying wreaths on her body that was kept for a couple of days at her residence before the funeral took place. While people streamed in to pay their homage, one could hear in the background shouts calling people to avenge her death. Soon there were reports of Sikhs being butchered in many parts of the country, with the situation in Delhi being horrendous. My Sikh, and even some Hindu, friends would say this was a classic political strategy to exploit the fears and insecurities of a majority to garner votes. Whip up emotions and bring the nation together against a perceived enemy, the Sikhs. I must confess, I did not like what I was hearing, an inbuilt conditioning resisting the complexity of a narrative I had believed was straightforward. Now a multi-layered assault of conflicting viewpoints left my mind in confusion and disarray. In the national elections that followed Indira Gandhi's assassination, Congress Party, led by her son Rajiv Gandhi, won a landslide victory, bagging an unprecedented 414 seats. India's majority had never voted so unanimously for one party ever.

Despite the growing mistrust, the miracle in Punjab was that no communal riots took place. Life went on, including our jobs and cricket and various other sports. The Punjab Ranji Trophy team was a mix of Hindus and Sikhs and I can't remember any incident that might have indicated that this atmosphere of mistrust had affected relationships among the players. They would travel, play and interact with each other as if nothing untoward was happening around them, and so would the journalists.

Communal and Caste Politics

As if the terror in Punjab was not enough, the Mandir–Masjid politics then began to create further divisions in the country. On 5 August 1990, fresh trouble arrived when the Mandal Commission report was implemented. It proposed 27 per cent reservation in government jobs for the Other Backward Classes, which represented around 52 per cent of India's total population. Massive disruptive protests from the entrenched classes brought northern India to a standstill.

Adding to these issues of Khalistan, Mandir–Masjid and Mandal Commission was the simmering Kashmir problem that all of a sudden erupted like a volcano. My homeland was in flames. Kashmiri Hindus, called Pandits, found themselves caught in the crossfire. Most of my relatives had already left the Valley much earlier, in more peaceful times, but a few of them were still living in Srinagar at that time. My cousins and their families abandoned their sprawling homes and, like lakhs of other Hindus, fled the Valley and scattered across India.

By then, V.P. Singh, a popular and important member of the Cabinet, had rebelled against Prime Minister Rajiv Gandhi on issues of corruption and formed his government in 1989 with the support of both left and right parties. Singh soon had to deal with the contradiction of this unlikely alliance in the context of the Ram Temple agitation. Interestingly, he had during his election campaigns openly espoused a secular ethos for the country and been critical of the rise of the right wing, despite the fact that his party was in alliance with them. The India of the late '80s was resounding with the slogan '*Kasam Ram kee khatey hain, Mandir wahee banayenge* (We swear by Ram that we will make his temple at the same spot)', as the BJP threatened to launch a nationwide movement to build the Ram Temple at the spot where Babri Masjid stood in UP's Ayodhya town.

I still remember listening to the speech VP gave after he was sworn in as the Prime Minister in 1989. Kamal Dhaliwal, expansive in all his habits, be it drinking or expressing an opinion, was at the Chandigarh Press Club with me that day. Listening to the PM's speech, that alluded to the marginalized and their aspirations with the words: '*Hum gaon kee dhool in galyaro mein le ke aye hain* (We have brought the dust of the villages into these mansions)', Kamal all of a sudden said: 'Mark my words, this man is no ordinary politician. He is destined to change India's history.' Kamal, with a fecund imagination and a photographer's eye for the unusual, gave reasons for passing this definite judgement on the man: 'Look at his choice of words, his theme for the speech and more importantly for me, he has a wonderfully innocent face that reflects sincerity and great resolve.' These words were to turn prophetic, even if the upper castes hate VP for what he did. He did change the course of Indian history.

VP's election campaign speeches always referred to 'social justice' as his main promise, and he would repeatedly assure his electorate that if voted to power he would implement the Mandal Commission recommendations.

When V.P. Singh carried out his pledge, it created a wedge between the 'quota' supporters and those against it. I once again was in a position of ambivalent neutrality, unsure of which side I belonged to. All around me, friends and relatives were furious, feeling betrayed by a man who they had believed was one of their own. Agitations, rioting and protests became commonplace as the middle and upper classes came onto the streets.

The world around me existed with all its caste differences and I till then didn't question why it was so. The four-division hierarchy was simply a fact of life in our homes and apart from a few half-hearted debates among some of my friends and relatives of it being a cruel form of exploitation, life went on as usual. Until VP's decision on caste-based quotas, the only divisions confronting me were based on religion—Muslims demanding Azadi in Kashmir and Sikhs an independent Khalistan state in Punjab.

Newspaper headlines declared their support for the anti-Mandal agitation as protests raged across the country. Many doctors lived in my neighbourhood in Chandigarh, and every evening they would step out on the streets in a candlelight protest. They would even bring brooms and sweep the streets in a mock exercise that symbolized what their plight would be after the implementation of the Mandal commission recommendations. I saw the pain and hurt in the eyes of the neighbourhood cobbler and other poor workers when they saw these protests. Ironically, their children would innocently repeat the slogans of *'Mandal Hai, Hai, VP Hai, Hai* (Down with Mandal, down with VP)', oblivious to the fact that those reservations could benefit them the most in the future.

My daughter Aakshi was around four years old then, and reacted to the images of these protests with questions like, 'Why are these uncles and aunties so angry?' Even while the protests were on, there was construction work on a four-storey apartment block ongoing next door. Aakshi would watch the construction work with intense curiosity and ask me what they were doing. On being told that they were building houses, like ours, she assumed that those who were building them would also live in them. When I explained that wasn't the case, she was confused and could not understand why would anyone build a house in which they wouldn't live themselves. This innocent query, in the context of what was going on around us, raised a more fundamental question for me.

Suddenly, the image of my schoolmate Suraj's cold, piercing look while ignoring my presence on the streets of Yamunanagar acquired a new meaning for me. It hit me that let alone not having a single Dalit or even an OBC friend, I may not have even known one—apart from those who were performing the jobs which their castes 'ordained' them to do, such as the cobblers, scavengers and dhobis.

Whether or not reservations are the right way to correct the wrongs of history is a complex debate but the disdain that my own class had for those at the bottom rung of the hierarchy was evident in their method and manner of protests. The overriding reason for their protests was to protect their own and their children's interests, with a complete lack of compassion for lower castes. The words *'bhangi'* and *'chuhra'*, derogatory terms used for manual scavengers and sweepers, were used with venom for all those coming within the ambit of reservations.

Most newspaper editors slammed VP for his divisive politics, and some even went to the extent of naming the protests as India's second independence struggle. The unrepentant and unrelenting VP was cast as a villain. As a counter to this uprising, BJP leader L.K. Advani began a rath yatra from Somnath Temple in Gujarat to the Babri Mosque in Ayodhya. His yatra left behind a trail of communal riots, creating fresh wounds that worsened almost three decades later when, in 2020, the Supreme Court decided in favour of building a temple at the exact spot where the mosque had stood. To my Sikh friends, who took pride in the fact that Sikhism was founded as a counter to Brahminical caste tyranny, the anti-reservation agitation was one more example of how self-obsessed and selfish India's upper castes were.

The BJP withdrew its support to V.P. Singh's government and he was removed from office by a majority vote. Before the vote, he had made an impassioned speech in Parliament, where he had told the elected members that they were not just exercising their vote on his government but on the future of the country: was it to be divided on religious and caste lines or stay united as an inclusive, caring society? The lack of support for him despite the issues he raised that day reflected the cynical, opportunistic politics of those who claimed to swear by the Indian Constitution but on that day sided with the right.

V.P. Singh's short but tumultuous stint as India's PM may have been a terrible failure, yet it had changed the course and nature of Indian politics forever. However, the rise of the right that he had checkmated through his Mandal politics, became unstoppable in 2014 with the BJP, led by Narendra Modi, getting a strong majority of its own. I still remember what my senior colleague and friend A.V.S. Namboodiri had to say at the height of the anti-Mandal agitation: 'Brahmins will overcome even this threat to their dominance as historically they have had a way to emasculate all rebellion and make readjustments through subtle, clever means, where all protesting strands become part of the mainstream in the long run.'

Cricket in Times of Social Unrest

In this period, I covered mostly Ranji Trophy matches held in Punjab or Haryana and the odd international match that was held in that region. But change came when *The Indian Express* appointed a national sports editor for the first time. The soft-spoken and well-regarded Ramu Sharma was chosen for the role, and he immediately decided to create a pool of writers on various disciplines, choosing reporters from different editions. Reporters were no longer confined to a territory.

I was sent to Assam to cover India's inter-zonal competition, the Duleep Trophy. My first experience in a northeastern state was a memorable one. Besides Sachin Tendulkar, I also saw the young players Vinod Kambli and Sourav Ganguly exhibit their rich promise and talent in the match between the West Zone and East Zone teams. In Guwahati, I was struck by the complete absence of political discourse regarding the reservations issue that was still ravaging northern India. On the train to Guwahati from Delhi, I realized that the North-east region had a different set of problems. Similar to Kashmir, alienation from the rest of India was one of its main issues. Other problems included the fear of Muslims migrating in large numbers from Bangladesh and the differences between the natives and migrants from Bengal.

During the match, Kambli, the prodigy who along with his schoolmate and close friend Tendulkar, was once seen as the future of Indian cricket, played a scorching innings for West Zone. It was the first time I was seeing the left-hander bat, and his stupendous hitting left me almost speechless. Those who witnessed his innings that day in Guwahati were left in little doubt that Kambli was ready to explode on the world stage.

Unlike Tendulkar, Kambli came from a modest background, belonging to the lower caste community. Many believe this made him less acceptable in the Indian dressing room, which may have resulted in his not lasting long in the Indian team despite his tremendous ability. What did not help was his own behaviour, with many having problems with his poor discipline. Before his career could really take off, he was stigmatized for being too 'fun-loving' when a picture of him dancing with cheerleaders on the field during a rain-ruined 1992 World Cup match in New Zealand appeared in the media.

In the 1996 World Cup, where Kambli was a key member of the team, one of the officials associated with the team told me that he felt that the manager, Ajit Wadekar, needed to rein in Kambli and not encourage his 'spirited' habits. The angry young man of Indian cricket, if one could call him that, had a rollercoaster ride. The abiding image of Kambli in my mind is him crying inconsolably at the crease while the crowds in the stadium erupted against the Indian team during the 1996 World Cup semi-final against Sri Lanka at the Eden Gardens in Calcutta. He had once famously remarked that he had to take the stairs to the top whereas Tendulkar took the lift.

That day in Guwahati, another youngster also put his skills on show. The nineteen-year-old Sourav Ganguly played a thrilling innings for East Zone, hitting mammoth sixes that landed outside the ground. It was hard to choose which of the two played better. But there was an incident in the match that revealed that the youngster from Bengal had a short fuse and could express himself in other ways besides his batting.

In a rare occurrence on a cricket field, Ganguly was given out on a ball which bounced twice before hitting him on the pads. According to the laws of the game, if this happens, the umpire should call a no-ball. But that did not happen. In protest, Ganguly dragged his batting partner with him to the dressing room. The entire East Zone team shut shop and refused to participate further in the match. It would have resulted in a forfeit.

I had known Ashok Malhotra from his Chandigarh days, as we had been regular squash rivals on Chandigarh's Sector 7 courts. This gave me the confidence to barge into the East Zone dressing room without fear of being ejected. I remember seeing an adamant Ganguly sitting on the floor and Ashok, who was leading the East, trying to pacify him. This was my first close glimpse of the man with whom I would have many informal interactions over the course of my career. I was privy to many of his dilemmas and witness to his many great moments as he led the Indian team with distinction in the first decade of the twenty-first century. My first impression of him that day was that of a young man with tremendous self-belief and a short temper. I was told that he belonged to a rich family and that his father was a close associate of Jagmohan Dalmiya, the man who ruled Indian, and even world, cricket for considerable length of time. Ganguly finally relented that day after the umpire changed his decision, and the match resumed.

He was later picked for the Australian tour preceding the 1992 World Cup, where he had a forgettable One-Day international debut against the West Indies in a tri-series match. It is believed that the tour manager, Ranbir Singh Mahendra, the president of the Haryana Cricket Association, was already miffed with Jagmohan Dalmiya and resented the presence of Ganguly in the team.

Soon stories started appearing that Ganguly was a spoilt brat and had even refused to take drinks for the players in a match, feeling slighted at being treated like a servant. It is hard to believe that he would have belittled a long-standing cricketing tradition where the twelfth man takes drinks to the field for his teammates during breaks in the match. Ganguly's nickname at home was 'Maharaj', and it became a term of ridicule. His reputation was sullied even before his career had really started. Subsequently dropped from the team, Ganguly would have remained a footnote in the history of Indian cricket but for his surprise recall for the 1996 tour of England.

Even though the media unanimously condemned his selection for that tour, his elegant century in that Guwahati match still lingered in my mind and made me more charitable in my judgement. Though critical of his selection, I added the qualifier: '… though there is no doubt he has the talent to surprise all of us'.

From Guwahati we moved to Patna, the capital of Bihar and a hotbed of caste politics. In the backdrop of the new quota system, Lalu Prasad Yadav, who belonged to the most powerful of the OBC communities, had become the central figure in Bihar politics. He was marshalling resources to fight the midterm polls after the fall of V.P. Singh, the man he had sided with while ditching his own leader, Chandra Shekhar.

The discord and divisions were visible even on our train journey from Guwahati to Patna, where passengers talked of nothing but the vicious caste divide and how the new reservations policy would affect the election results. V.P. Singh was derided and ridiculed by most of the passengers, who evidently belonged to the upper classes. I still remember two elderly people discussing the rise of the lower classes, saying, 'Why blame others, when our own man has betrayed us?' They perhaps belonged to the Thakur caste like V.P. Singh and believed that they had been stabbed in the back by one who they had trusted as their own.

Patna, whatever I remember of it, was a bit of a shock, especially for someone from the sanitized environment of Chandigarh. I felt that life in Patna must be an ordeal, with its unruly traffic, terrible roads and crowds jostling for space in the heavily congested city. It was here, at the Moin-ul-Haq Stadium, that the Duleep Trophy semi-final between Central Zone and North Zone was to be played.

The match became a platform for another young lad to showcase his outstanding talent. It was Praveen Amre, a Maharashtrian representing Rajasthan in the Ranji Trophy, who scored a hundred that day against the North's famed pace attack led by Kapil Dev. Amre would go on to play for India and score an exceptional century in his debut Test in 1992, against South Africa in Durban. However, despite his talent and runs, Amre had a limited international career. He was always seen as someone lacking in Test match 'character' and 'class'.

Raj Singh Dungarpur, who was one of the most influential administrators in Indian cricket, had no qualms in declaring that 'Amre lacked the class to be part of the Indian team'. Amre's inclusion in the team had dislodged a player from the influential Bombay team, Sanjay Manjrekar, and this was perhaps not a popular decision. Amre was not bred in the city manners of the middle-class, unlike the majority of players in the team. It is hard to say what made him so unwelcome, though there were definite signs of his being discriminated against.

I remember that on the 1994 tour of New Zealand, where Kapil played his last Test, Amre approached me on the eve of a One-Day match. He claimed that he was being left out of the playing XI on the pretext that he was not well. 'I have been telling them I am fit to play,' he said, 'but they don't believe me.' This attempt to seek 'help' from a scribe, was a cry of desperation and reflected the frustration of a player who knew the threat to his career was serious. I had no means to check the authenticity of his claim, but this incident combined with other circumstantial evidence convinced me that Amre was being treated unfairly by the team selectors. There may not have been prejudice of caste here, but there certainly was one of 'class'.

Even as hatred grew in a society divided on caste and religious lines, the campaign for the 1991 Lok Sabha elections was in full steam. A fortnight after Haryana won its maiden Ranji Trophy in Bombay, Rajiv Gandhi was assassinated by a suicide bomber while campaigning in Sriperumbudur, Tamil Nadu.

One and a half years later on 6 December 1992, the eve of a Punjab–Haryana Ranji Trophy encounter in Jalandhar, I heard the news that the Babri Mosque had been demolished by the 'kar sewaks' in Ayodhya.

4
Money Games

As the 1980s came to an end, one of the brightest young talents in the history of the game emerged on the horizon.

It was a pleasant September day in Himachal in 1989 when I reached Una to cover the Deodhar Trophy match between West Zone and Central Zone. My colleague Vineet Joshi had accompanied me on the assignment. At the time, a sixteen-year-old was generating a lot of excitement among cricket fans.

On the eve of the match, as we were having chai at a roadside shop, I spotted the boy. His innocent face showed a child's curiosity as he sipped tea with his teammates. This was a face yet to become familiar to the Indian public, though his sensational batting skills had already received some coverage in newspapers. The boy was Sachin Tendulkar, and with his schoolmate Vinod Kambli, he had shared a record-breaking 600-run partnership in an inter-school match in Bombay.

I recall telling Vineet to record that moment carefully in his memory, as a time might come when we would be able to tell our grandchildren that we had seen Tendulkar as a kid, sipping tea at a roadside dhaba in a nondescript town in the interiors of Himachal! I do not remember any sportsperson in India who was already talked about as a great player before achieving any major success at the highest level. But it was taken for granted that this boy, overflowing with natural talent, had his destiny written in bold, golden letters. His far more accomplished teammates were already in awe of him.

Despite his age, Tendulkar had been in the running for the Indian team that had toured the West Indies at the beginning of the year. It was said that the then chairman of the selection committee, Raj Singh Dungarpur, did not want to expose the young player to the battery of fast bowlers in the Caribbean, as it might possibly leave psychological scars. In the match at Una, he scored a mere ten runs. However, Tendulkar could not be denied for long, and a month after that Deodhar Trophy match in Una, he was chosen for the Indian team to tour Pakistan. He made his debut in the Karachi Test on that tour.

Cricket Board vs Players

Even as Tendulkar was taking the first steps of his eventually glorious career, the future of Indian cricket was looking bleak. Days before the Una match, the BCCI was forced by the Supreme Court to lift a ban on six top Indian cricketers—Kapil, Vengsarkar, Shastri, Azharuddin, More and Arun Lal—for having played in an exhibition match in the USA without their permission. The ban had shocked the country and had pit the players against the Board in public. It was the culmination of a long-drawn battle in the years after the 1983 World Cup win, which had opened new avenues for the players to enhance their earnings.

The star status of top cricketers led to their being sought out by top business houses to endorse their products. From 1984 to 1989, there were many skirmishes between the players and the Board, the issues ranging from the use of logos on their clothing and bats, writing newspaper columns to their playing in privately sponsored exhibition matches. At the heart of the dispute was the money which the players were making independent of the Board and in the absence of any regulatory checks. This had resulted in the rising power of the players, who had formed their own association to negotiate better deals for themselves, and a miffed Board feared loss of control over the finances of the game. These money games had the potential to not just turn the Board against the players but also to cause heartburn among the players themselves, as those with greater star value would be paid considerably larger sums than their teammates.

I was not personally witness to any of these squabbles, but senior reporters would regularly file reports on how some of these money deals were vitiating the harmony of the cricket fraternity. It wouldn't be wrong to say that these money disputes and the defiance of the players played a significant role in the Board changing the captain three times in the two-year period from 1987 to 1989. Kapil, Vengsarkar and Srikkanth were the participants in this game of captaincy musical chairs. Soon, images of cricketers being presented huge cheques or luxury cars as prizes by sponsors at the end of tournaments were being beamed live into our bedrooms, and they became the symbols of a new emerging India where display of wealth was becoming the norm.

With cricket's commercial value enhanced, the players, led by Kapil and Gavaskar, were not willing to forgo what they believed was their just share. After India's disastrous tour of the West Indies in 1989, where Vengsarkar even accused some of his players of running shy of the West Indies pace attack, members of the Indian team defied the Board diktat and went to play in America in a privately sponsored series of 'masala matches', which were games organized by private entities between teams comprising the best Indian players. This led to six players being promptly banned by the Board for a year. The players challenged the decision in the Supreme Court, which made scathing observations in their hearings against the Board. Sensing the mood of the public and the court, the bans and fines imposed on the players were withdrawn by the Board.

Even before India won the 1983 World Cup, there were some companies that had recognized the commercial value of the game's popularity and had begun paying players to wear shirts displaying their logos. These were deals the Board was presumably not aware of. The sponsored shirts were first seen on the Indian team's tour of Pakistan in 1982. Some of the players who played in that series say they were promised Rs 25,000 each by a senior player who had negotiated the deal with the sponsors. This was a huge sum in those days, equivalent to the amount each player was paid by the Board for an entire series. However, the players never received the money promised by the sponsor.

After the World Cup win, the commercial value of Indian cricket and its star players greatly increased. The players would sign individual contracts with sponsors to display logos on their clothing and bats. There were no rules and regulations governing such deals at that time, and stories began floating around that players were getting greedy. There was jealousy and competition between players, each trying to get the best deal for himself. A situation of conflict and confrontation was emerging and the Board was forced to write player contracts that included clear rules regarding sponsorship.

The eighties saw the emergence of another avenue for players to make money—the so-called 'masala matches'. These matches would draw huge crowds in small cities across India. Bharat Reddy, who had played for India against England in the 1979 Test series, organized many such masala matches from 1985 to 1989. Reddy says that because of his good relationship with the players he could easily persuade them to play in these matches. According to him, many start-up businesses or those opening big showrooms in a city would come forward to sponsor these matches. The games would be played in towns and cities such as Durgapur, Varanasi, Ludhiana, and other smaller venues across India. They were televised live on the local DD channels wherever possible.

Star players such as Kapil, Gavaskar, Vengsarkar, Azharuddin and Shastri would be paid a fee ranging from Rs 30,000 to Rs 50,000 each, with the rest receiving between Rs 10,000 and Rs 15,000 per match. These amounts can be put in perspective when one learns that a player's fee for a Test match in that era was about Rs 3500 in 1984, rising to around Rs 7500 by 1989. Though media stories speculated that the lack of transparency and parity in the sharing of the money was causing differences among the players, I know that some of the lesser-known players were happy enough to get their ten to fifteen thousand rupees. They were not concerned with what the star players were receiving.

The issue of wearing logos came to a boil during the 1987 World Cup. At least seven of the senior players had sponsors who were willing to pay each of them around a lakh for wearing their logos during the tournament. The World Cup was sponsored by Reliance and its name was prominently on display on the shirts the players were going to wear. The players refused to sign a contract that barred them wearing any other logo, leading to a fresh row. The Board even threatened to field a second-string team if the players didn't relent, but eventually gave in themselves. Those senior players who had secured their own logo deal with a sponsor went ahead and displayed the logo on their shirts.

This incident was followed by the one in 1989 when some players decided to play masala matches in the USA and Canada on their way back from the West Indies tour, despite the Board having specifically given written instructions not to do so. Millions of cricket fans followed the ensuing drama with keen interest. Vengsarkar was promptly stripped of the captaincy, and Kris Srikkanth was appointed in the hope that he would be a captain who toed the Board's line. Though Srikkanth led the side admirably on India's tour to Pakistan in 1989, handling the off-field tensions of a difficult tour well, the Board decided he was not the right man as he was seen as being too close to Kapil and the other rebellious senior players.

The Board now wanted the players to sign fresh contracts, but the players felt they had clauses that restricted their earnings. The major bone of contention was the logo of the sponsor: the players could only wear a logo with the consent of the Board and the revenue from this would be shared. There were also other conditions that the players found stifling, and they refused to sign.

With Srikkanth being viewed as siding with the players and not the establishment, the Board, wary of player power and not wanting to give the captaincy to any senior player, made a very radical move, offering the captaincy to the shy, introverted Mohammad Azharuddin. The wristy, elegant Hyderabadi—who had made a stunning debut against England in 1984 by scoring centuries in his first three games—was viewed by the Board as less confrontational and perhaps more pliable, in spite of the fact that he was among the six who had recently been banned.

What an irony that a decade later Azharuddin's phenomenal career ended in shame and embarrassment, after he was found guilty of match-fixing and banned from playing cricket for life.

The Money-spinning Deserts of Sharjah

The last decade of the twentieth century started on a positive note for me, as I was assigned to cover a One-Day Australasia Cup at the neutral venue of Sharjah in 1990. Cricket had become a money-spinning exercise for Sheikh Abdul Rehman Bukhatir, a businessman from the oil-rich emirate. This was a venue that offered loads of money as rewards for cricketers, be it in fees, prizes or one-time purses for retired cricketers.

Players and officials from India and Pakistan had no compunction about participating in these matches, as the two bitter subcontinent foes were finding it difficult to play regularly in each other's territories due to deteriorating diplomatic relations. Sharjah filled this vacuum, enabling millions of people—possibly the largest fan base of any sport in the world—to watch the two arch-rivals compete with each other without fear of bitter political feuding playing spoilsport.

Live feeds of the matches were beamed by the state-owned Doordarshan in India. The war minus the shooting—as George Orwell famously described sporting contests—started playing out in the deserts of Sharjah, with thousands of Indian and Pakistani expatriates, most of them unskilled workers, screaming at each other in visceral hatred. Money was not a problem, nor was there any resistance from the two Boards, whose officials were invited to the venue and treated like royal guests. Dilip Doshi, the left-arm spinner, wrote in his book *Spin Punch*:[5] 'Organisers of such tournaments as the one in Gulf lay out fabulous hospitality with lavish gifts thrown in, and the elder statesmen of Indian cricket will do well to maintain a sense of proportion about what they accept and what they turn down.'

Bharat Reddy, the masala match organizer, was part of one of the teams that played the first Benefit Series matches in Sharjah, during which former Indian and Pakistani players were presented with a one-time reward for their contribution to cricket. The sum then was around $15,000 each, increasing to $50,000 by the time these matches were eventually stopped after the match-fixing scandal in 2000.

The first match in Sharjah was organized for the benefit of Madhav Mantri. Reddy remembers a pay dispute arising on the eve of the match. He does not remember the exact amount the players were promised. 'Probably around $700,' he recalls. The teams wanted to be given this amount a day before the match. Former Pakistani captain Asif Iqbal, who organized these matches for the Sheikh, agreed and the match went ahead on schedule the next day.

Among the many stand-out moments that have remained in the minds of people who watched the matches played at this offshore venue is the six hit by the mercurial Javed Miandad off the last ball of a game, which took Pakistan to an unlikely victory. Another is India's success in defending a measly total of 125. Both matches were played under the leadership of Kapil Dev.

However, before the cricket even started, a major controversy surfaced in 1982 when Dilip Vengsarkar, who had arrived to play in an exhibition series against a Pakistani side, was deported after landing at Dubai airport. What had disturbed the sporting fraternity more than the behaviour of the customs officials at the airport was the complete silence of the other Indian players, none of whom protested on behalf of their teammate. No one knows what exactly transpired that led to Vengsarkar's deportation via Cochin, but a blog written by Abhishek Mukherjee sheds some light.

Mukherjee states that a group of movie stars were on the same Gulf Air flight to Dubai as the cricketers. The actors were behind the cricketers in the immigration queue. Recognizing the actors, the immigration officers asked them to come to the front of the queue. If this upset the cricketers, most of them did not show it. But Dilip Vengsarkar, never the greatest of diplomats, passed a comment.

Mukherjee continues that it is not clear exactly what Vengsarkar had said, but surmises that it was probably a joke, with a touch of sarcasm. He quotes *Indian Cricket Controversies*, by K.R. Wadhwaney:

'He made an observation, which should have been laughed at.' But the officer was not amused, and he denied Vengsarkar admission to the UAE on the grounds that the latter 'had made a nasty remark in Marathi'.

Incidentally, Wadhwaney was the sports editor of *The Indian Express* in Delhi while I was in Chandigarh, and had written a lengthy piece about a bitter fight between Sunil Gavaskar and Kapil Dev over the distribution of money for an exhibition match that was played in Ranchi. The story had made it very clear that these masala matches were causing a deep divide among India's team members.

The Vengsarkar incident also exposes how the lure of money affected the behaviour of the rest of the team. The huge prizes for those games and the many expensive gifts that wealthy expatriates in the Gulf would shower on their 'idols' probably caused the players to remain silent and abandon their teammate rather than risk deportation and loss of earnings themselves.

Sharjah's other legacy is match-fixing. Though no one was ever caught in the act, many doubts were raised at some of the matches that produced unusual results. Lending substance to the suspicions was the presence of a large number of wheeler-dealers who had become patrons of cricket in the UAE.

Dawood Ibrahim was a regular visitor at Sharjah, even having a box reserved for him at the stadium. Before the 1993 bomb blasts in Bombay, Dawood was one of the many Indian 'businessmen' who had large investments in the Gulf, particularly in Dubai, and was considered a great patron of Indian films and cricket.

It's only now that I understand the hypocrisy of the BCCI, which fought over money with the players arguing that their greed led to unethical practices, but then let them play in Sharjah purely for earning more money. At that stage of my career and life, these issues of money and greed and the player–administrator confrontations were simply side stories to the main thrill of covering a cricket series outside India. I remember the opulence of that desert city, the lavish spreads of lunch and tea at the ground and the smug feeling that came from being a part of something so grand. I also remember being brought down to earth by a comment made in innocence and bewilderment by a Pakistani taxi driver.

The Sharjah press box had a limited number of fax machines and could not cope with the rush from journalists to send their reports after the match. A reporter from the *Deccan Herald* had discovered that it was easier to go to a state-owned telecom centre nearby and send the report from there. So each day after the match, we would take a taxi to that telecom centre. On one such occasion, as the taxi driver drove past the huge crowds leaving the stadium, he asked us what was going on. The man had recently arrived in Sharjah from a village in Pakistan, and couldn't understand why such a large number of people would be so enthusiastic about a cricket match, and pay money to watch it. It surprised him even more that we had come all the way from India to write on these matches. He was curious to know who had paid for our visit, and was stunned on being told that all our expenses were paid by our employers. He was struggling to make a living, and had left his family and home country to do so, and here were two young men being paid for something as trivial and meaningless as reporting on a cricket match! This was beyond his comprehension. All of a sudden, his bewilderment gave way to an uncontrolled burst of laughter as he uttered the words which are stuck in my memory: '*Achha ji, duniya mein aisa bhi hota hai* (Oh, so such things also happen in this world)!'

The cricket played at the Australasia Cup in Sharjah was not too exciting, though Waqar Younis, who had made his Test debut for Pakistan a few months earlier in the same match as Sachin Tendulkar, was displaying the skills that distinguish a rare talent from an average player. Batsmen had no answer for his searing pace and toe-crushing yorkers, and India was knocked out early. From a larger perspective, the significant event of that series was the debut of a bespectacled, tall engineering student from Bangalore, Anil Kumble. Bishan Singh Bedi, the manager, introduced the newcomer to journalists as someone who could develop into a useful all-rounder, especially in One-Day matches.

The shy youngster did not make much of an impression with his bowling, which was mainly fast leg spin, though the balls hardly turned. No one at the time could predict that this young man would end up with the most Test wickets taken by an Indian. That he defied all predictions and laboured his way up the cricketing ladder to reach the very top shows that determined effort and hard work are as essential as talent in the making of a great sportsperson.

What caught my imagination in Sharjah was not the cricket played but the rivalry and bitterness between the expats from India and Pakistan at the stadium. During a match between the two fierce rivals, the atmosphere at the ground was very tense. The two sets of loyal fans were at each other's throats, screaming and shouting with frightening passion and keeping the security personnel on their toes.

Even considering the soured relationship between the two nations, it was still shocking to see the fans behave in a such a crude manner, waving their respective flags in the air like rifles. Even children took part in this vicious behaviour. This was not a crowd enjoying their cricket or appreciating a good performance. On my extensive cricket reporting from various parts of the world, including Pakistan, I have never seen a crowd as hateful as the one in Sharjah in 1990. Sharjah may have been a great venue for players and officials given the financial benefits, but it was an unmitigated disaster when it came to building bridges between the two nations.

Why was the Sharjah crowd so hostile? After interacting with people of Indian origin in England, Australia, South Africa and the West Indies, I understood that many immigrants feel nostalgic about their roots mixed with a sense of guilt at having abandoned their homeland. That makes them express ultra-nationalistic feelings when a sports team from their country of origin comes visiting their adopted country. They somehow feel the need to be more voluble in their support for them. So the expat Indians come to the ground with Indian flags even if they are no longer Indian nationals, taunt the home team of their new country and make no bones about where their loyalties lie. And when it is an India–Pakistan match, expats from both countries prepare days in advance, as if they are getting ready to fight a bloody war.

I have often asked these great 'patriots' whether they are not being disloyal to the country of which they are citizens when they support India. They have many arguments to justify themselves, the main being that this is only a sporting contest and not a war. This longing for home makes many Indian-origin families cling strongly to symbols from their cultural past, fearing their children may lose their way in the country of their adoption with different set of values from what they believed in. During my visit to Australia, I stayed with an Indian couple who had two small children. At their home a recording of the Hindi film *Hum Saath-Saath Hain* would be constantly playing on the television. Many in India had found this hit movie too steeped in the outdated morality of the past, using religious symbols to buttress its point, but in faraway Australia, an Indian immigrant family was using the film to make their children aware of 'Indian culture'.

In Guyana in 1997, I had another such encounter with a family whose forefathers had migrated from India to the West Indies as indentured labourers in the nineteenth century. My host had invited me to his home for dinner. After our meal, he put on a Lata Mangeshkar tape. As Lata's mellifluous voice swept through the room, a powerful sense of loss hung heavy in the air. This emotion overwhelmed my host so much that tears flowed down his cheeks. Till then my interaction with him had been in English, so I said, 'I didn't know you understood Hindi.' He replied, 'I don't.' Watching the couple deeply immersed in Lata's singing in a language they did not comprehend, yet somehow related to as a cultural link to their roots, I understood how lonely people can feel without holding on to something they can call their own.

In Sharjah, I had no such opportunity to interact with Indians or Pakistanis who were part of the crowd. In the UAE, getting citizenship is not an option for most of the Indian and Pakistani diaspora. The majority lived there on work visas, without their families. It was a regimented life in a foreign country, where the laws of the land are strictly implemented and even a minor offence can lead to deportation. In this stifling atmosphere, an India–Pakistan cricket match can become a perfect opportunity to let off one's frustrations through aggressive behaviour towards a perceived enemy. This high decibel expression of hatred could have culminated in physical violence, but in Sharjah the fear of deportation ensured no riots took place at the stadium.

The players were not immune to this pressure. At that time India did not have a team that could match the formidable Pakistan team, and with each defeat in Sharjah, the chorus against the Indian team would grow. Friday is a holiday in Muslim countries, and matches were usually scheduled for that day. Many Indians believed that Pakistan played with greater verve and motivation on Fridays, so there was a demand from many, including a few players, that India should not agree to play Pakistan on a Friday.

If this argument appears outlandish, it gets better: 'The Pakistani players' strong motivation comes from having one national religion that unites them. It is time for India to do the same, if they want to beat them on a cricket field.' This view, from an Indian player of the time, echoes a right-wing sentiment that has now gained official currency.

Movie stars from both India and Pakistan were regular visitors to the Sharjah matches during the eighties and nineties. And there was one man whose popularity in Sharjah rivalled that of the actors and even the players themselves. This was Henry Blofeld, the British television commentator. His celebrity status did not stem from his nuanced cricket commentary on television but his vivid descriptions of the outfits worn by the stars watching the match. Such was Blofeld's popularity that celebrities in VIP boxes were pleased to be spotted and described by him.

Were the matches in Sharjah fixed? This question was to surface later, though at that time no one in officialdom cared what was happening off the field as long as the organizers remained good hosts. It was only when the Justice Qayyum report on match-fixing in Pakistan cricket was released in 2000 that Sharjah was identified as one of the places where matches were fixed. Salim Malik, who was given a life ban from cricket for his role in the affair, was quoted in the report saying that betting in cricket and possibly even match-fixing was rife in Sharjah in the nineties. Aamer Sohail had also reported this, though nothing has been proved so far. Kapil Dev has gone on record to say that he threw Dawood Ibrahim out of the Indian dressing room when he came in to offer huge gifts to the players if they won their matches against Australia and Pakistan.

However, it must be said that no one offers money or gifts to a team or players for winning, as no one can guarantee a positive result. It is underperformance that a player can ensure, and when I was in Sharjah, stories of players being given major gifts by businessmen were rife. Were they linked to fixing? That is a big question, which has not been convincingly answered, though doubts persist. This was all the more so after the fixing scandal in 2000 led to life bans from any form of cricket for Mohammed Azharuddin and South

African captain Hansie Cronje. Many began to feel that Sharjah was a venue that was permanently scarring the integrity of the sport.

Encounters with Bedi

Sharjah also introduced me to one of the most fascinating characters of Indian cricket, Bishan Singh Bedi. He had been given the dual role of manager and coach to assist the new captain, Azharuddin. It was an unlikely combination, as Bedi was a man of strong opinions and not one to mince words, whereas Azharuddin was quiet and reserved. Most understood that the Board had appointed a proxy captain and it would be Bedi who actually ran the team. This theory gained credence when Bedi was appointed manager for three successive series, in New Zealand, Sharjah and England.

Bedi, whose training methods could be somewhat unconventional, was a strict disciplinarian who valued the traditions of the game. He put the team through a much-needed fitness drill that most found difficult to complete. Soon, there were grumblings from the players, who began to convey their displeasure to the media.

Bedi's working relationship with the captain was bound to be problematic. The differences had cropped up in Azharuddin's first assignment in New Zealand, where the team had put up a poor performance. Bedi had been quoted as saying that the team should be 'thrown into the Pacific'. He later clarified that all he had said was, 'If somebody wants to commit suicide by jumping into the sea, I won't stop him.' Later, on the tour of England, Bedi publicly criticized Azharuddin's decision to put England in to bat after winning the toss. Bedi declared that his captain lacked the courage to bat first even as Graham Gooch scored over 300 runs off his own bat.

I had heard a lot of stories about Bedi and his courageous fights with the powerbrokers of the game, especially his battle with R.P.

Mehra, who was the honcho of the Delhi cricket administration in the eighties. Bedi had changed teams from Punjab to Delhi and had been appointed captain of his new side, leading them to many famous victories. In the latter part of his career he launched a players' rebellion against Mehra and succeeded in ousting him. This kind of stand against the autocratic functioning of officials by an active player was unheard of in Indian cricket.

I got to know Bedi better a year after his stint with the Indian team, when he was appointed manager of the Punjab team. Bedi was given unbridled powers to run the team with the assurance of no interference from the administrators. To Bedi's tremendous credit, he transformed the fortunes of the team within a year and Punjab won their first-ever Ranji Trophy in 1993.

During the course of that Ranji campaign I spent a lot of time with Bedi in cities like Amritsar, Ludhiana, Jalandhar and Patiala when they would host Punjab's matches. Bedi's appointment meant trouble for those who used team selections as a vehicle to promote their own interests, leading to resentment within the association. He was termed an 'outsider' by his detractors as he lived in Delhi. He would only join the team for preparatory camps and for matches.

I remember doing a critical story on him in which I wrote that Bedi needed to be present in Punjab to see its cricket structure firsthand if he was to understand what was needed for improvements. I also hinted that some wrong selections were made because Bedi was misled by Punjab officials. The morning my story appeared, Bedi barged into my room, turned his backside towards me, bent over and in a tone more sarcastic than bitter, said in the crudest of Punjabi: '*Maar lo, jinney marney hai maar lo*' which roughly translates to 'Hit me as much as you want'. This was his characteristic manner of expressing hurt at being unfairly targeted.

Over the years I have got to know Bedi well and I have seen him at his best and, I daresay, at his worst. I have little hesitation in saying that Indian cricket has never seen, and will probably never see, a more large-hearted, well-meaning and honest person. Yet, his strong opinions that many a time cross the line of social niceties continue to be unfairly interpreted as the rants of a jealous man. He can lash out at his critics, especially if he believes a wrong has been done. Everyone feared his temper and tongue, and players who benefited from his support have often distanced themselves from him later, fearing retaliation from the establishment.

Bedi's commitment to what he believes is the right cause is unrelenting and is not driven by personal aggrandizement, though you could at times question his judgement of people. He can also be obdurate and a difficult person to negotiate with.

A player Bedi had immense respect for was Tiger Pataudi, as he believes it was under Pataudi's leadership that India for the first time became a united team, and regional, parochial divisions were not allowed to surface. He never hid his dislike for the Bombay players, who he believes were the most parochial and selfish of all. I interviewed him for television in 1997, and in that interview he is on record saying, 'The Maharashtra players are the most parochial and Ajit Wadekar, who replaced Pataudi as the captain of the team for the 1971 West Indies tour, did the most harm to the team spirit that had been built by Tiger with so much effort, understanding and care.'

He had a special love–hate relationship with Sunil Gavaskar. It was obvious that the two shared terrible vibes, especially at the twilight of Bedi's career; the master spinner felt he could have played a little longer had Gavaskar treated him fairly on the field and accused him of playing favourites when he was captain. Despite airing his views against Gavaskar in the press and in public, the few times I saw the two at the same gathering, they made every effort not to come face to face with each other.

However, Bedi named his first son Gavasinder, after Gavaskar. Bedi's admiration of Gavaskar's batting skills remained undiminished, despite his personal dislike for the man. On a visit to his hometown, Amritsar, Bedi took me to his ancestral house. In one of the rooms newspaper cuttings of his exploits were framed on the wall. One of them had a picture of his first wife, an Australian, and Gavasinder. The picture brought tears to Bedi's eyes in a rare show of emotion and vulnerability.

Though himself never the fittest of athletes, Bedi demanded utmost discipline and hard work from those he trained. A very strict disciplinarian, his training mantra was practice and more practice. He never tires of narrating his favourite sporting anecdote. Golf legend Gary Player once sank a putt from a very difficult angle. Someone from the crowd remarked, 'What a fluke!' Gary immediately retorted, 'Yes, the more I practice the more such flukes I hit.'

The Punjab players were in awe of him and responded well to his demands. The rigorous training schedule and the increasingly fit players had resulted in exceptional athleticism on the field, one of the key factors in their Ranji triumph. I think the Punjab team was among the best fielding sides I have ever seen in my decades of covering cricket. Vikram Rathour, who later went on to play for India and is at present the Indian team's batting coach, was particularly brilliant in the slips.

Bedi laid extra emphasis on fair play and respect for the umpire. He would accept the umpire's decision, even if it was a terrible one and went against his team. He would admonish and punish his players if they showed dissent on the field against an umpiring decision, though at the end of the match, and in private, he would let the umpires know what he thought of those mistakes.

Ironically, Punjab's Ranji title led to a deep divide between Bedi and the administrators. Bedi didn't give a damn about the officials and did what he thought was in the best interest of the team, and this attitude had made him enemies. I am not privy to what actually transpired that eventually led to Bedi's ouster. However, I do know that Bedi's questioning of some of the financial dealings and expenditure of the officials made everyone in the Punjab Cricket Association uncomfortable.

I recall meeting him at a match during this period and escorting him to the lunch table at the Mohali cricket ground's magnificently built facility. His knees were wobbly due to overuse and he would be often seen walking with weights tied around his ankles on medical advice. His walk was a bit more unsteady that day, his low spirits contributing to his faltering more than normal. He was angry at the manner in which he was being treated by the Punjab Cricket Association. No official wanted to be seen with him.

We both had lunch in the presence of a large gathering who did not acknowledge his presence. Bedi was largely responsible for Punjab's first major domestic triumph and without doubt its greatest player ever, but was now reduced to a lonely figure shunned by all. Not that he cared. From his point of view, he had done no wrong and the wily, foxy administrators needed to be shown the mirror. He was willing to pay the price.

I had by then spent almost fifteen years in journalism and my career graph was heading nowhere. I had a set routine of late nights at the Press Club and mornings spent playing squash and tennis. I was completely bored with the repetitiveness of my daily life while waiting and hoping to get an important assignment to cover.

I felt trapped, and this had a strange impact on my psyche. One day I had gone to meet a friend and when I came out of his house, I suddenly felt unable to identify my surroundings. It was a feeling very similar to when you wake up after a deep sleep and look around trying to figure out where you are and what time of the day it is. Except that I was wide awake, standing in the sun and still wondering where I was.

The offer of a transfer to Delhi with *The Indian Express*, with a promise of heading the sports department, could not have come soon enough for my well-being. I clutched on to it as if I was being rescued from drowning without a trace.

5

Capital Times

It was 1993 when I received a call from Suresh Menon, the national sports editor of *The Indian Express*. A friend more than a boss, Suresh and I had started our careers almost at the same time. He was among the best cricket writers in the country, but had decided to move to Dubai. He told me he had recommended my name to the editor, Prabhu Chawla, as his possible replacement.

About the same time, the Hero Cup was being organized by the Cricket Association of Bengal to commemorate its diamond jubilee. Five teams were to participate—India, South Africa, the West Indies, Zimbabwe and Sri Lanka. For the first time in the country, a private channel, Star, had been given the right to beam the matches live. It ended the monopoly of the state-owned DD, which until then had, as a matter of right, broadcast all live matches held in India.

DD had challenged the decision on the grounds that it was against the Indian Telegraph Act 1885, which stipulates that the up-linking of an event can't take place outside India. Star was doing it from Hong Kong. DD's refusal to relinquish its monopoly over cricket coverage was also casting a shadow over India's hosting of the 1996 World Cup. The courts gave interim relief to the BCCI, allowing Star to go ahead with the telecast of the Hero Cup. Finally, in a landmark judgment two years later, the Supreme Court declared that broadcasting rights can't be treated as public property. It was this judgement that turned the fortunes of Indian cricket, slowly but surely making the Indian Board among the richest sports bodies in the world.

This was also a period when India shed its pretence of being a socialist country, and opened its doors to foreign investment. The national elections had once again resulted in a hung Parliament, with Congress emerging as the single largest party. P.V. Narasimha Rao, a Congress veteran from the Telangana region, was sworn in as Prime Minister with the support of the left. During his five-year tenure, unprecedented economic reforms benefited the cricket fraternity immensely.

Until its monopoly was broken, DD not only paid nothing for the broadcast rights but also charged the BCCI for the broadcasts. The host associations could make money only through ticket sales and advertisement boards inside the stadium. For hosting an international match, a host association had to pay guarantee money to the BCCI, which by 1990 had gone up to Rs 20 lakh from around Rs 2 lakh in the early eighties.

The sale of broadcasting rights transformed the face of the Indian Board's finances and from 1994 onwards money started pouring in. In 2000, DD paid the BCCI around Rs 240 crore for a four-year period. Almost decades later, Star Sports signed a Rs 6138 crore deal for broadcasting all international cricket for a five-year period. This money is shared in the ratio of 70–30 between the state associations and the Board. Add to this the whopping Rs 16,347.5 crore deal Star signed with the Board for the broadcasting rights of the IPL in 2017 for five years. On an average, a state unit now gets around Rs 25 to 30 crore as yearly subsidy from the Board. The revenues generated from IPL are divided 60–40 between the team owners and the Board. Of the 30 per cent the Board keeps from international cricket's broadcasting rights, 26 per cent is spent on paying the players, both international and domestic. This explains the reason behind the Board's bulging coffers and the huge jump in the earnings of the players, through match fees, yearly contracts and team sponsorship. Personal endorsements of the players are separate.

In that first-ever privately broadcasted tournament, the Hero Cup, India won a lop-sided final against the West Indies. It was the match in which Kumble showed how lethal his accuracy and variations could be, by taking 6 wickets for 12 runs. I remember interviewing Kumble a few days after the match and being struck by his articulation and fluent language.

Kumble told me that he had started out as a fast bowler because of his height and build. Unfortunately, he discovered that he had a faulty action and was chucking the ball. At that moment of crisis, he was advised to try bowling leg-spin. The rest is history.

Detour to New Zealand

Professionally there was disappointment in store for me, as the potential appointment to the position of national sports editor never materialized. Around February 1994, my friend Harvinder Ahuja, who had started his career in Chandigarh with me and was now a news editor with the Delhi *Indian Express*, called to ask if I would be interested in heading the Delhi sports desk. By then the paper had appointed Ashok Kamath as national sports editor. I was told I could join the Delhi office after covering India's short tour of New Zealand that was to begin in a month's time.

To an Indian, the first sight of New Zealand can be a shock. You see more sheep on its undulating fields than people around, something that can be unnerving for those used to jostling for space in the overcrowded cities of their own country. India's tour comprised one Test and four One-Day internationals. It was on this tour that Sachin Tendulkar was tried as an opener for the first time, the position that speeded up his march in becoming one of the best One-Day batsmen ever. The Test match was to be Kapil's last, though we did not know it then.

There was no hint till the morning of the One-Day match at Auckland that Tendulkar would be opening. On hearing that regular opener Navjot Sidhu had woken up with a sprained neck and wouldn't be playing, Tendulkar requested the manager, Wadekar, to let him open. His wish was granted and he went on to play an innings of brutal aggression that a capacity crowd rose as one to cheer. He finished with 82 runs off 49 balls.

In the post-match press conference, Tendulkar was asked whether he regretted playing a wild heave and getting bowled when he was nearing his first One-Day century. Tendulkar's answer showed no trace of regret but only his immense self-belief. He said, 'Had I connected with that ball, it would have gone for a six and you would not have been asking this question.' He almost appeared to be chiding the reporter, saying, 'Come on man, be happy with how I played instead of finding faults.' Sachin may have been shy and reserved but right from his younger days, he would never take it lying down if anyone picked faults in his batting.

The only Test match of that tour was played at a very windy, chilly Hamilton, another picturesque venue. That this turned out to be the last time Kapil Dev played a Test for India was not by design. By then, Kapil had become the world's highest wicket-taker. However, there was little doubt that he was no longer the bowler he once was, not only having lost a yard or two in pace but also his penetration and swing. It was widely reported that captain Azharuddin was not too happy with Kapil's unwillingness to retire from cricket. Richard Hadlee, whose world record for Test wickets had been broken by Kapil, had already called it quits. Even the New Zealand newspapers were wondering why Kapil was still playing.

It was apparent that his shoulder was troubling him. In one of the practice sessions, he asked me to touch his shoulder, indicating that it was swollen. A young bowler named Venkatesh Prasad had joined the team for the One-Day matches, and was bowling at the nets at that moment. Kapil expressed his joy at seeing a new talented face. I wrote an article the next day that included his quote about how good it was to see new faces, and ended it with the conclusion that it was high time Kapil realized that he himself needed to make way for a fresh face.

Another memory of that tour is of the heated monologue aimed at Gavaskar that was delivered by the late journalist Rajan Bala. It was Wadekar's birthday and he had invited us to his hotel room. Bala was one of the best-known names in cricket journalism at the time. I had once seen him give Tendulkar advice on batting technique during a Test match and even here on the eve of the Hamilton Test he was seen giving tips to Nayan Mongia on how to improve his wicketkeeping. He couldn't care less about what the players thought of his suggestions, so confident and consumed was he in his own knowledge of the game.

When sober, he was generally a soft-spoken man even if provoked, but a few drinks down, he would transform into a boisterous, aggressive talker. A fine singer, mimic and storyteller, with loads of cricketing anecdotes to narrate, his voice would drown out all others in an evening gathering. If provoked he could be very acerbic, even if he happened to be talking to a player of great stature. That night at Wadekar's celebration he targeted Gavaskar, accusing him of being selfish. This embarrassed Wadekar and the rest of us present in the room. I admired the remarkable patience Gavaskar demonstrated, even though the provocation was strong. Later, I escorted Gavaskar to the hotel lobby when he left, feeling apologetic for having been a silent spectator, just like the others, to Rajan's haranguing.

This incident stayed with me for long, not because of what was said or not said, but purely as an example of how a journalist–player relationship gone sour has the potential to not only create unpleasantness but more disturbingly also to affect one's objectivity in reporting and writing.

On that New Zealand tour I struggled to find stories that would satisfy the demands of my office. The new editor would berate me almost every evening for my inability to file something more than just a cricketing report. 'Barge into the dressing room and find something extra, I don't care how you do it,' he would yell over the phone. I began living in dread of the phone ringing in my hotel room, a dread that reappeared on many future tours.

On that tour I understood how mutually beneficial the relationship between the Indian diaspora and the Indian players and journalists was. Indians settled abroad would invite the team home for dinner during tours, and also bring food to the ground for not just the players but us journalists as well. We called these hospitable folk 'Mamu' (a term used for one's mother's brother) and we would look for them on every tour. Over the years, players and journalists have forged lifelong ties with local Indian communities in almost all the cricket-playing nations. The Mamus went out of their way to make the guests from back home comfortable, treating them to lavish home-cooked meals and even inviting journalists to stay with them.

The benefit Mamus would get from showering kindness on journalists was introductions to their favourite players. But to reduce this relationship to just that would be grossly unfair to the overseas Indian community which over the years has grown in numbers and influence. Wherever the Indian team goes now almost becomes their second home, given the large number of compatriots that fill the stadiums whenever a match is on.

Delhi Days

Back home, things did not pan out for me as planned. Instead of being put in charge of the Delhi department, I was told that I would have to prove myself before I got a major assignment. I had uprooted myself from the mechanical routine and comforts of Chandigarh, a place where I had lived and worked for almost seventeen years, and Delhi appeared cold, aloof and unforgiving to an outsider.

I was mostly given local assignments to cover, such as a basketball league organized by Delhi University or some other minor event that would usually get no more than a brief mention in the paper. Most of my time was spent at the desk, editing copy and making pages. I decided to look for a new job and began desperately trying to contact people to find suitable openings.

It was towards the end of 1994, and the West Indies team was scheduled to tour India. It was a team on the decline, a far cry from the invincible outfits led by Clive Lloyd and Viv Richards. Brian Lara had made a huge impact as a batsman after his debut in 1990, but was going through a lean patch. He had decided to join his team in India a few days late. There were many stories floating around that were critical of his attitude, and he was being painted as an arrogant man who cared more about his earnings than about playing for his country.

I was assigned to cover his arrival at Delhi airport and get a few quotes from him. The waiting lounge was teeming with print and television journalists. Lara arrived and all of us rushed towards him. Sunglasses on, he betrayed no emotion and was obviously in no mood to oblige the waiting press. However, I knew the BCCI's travel agent, Ajay Duggal, who was present at the airport to receive him. Understanding my desperation to talk to Lara, he arranged for me to sit on the front seat of the car that was to take Lara to his hotel. He said it was up to me to make Lara talk. I took my seat, waiting for Lara to get in.

A few minutes later, Lara was escorted to the car, the press and television cameras still chasing him. He slumped on to the backseat as soon as he got in. When he took off his sunglasses, I saw his face had turned pale and he was breathing so heavily that I thought he was having a heart attack. He was no longer the man who had appeared cool and indifferent to his surroundings a few moments before. In panic, I asked him, 'What's wrong?' He only said, 'Pressure, man, pressure.'

Unfortunately for me, I could not speak with him any further as his golf kit had to be placed on the front seat I was occupying. But I had landed this interesting story, and it went on the front page of the paper. I finally had something different from the small-time stories I was getting sick of.

My ego and self-esteem took another blow while reporting on the One-Day international between the West Indies and India played in Faridabad. That day, Kapil bowled what must have been one of his most embarrassing spells ever. It was apparent that he was unfit; he could not complete his full quota of 10 overs. The West Indies batsmen thrashed him. His figures in that match were 5–0–37–0. He never played international cricket again.

My report was so scathing in its criticism of Kapil that I was accused by my bosses of having an agenda against the player. I had focused more on Kapil and directly commented that it was time for him to retire instead of embarrassing himself and marring his great legacy by extending his career. I believed I was right but the bosses in the office did not agree. Among the confusing signals which we reporters used to get from above, one was that since people watched the match on television, we need not describe the details but should enhance the watching experience by discussing the talking point of the day at length. That day I had picked the Kapil issue, even though he was one of the greatest Indian cricketers ever and also a person I knew personally.

The next day Kapil announced his withdrawal from the remaining matches, and a few days later retired from the game. An outstanding career had come to a rather tame and unplanned end. Kapil, like many Indian cricketers past and present, had succumbed to the temptation of prolonging his stay in the team, despite body signals to the contrary, and had to finally go without being mentally ready for it.

Despite being vindicated, I still suffered from the criticism of my match report. It only increased my conviction that professionally I was going nowhere. The boredom and despair that I thought I had escaped from had followed me here. Like in Chandigarh, Delhi's Press Club became the place to look forward to every night after office hours.

In my quest for a new job, I sought the help of my friend Shekhar Gupta, who was at that time a senior editor with *India Today*. He told me to stay put for a little while more. I took his advice. A few months later, much to my surprise, Shekhar took over as the editor of *The Indian Express*, replacing Prabhu Chawla. It was the most welcome news I had heard in years.

In the newsroom, the moment it is known that a new boss is on the way, uncertainty pervades the atmosphere. Friends and foes change their attitude to each other and become more careful and cautious in their stated positions. The favourite of the previous editor could now be removed from the plum assignments and someone languishing in oblivion could be back in favour. My own experience, backed by almost four decades of working in various organizations, has been that even if a journalist produces outstanding work, they also need to be on the right side of the boss to keep getting opportunities to showcase their worth. Such are the insecurities and personal ambitions of the bosses that 'loyalty' in one's subordinates at times becomes more important than talent.

Shekhar's joining the paper coincided with the 1996 Cricket World Cup. The tournament was going to be held in India, Pakistan and Sri Lanka, and the accreditation forms for the journalists covering the event had to be filled in even before Shekhar took over. To my utter surprise, I was told that I would be following the Indian team during its campaign. In the past two years, I had been assigned just two international matches; now, all of a sudden, I was being asked to cover the most important matches an Indian journalist could aspire for.

Shekhar told me that he had done nothing to push my case except to instruct the sports editor to send his best cricket writer to cover the Indian games.

World Cup and a New World Order

The 1996 World Cup was a reflection of the shifts in power in world cricket. The opening up of the economy and the advent of satellite TV had launched a money-spinning revolution in Indian cricket. India was now in a position to assert itself in the cricket hierarchy that had till then been controlled by the England–Australia nexus, disturbing the traditional balance.

At this crucial moment of transition, Indian cricket was being directed by two contrasting figures. One was Jagmohan Dalmiya, the wily Marwari businessman from Calcutta who understood the power of money. He was adept at complex negotiations. The other was his trusted lieutenant, Inderjit Singh Bindra, the urbane Sikh from Punjab who was fluent in the English language. He knew how to get the influential sections of the international media on his side, and became the public face of the new, powerful Indian cricket.

India, Pakistan and Sri Lanka had promised to pay the World Cup associate members 100,000 pounds each, compared to England's offer of 60,000 pounds. This played a decisive role in the World Cup being awarded to the subcontinent despite scepticism over the organizational abilities of these three countries.

This new-found power of cricket to fetch profits for those associated with it was visible everywhere, most evidently in the media. I remember that Shekhar, who had by then taken on his new responsibilities, was keen to use this opportunity to help the paper with its revenues. He used his experience with the more professionally managed *India Today*, which even today remains the country's best-selling weekly, to come up with new ideas. One of them was to have some leading former cricketers to write opinion pieces on crucial issues and matches during the event.

In that era, it was still not common to see players airing their views in the media. There were a few management companies that had signed players to write exclusively for them, and who in turn would sell these columns to the highest bidder in the newspaper industry. Sometimes they would get a corporate house to sponsor the article. The newspaper would create an advertisement space within the article and sell it, or the player or the agency would sell the article with a pre-sold advertisement (called the 'logo') to the paper. The arrangement worked for everyone. The player would get his fees, the paper would make money from selling the logo space, and the agency would take their cut.

This practice is widespread now, though most of these articles are ghostwritten as the players themselves usually don't have the time or the language skills to write their own articles. While there are a few who do it for the sake of expressing their strong opinions, there are also those whose motive is purely commercial.

Back in 1996, Shekhar was convinced that columns written by legends of the game would make our World Cup coverage more interesting for readers while also making a bit of money for the paper. We approached Kapil to write for us and were shocked to learn that his writing fee per column was around Rs 70,000. He made it clear that he did not write very often and the World Cup was one such rare occasion when he thought he should share his cricketing acumen and knowledge with his fans. He had deliberately kept his writing fee very high as quality and not quantity was more important for him.

Not wishing to lose this opportunity, our marketing department started hunting for potential advertisers who would want to sponsor Kapil's column. But it was difficult to find someone willing to pay that kind of money. Kapil, sensing our difficulty, made us a business offer. He was willing to find a sponsor on his own, even to sell an entire page for the paper with a revenue-sharing model that would benefit us both. He did succeed in finding a potential sponsor who was willing to buy an entire page that had World Cup stories, provided the company was prominently advertised on the page. The company was willing to pay a huge amount.

The deal fell through—not because of any differences about money but for 'ethical' reasons. The company sold gutkha and paan masala, and Shekhar did not think it appropriate to associate the paper's World Cup pages with tobacco products. Those who followed the 1996 World Cup would perhaps remember that Kapil and the paan masala company did eventually do a campaign called '*Sabse bada khiladi* (the greatest player)'. It was an interactive campaign in which viewers could participate by predicting the best player for each match. This incident taught me how big business deals are involved behind what I thought was a simple matter of a player airing his views.

Kapil, probably happy with his deal with the other company, finally did write for us for a much lower fee. In one of the first pieces he wrote, he created a sensation by revealing that Ajit Wadekar had prevented Kapil's mother from visiting him in his hotel. Kapil was making a case for allowing family members and wives of the players to meet them during tours, and cited this example as a very humiliating experience for him. There was a rule against players having women in their rooms, and in Kapil's case, even his mother was not given permission to meet him.

The 1996 World Cup was my first major cricketing assignment. I travelled from Cuttack to Kanpur, Delhi, Bhopal, Mumbai Bangalore, and finally to Calcutta, while reporting on India's progress. I remember clearly the sea of humanity jostling inside and outside each of the venues to catch a glimpse of their stars. The chaos at Cuttack's Barabati Stadium could not match the unruly scenes in Bhopal's Roop Singh Stadium, where to my horror and shock I heard people in the crowd calling the West Indians 'bhoot' (ghosts), presumably because of the dark colour of their skin.

In Kanpur, we visited the home of the paan masala merchant whose brand was now one of the major World Cup advertisers. During that dinner I heard whispers about Vinod Kambli having a drinking problem. Not among the most popular players in the Indian team, it was becoming obvious that he was seen as a problem child who needed to be disciplined. One of the officials associated with the Indian team was a bit upset that Kambli, instead of being restrained, was being almost encouraged by the manager to stick to his habits. 'They both love their evening drinks and this is not helping the player,' he muttered. 'This needs to be corrected.'

India's encounter with Australia at Mumbai's Wankhede was perhaps a great example of two batting superstars showcasing their skills. For Australia it was the graceful elegance of Mark Waugh, whose wristy caressing of the ball on the way to his hundred was very much like the Indian tradition of batting; for India it was the power displayed by Sachin Tendulkar's shots, closer to the Australian approach to batting. Though Tendulkar fell short of a century, his tremendous assault on the Australian bowling led by Glenn McGrath, secured a narrow win for India.

It was all heady stuff and India was on a roll, and next was the quarter-final, in which they were to meet Pakistan in Bangalore. A sea of saffron, white and green covered the Chinnaswamy Stadium. People had been lining up in thousands well before dawn. Just before the match was to start, it was announced that Wasim Akram had withdrawn from the match because of a stiff back. The large Pakistani press contingent was in shock.

Even today, over two decades later, questions are asked about the real reason for the last-minute withdrawal of Pakistan's captain. Was it simply an injury or something more suspicious? Akram's detractors claim he was not above board, as Justice Malik Mohammad Qayyum's report on match-fixing in Pakistan cricket had raised doubts over Akram's integrity. In his report, which came four years after that match at Bangalore, Qayyum stated: 'It is only by giving Wasim Akram the benefit of the doubt after Ata-ur-Rehman changed his testimony in suspicious circumstances that he has not been found guilty of match-fixing. He cannot be said to be above suspicion.'

In an interview to ESPN Cricinfo five years after the report was made public, the judge said, 'I had a soft spot for Wasim. He was a very great player, and I was his fan, and therefore that did weigh on me. I didn't want that cricket should be deprived of his participation, and I also didn't want that towards the end of his career he should be banned. My mission was not to find people guilty and then punish them. It was that I had to do something to put an end to the practice in future. What had happened had happened. You couldn't turn the clock back but you had to make sure they wouldn't repeat what they had done.'

I refer to this report not to malign one of the greatest players ever, who is also a tremendously polite and decent person, but to just highlight the fact that if cricket was being viewed with suspicion during that World Cup, the reasons were grounded in reality.

Akram's absence, however, did not deter the Pakistan team. The openers Aamer Sohail and Saeed Anwar put on 84 rapid runs while chasing India's score of 287. But once Sohail lost his cool and his stumps, India rolled the rest of their side and made it to the semi-finals with ease.

Calcutta was the next destination and there was hardly any Indian who was not confident that the World Cup was now as good as won. It was a sentiment so widely shared that one feared what would happen if the script went awry. Calcutta crowds had a history of violent reaction to anything that did not follow the expected pattern.

Among the myriad memories I have of that World Cup, the one that stands out is the sensational turn the India–Sri Lanka semi-final took in the simmering cauldron that was Eden Gardens that day. The Indian progress was backed by the incessant advertising blitz that emphasized day in and day out the invincible strength of the host team. It was being drummed into the minds of the people that an Indian win was almost certain as they marched into the semi-finals.

Their only defeat in the league stage had come against the surprisingly aggressive and ebullient Sri Lankans at the Kotla in Delhi. That victory had made Sri Lanka's semi-final berth a certainty as Australia and the West Indies had conceded their matches to them, refusing to play in Sri Lanka due to security issues. They had stunned all their rivals in that tournament by unleashing the Kaluwitharana–Jayasuriya opening combination. The pair redefined the opening strategy in One-Day matches by slogging mercilessly in the first 15 overs to take the bite out of the opening attacks.

Normally, my front page article would have discussed the prospects of the match from purely a cricketing angle. But in a sign of changing priorities of the times, I was told to write more about the celebratory mood in Calcutta and the rest of India, and which celebrities and VIPs would be watching the match at Eden Gardens. It is the kind of reporting a cricket writer is ill-suited to perform but, given the instructions from the top, I had no choice but to acquiesce.

Eden Gardens, where the opening ceremony had been held, was all dressed up for the gala. However, doubts were being raised about the wicket, which many feared might not hold up. That was because the main square had remained covered for nearly a month during rehearsals for the opening ceremony. It was feared that the wicket might be underprepared. Under the circumstances the toss became a crucial factor. When Azharuddin called correctly and decided to bowl, tongues started wagging as most teams, given the uncertainty over the nature of the wicket, would have preferred to bat first.

India made a fantastic start, getting rid of Jayasuriya and Kaluwitharana in no time. Had Aravinda de Silva, perhaps the most elegant of the Sri Lankan batsmen, not produced an innings of outstanding maturity and grit, India would have bowled out their rivals for far less than their eventual total of 258. De Silva scored 66 on a track that appeared to have a lot of turn in it.

There was no sign of the impending disaster awaiting India when during the chase Sachin Tendulkar and Sanjay Manjrekar took the score to 98 for the loss of just one wicket. But a dramatic collapse followed, leaving the crowd stunned. The ball was turning and in the glare of the floodlights the batsmen crumbled under the weight of expectations. All of a sudden, India was hurtling towards defeat. The crowd got angrier and angrier.

The first signs of trouble were the empty water bottles hurled at the ground, the Sri Lankan fielders being the unwitting targets of those plastic missiles. The anger of the crowd was now manifesting in dangerous ways. When play was stopped a battling Vinod Kambli was at the crease but India had lost seven wickets for the addition of 22 runs. By the time the players went off the field fearing for their lives, a part of the stands had become one big bonfire, which the crowd was feeding by throwing in newspapers and empty bottles.

What a frightening and heartrending sight it was to watch Kambli walk dejectedly towards the pavilion, his face drenched in tears, while thousands in the stand were raging and shouting slogans against the Indian team.

Our submission deadline was fast approaching, but none of us journalists could know for certain what would happen. A restart looked impossible; whether the game was to be continued the next day or declared abandoned was not known. I rushed down and somehow managed to get into the umpires' room on the ground floor. The two umpires, Steve Dunne and Cyril Mitchley, were literally shaking, and seeing a stranger entering their room they panicked. One of them screamed at me, ordering me to get out even as I was apologetically explaining to them that I was no threat but just a scribe doing my job. At that moment, Clive Lloyd, the match referee, walked in. He was composed and unruffled and told everyone to calm down. In a firm but polite tone, he ordered me to leave the room, saying an announcement would soon be made on the fate of the match.

At 120 for 8, with only 15 overs left for play, it was not likely India could achieve their target of 258. The game was finally abandoned and the match awarded to Sri Lanka. It was a tragic end for India, the disastrous exit embarrassing the country as much for the cricket they displayed as for the shameful manner in which the crowd behaved.

Sri Lanka, who till then had never tasted a major win, went on to beat Australia at Lahore's Gaddafi Stadium to win their first World Cup, while in India we were tearing our hair out and debating the reasons behind the defeat and the crowd behaviour. There was one bizarre explanation that most scoffed at, but a few believed. This was that the bookmakers had put so much money on an Indian win that they had engineered a riot in the hope that the match would get abandoned and a replay ordered.

Like in Bangalore, where the last-minute withdrawal of skipper Wasim Akram had given rise to much speculation, cricket circles were rife with rumours that the game had been infiltrated by the betting industry. Rumour had it that matches were routinely being fixed and many big names, especially in India, were on the payrolls of the bookmakers.

All this sounded like imagination gone rogue at the time, but subsequent events were to prove that cricket was not as pristine as we all had believed it to be.

6
Fixers and Fixing

The shattering of India's World Cup dream in 1996 and the unsporting rowdiness of the Indian crowd was a grievous wound for Indian cricket. As would be expected, recriminations followed.

Though it was widely believed that Azharuddin would be made the fall guy and removed from captaincy, the axe fell on Vinod Kambli. Despite having shown an undeniable capacity for big scores, and boasting an average of over 50 in Test match cricket, Kambli could not find a place in the Indian team that was to tour England after the World Cup. The man whose sobbing, desolate figure encapsulated the image of a despairing India in that semi-final probably paid the price for previous indiscretions and accusations of indiscipline made against him. While his close friend Tendulkar was now the toast of the nation, Kambli slipped off the radar.

Despite massive criticism in the media, Azharuddin survived as captain, perhaps because the selectors thought Tendulkar was still too young to shoulder that burden. Also named in the squad of sixteen for the England tour were Sourav Ganguly and Rahul Dravid.

Dravid's selection was welcomed by most experts. The unanimous opinion was that the batsman from Karnataka was tailormade for Tests, as the foundations of his batting were rock-solid technique and loads of patience. However, the name of Ganguly raised eyebrows and invited much criticism. He had lived a life of oblivion after being dropped from the Indian squad in 1992, playing First-Class cricket without any spectacular results. He was consistent without being outstanding and no one had imagined he would make a comeback to the Indian side.

The Prince of Kolkata's return was being attributed to the backing from India's most powerful administrator, Jagmohan Dalmiya, and was largely panned in the press. I too could not resist the temptation to take a dig at his selection, writing in *The Indian Express* that no Indian team was complete without a joker in the pack.

I remember that day at Lord's when Ganguly hit a century on debut in the second Test of the tour. When he later met a few of the Indian journalists covering the tour, he was courtesy and politeness personified, expressing his happiness and thanking the media. On my asking him how he could be so gracious after what we had written about him, he replied with a genuinely warm smile: 'I don't know what you guys had written as I did not read it.'

England 1996

That tour of England in 1996 was my first major cricketing assignment outside of India. Before the Indian team left the country, I tried to get an interview with the Indian captain. To my disappointment, Azharuddin refused, mumbling in his usual style that he did not speak to the press on the eve of a tour. Despite maintaining a low profile and shunning the limelight, he had the knack of being always in the news. Cricket fans and critics alike gushed at his silken smooth strokes or his brilliance as a fielder, while off the field they were obsessed with his flashy, expensive attire and rumours of a second marriage, to actress Sangeeta Bijlani.

As captain, Azhar had created an aura of invincibility on wickets that suited his spin bowlers, and in partnership with his astute manager Ajit Wadekar, had created a team that was difficult to beat in home conditions. Away from home, however, they could hardly win a match, an unenviable characteristic that has dogged Indian cricket for ages.

On that tour of England, he did not have his trusted strategist Wadekar to help him. India had a new team manager, the dashing Sandeep Patil. As a player, Patil is remembered for his brave, aggressive century after having been hit on the head by a Len Pascoe bouncer during India's 1981 tour of Australia. Patil was assistant to Wadekar during the 1996 World Cup, and there was speculation that his promotion to manager was made to curtail Azharuddin's control over the team.

Azhar, even to his friends in the media, was an enigma who preferred his own counsel and rarely let anyone into his inner world. During interviews, he would talk in monosyllables, mumbling a few words that left the interviewer rather frustrated. Despite his dashing image, he was a devout Muslim and read his namaz (prayers) five times a day. It is hard to figure out who the real Azhar is: a simple loner who got caught up in the trappings of a world too complicated for his understanding, or a sharp, scheming individual plotting to gain power and wealth.

During a chat I had with him in New Zealand in 1994, Azhar told me that his wristy, unconventional style was not due to any effort or coaching, because for as long as he could remember he had always batted the way he did. 'It is only after I started reading that I bat in a special, unconventional manner did I begin to wonder if it was true,' he said. On his style of functioning as captain, he said he did nothing unusual, letting the players make their own decisions and never interfering in their personal lives either. If we believe him, the mantra of his success was simple: let events take their own course. It was hard to fathom if he really meant what he said.

On the 1996 tour of England, reporters had to fill in long gaps between matches with newsworthy reporting. I quickly realized that unless one had access to the team, it would not be an easy job. One could write match copy, make cricketing analysis, praise or criticize a player or the team, but to report on team developments, selection problems and injury-related issues, one needed to have a trusted contact, an insider who could tell you what was going on with the team behind the scenes. Sports reporting in print was becoming challenging as live television coverage expanded, hence the need for scoops was greater.

Unable to find such a source, I remained unaware of a major altercation brewing in the team between Navjot Singh Sidhu and Azharuddin. On the eve of the Oval One-Day match, *The Hindu* carried details of what was to come. It was picked up by the news agency PTI and became a talking point in India, but due to my lack of awareness *The Indian Express* made no mention of it. It was a bad miss on my part, and luckily for me my editors did not make an issue of it. Had such a thing happened in present times, I would probably have been given marching orders.

Even on the morning of the match, I was sitting in front of my laptop, oblivious of the convulsions shaking the dressing room, when R. Mohan of *The Hindu* apprised me of developments and told me to meet Sidhu, who was to address Indian journalists in front of the dressing room. I rushed there to see Sidhu in tears, announcing his decision to quit the tour and go home. It was an unprecedented decision. One had known of players having been sent back on grounds of indiscipline—like Lala Amarnath was from England in 1936 for 'insubordinate' behaviour towards the captain—but here it was the player who had decided to return, citing his differences with the team management as the reason.

Sidhu was then not the loquacious personality he became in his post-retirement broadcasting career. He was a quiet, reserved guy, the last man one would expect to rebel and take a career-threatening decision. Yet there he was, tearfully citing self-esteem, pride and his father's name, saying he would rather die than compromise his dignity and sully the family name. He would go no further.

Despite reporters knocking at his hotel room door and pleading for a quote, literally stalking him in England till his departure for India, Sidhu did not reveal the reason behind his outrage. From the little the players and the team management were willing to reveal, it seemed that the relationship between the captain and Sidhu had soured beyond repair. It was said that Azhar had made extremely harsh and derogatory remarks against Sidhu, which had humiliated the player and broken his spirit.

More than two decades have passed, but the truth has never come to light. Neither of the protagonists made any public or private confession to throw light on what actually caused Sidhu to take that drastic decision. Was there a more sinister explanation that the two did not wish to reveal? No one knows. The exchange that transpired in the dressing room between Sidhu and the Indian captain remains a mystery even today.

The dramatic exit of Sidhu from the Indian team was forgotten after a Tendulkar masterclass in the first Test, played in Birmingham. The wicket was seaming and not easy to bat on. England may not have had the best of attacks, but there is little doubt in my mind that Sachin's knock would rank among the best he has ever played. However, his century could not save India from a defeat. For us

Indian journalists, watching India lose was neither shocking nor depressing, just a reaffirmation of the fact that they were no good in those conditions. What we celebrated those days were exceptional individual feats.

More individual joy was to follow in the second Test at Lord's. Sidhu's exit and Manjrekar's injury opened up two batting slots, taken by Sourav Ganguly and Rahul Dravid. While that Test is always remembered for Ganguly's debut hundred and how fellow debutant Dravid missed that feat by five runs, it also showcased a memorable spell by the lanky Venkatesh Prasad. Prasad and his Karnataka teammate, the enigmatic and formidable Javagal Srinath, produced an outstanding performance to help India draw the Test.

The last Test of the series was played in Nottingham. Another smooth hundred from Ganguly proved that his successful debut was no fluke. Tendulkar also performed well in that Test, but the match ended in a boring draw.

For me the series had many interesting lessons, especially when it came to off-the-field interactions with the team and how these revealed the inner dynamics between the players and the coach or manager. My own lack of access made me feel insecure. I felt Azharuddin had, over the years, developed his own coterie among journalists, and they were the ones to whom he would reveal insider accounts of the team's activities. From the outside it appeared a cosy relationship in which these journalists would be the first to hear of team selections and other such details and in return they would be generally soft on the captain, even if an incident demanded more critical appraisal. Someone like me remained an outsider, clueless as to what was transpiring within the team.

This feeling of being left out made me very critical in an article I wrote about the captain's handling of the team, especially after the first Test loss and the Sidhu episode. I also wrote that as Azharuddin had his own favourites in the media and talked only to them, it was difficult for the 'neutrals' to assess what was going wrong with the team. Needless to say, it made me very unpopular in the media box, especially among the well-established journalists.

Like many who had followed Indian cricket in the eighties, I was a great fan of Sandip Patil because of his attacking batsmanship. Patil was the new team manager, and felt the team needed new vigour and energy. He was keen to make some key changes in the way it was being managed and trained. He chose to give me an 'explosive' interview in which he was very critical of the team's training methods and scathing in his comments on physio Dr Ali Irani.

The interview was published on page one of *The Indian Express*. Patil was quoted as saying that Ali Irani acted more like a loyal servant of the players and less like a trainer. 'He serves tea to some of the stars in the morning and tends to their personal needs,' said Patil, 'and the players don't care much for his training methods.' Advocating radical changes in the team's fitness regimen, Patil said that unless this was done the team would lag behind and never make it to the top. In that interview he was also critical of Azharuddin's style of leadership, though not flaying him as directly as he had Irani.

After the interview, he came to the press box and, with a mischievous grin, told a few journalists there, '*Aaj Pradeep ko bomb interview diya hai* (I have given an explosive interview to Pradeep today).' This, perhaps, was his way of conveying to everyone that he was forging new alliances in the media instead of simply trusting the old establishment who were perceived as being close to Azharuddin.

I don't know whether this interview had the kind of impact Patil desired, but it did get me more access to the team, and surprisingly, to Ali Irani as well. Being part of the Indian team comes with its own set of insecurities, especially if a player has still not established himself as a key member of the team. Many of them keep a keen watch on media–captain–coach relationships and if any journalist is believed to be close to one of them, he is treated with care in the fear that he could adversely influence the management against them.

The day after the interview appeared, Irani sought me out and politely complained about what I had written. With a deadpan face I told him that I had only quoted what Patil had to say about him, and if he had a grouse, he should ask the coach-manager for clarification and not me. Irani, not wanting to annoy me, was very friendly and even offered tickets for the next Test for my friends in case I needed them.

I didn't really know Irani, having only watched his archaic training methods and, like most observers, wondered how he kept his role in the team. He was seen as someone very close to Azhar, but he retained his position even when Sachin Tendulkar became the captain later. There was an incident that revealed a lot about how important Irani was to the BCCI, who backed him even when the coach of the team wanted him out.

Like his predecessor, Madan Lal, the new coach, was unhappy with Irani's methods and had started supervising the team's training himself. But on the Sri Lanka tour the following year, in 1997, Madan was made to understand Irani's value to the Board. Once they had arrived in Sri Lanka, Irani handed over a letter from the Board to Madan, which the coach tucked away somewhere and forgot to read. But when Madan started to get involved in training, the trainer told the coach to lay off and follow the instructions in the Board's letter that had been given to him. Back in his hotel room, Madan found that the letter explicitly stated that the responsibility of training the team was Irani's and that the coach should not interfere in his training sessions.

Madan came to my room and sought my suggestions on how to deal with this humiliation. Feeling frustrated and angry, he even contemplated quitting his job. Eventually, he wrote a carefully drafted letter to the Board in which he expressed his displeasure but made no mention of leaving his post. That was because by then it was clear that Irani's role was that of an 'informer' to the Board officials. This was the reason behind his longevity in the team, despite both Patil and Madan having seen through his unprofessional training methods.

After Patil's interview, not only Irani but also Azharuddin started making friendly overtures to me. He suddenly remembered my request for an interview that he had declined before the tour had begun. I was invited to the players' dining room above the Trent Bridge dressing room. Azhar was waiting for me there alone. We began the interview and he talked to me at length on his leadership and why his record backed his claims to be retained as captain.

The interview took place while the third Test was meandering towards a draw. One loss and two draws in an overseas series was perhaps not a bad result in that era. But criticism of Azharuddin's aloof style of captaincy was growing at home. It became obvious to me that, fearing he could lose his job, he had decided to reach out to those sections of the media that were critical of him.

Azharuddin could be abrupt or charming, depending upon the circumstances. If he was in trouble, he would present his best face; if secure, he could be smug and even brusque. Two years later, when speculation was rife that Azhar could be involved in the match-fixing allegations that were flying around, he was once again at his gracious best.

Azharuddin's premonition that he was on his way out proved true. Tendulkar, who many believed was born not just to bat but to lead the country as well, was expectedly made captain after the England series. Reminiscent of the Gavaskar–Kapil captaincy exchanges and keeping with the unpredictability of Indian cricket, Tendulkar was removed as captain after just two years and Azharuddin found himself back at the helm. It made no sense to outsiders. Tendulkar was cut to size, his ego battered, while Azharuddin was back with his familiar swagger.

This was a period when the rumours of match-fixing were circulating widely as Manoj Prabhakar had alleged in a signed article in *Outlook* that he was offered Rs 24 lakh by an Indian player to fix a game in a One-Day series in Sri Lanka.

Not Quite Cricket

Though the BCCI would have us believe that the accusations of match-fixing were fictions created by demented, diabolical minds, many insiders had their own version of events and no one was sure what the truth was.

I myself stumbled into this minefield on India's tour of the West Indies in 1997, where Tendulkar was the captain and in the team was a disgruntled Azhar, stripped of his powers. The tour did not go well for India. In the Barbados Test, they were bowled out for 81 while chasing a mere 120 runs for victory. The defeat had stung Tendulkar so badly that he did not leave his hotel room for two days and even considered quitting the game, as he revealed later in his autobiography.

The final day's strip was a difficult one to bat on with its uneven bounce. Yet a target of 120 was very gettable and India's collapse, mainly from poor shots, had left everyone shocked. Azharuddin batted as irresponsibly as anyone, but his lack of interest was what stood out. But no one suspected anything sinister, putting it down to him being peeved at being removed as captain. However, a cloud of mistrust hung over the team and we in the media were not sure who was to be blamed.

It was during that tour of the West Indies that I was approached by a man who told me he was a cricket fan who had come all the way from Delhi to watch India play. He had a slight squint in one eye. Soon, he revealed that he was in fact a bookie, and was trying to get a few Indian players on his payroll. He was willing to pay large sums of money to anyone who could help him get in touch with a few key members of the team.

If his stories were to be believed, match-fixing was an international phenomenon and most of the players were already on the books of some syndicate or the other. Now his syndicate, based out of Delhi, was also trying to get into the business. Anyone—and that included me as well—who could introduce him to certain Indian players would be rewarded with a new apartment in Delhi. I played along, giving him the impression that I could fix the deal for him.

Before I left the Caribbean after the conclusion of the Test series, I requested an interview with Tendulkar in the hope of getting his view on this man who claimed to be a bookie and was willing to pay enormous amounts of money to establish contact with the players. At the team hotel in Guyana, Tendulkar appeared concerned when I told him about this man's approach. I feared he might explode in anger against me for bringing up this subject, but his reaction was far more pragmatic. He confessed that he too had heard stories like these and his advice to me was to not do a story immediately but to ask the police to shadow the man and tap his phones, so that they would know if he was in contact with anyone in the team. He also made it clear to me, and understandably so, that he was not going to say anything on record. I assured him that I would quote him as saying he was not willing to comment on these unfounded, baseless rumours.

The story was carried on the front page of *The Pioneer* and created a stir with its comparison of a bookie with a shark, loaded with money out to buy players. The story had nothing against the players and many, including the BCCI, dismissed it as 'a salacious bit of gossip to create a sensation'. However, around the same time, the Australian cricketers Shane Warne and Mark Waugh alleged that Pakistani cricketer Salim Malik had offered them money to throw a match. There were many other unsubstantiated tales of similar nature doing the rounds, and the cricketing world was spinning in a whirl of confusion.

A proper investigation required the cricket establishment to first acknowledge that there was a problem. Instead, the reaction of officialdom, especially of the BCCI, was to condemn those who were raising doubts and making these allegations. Funnily enough, cricket boards around the world believed that this was a problem only in the subcontinent and that their own players had nothing to do with it. And the BCCI would have the world believe that Indian cricket was being maligned by vested interests who were prejudiced against the rise of the hitherto 'exploited' and 'marginalized' nation.

Among the strangest reactions to my story was the BCCI issuing a show-cause notice to Tendulkar asking him to clarify if he had been offered money to fix matches and, if so, why he had not informed them of this. I was made aware of this startling fact by Tendulkar himself at Chennai's Chidambaram Stadium, where India and Pakistan were preparing to play a One-Day match. This was the match in which Saeed Anwar would score 194, which was the highest individual score at the time.

This was my first encounter with the Indian team after my bookie story from the West Indies. Though I was already apprehensive of any adverse reaction from the team, I was still surprised when Tendulkar himself rushed towards me after finishing his batting session in the nets. He was angry and wanted to know on what basis had I got him involved in all this and why had I written that he was offered money to fix matches. Tendulkar was clearly upset, both with the BCCI and with me. His anger subsided once I told him that the Board had wrongly inferred from my story that he had been offered money. I told him that the story had simply quoted him saying that it was 'beneath his dignity to respond'.

I offered to write to the Board and state that it was I and not Tendulkar who had been offered money. This seemed to please both him and the coach, Madan Lal. After the match the following night, I showed them the draft of the letter. It was only after Tendulkar had finished with his press conference duties did I get their approval on the letter.

This whole episode just goes to show that the establishment would rather target the Indian captain instead of trying to find out the truth. It was only a chance recording of underworld phone calls by the Delhi police in 2000 that blew the lid off the players–bookie nexus. Evidence was found of South African captain Hansie Cronje dealing with bookies to fix a few games in India.

It was clear once the scandal surfaced that the scourge had spread far and wide, and India was the epicentre. The players involved were defrauding the fans by compromising and manipulating their own performances, robbing the game of its true unpredictable nature. If the investigation was left to the cricket establishment, we would probably have never known what was going on. They would have stuck to their position that match-fixing allegations were simply attempts to malign the great game of cricket that was synonymous with 'gentlemanliness and moral conduct'.

Even while the shadow of match-fixing was stalking world cricket, the BCCI and the Indian selectors were busy with their politicking. Admittedly, India's performance under Tendulkar's captaincy was not earth-shattering and even his own form may have dwindled a bit. But he was still only twenty-five and had just two years of leadership experience. He needed to be backed and not dumped unceremoniously. Yet, not only was he removed as captain, he was also replaced by someone whose credentials were increasingly becoming suspect in the eyes of the world.

To everyone's shock and surprise, Azharuddin was reappointed captain for a One-Day tournament held in Dhaka in January 1998. On the eve of the final against Pakistan, I was invited by the Indian captain for lunch with his wife in his hotel. The couple were at their charming best. In the course of the conversation, Azharuddin referred to Prabhakar's allegations in *Outlook* and made a very revealing comment: 'Whoever he may be referring to, the world knows and I know what he has done.' Later, Prabhakar was found by India's Central Bureau of Investigation to be one of the key figures in the fixing scandal and was banned for life by the BCCI. But at the time I wondered why Azhar seemed to be defending himself when no one had yet accused him of anything.

The final ended in a thrilling, dramatic finish. In a chase of 315 (a world record at the time), Hrishikesh Kanitkar hit the winning boundary with one ball remaining. It was a moment as memorable as the last-ball six by Javed Miandad in Sharjah.

By beating Pakistan and winning that tournament in great style, Azharuddin should have been relieved, but in fact he was a worried man. The *Outlook* story on match-fixing with Prabhakar's allegations had not named any players, but then Pakistani player Rashid Latif was recorded in a sting operation stating that Azharuddin was on the books of a betting syndicate.

It was in 1998 that Karthika V.K., then one of the commissioning editors at Penguin Books India, approached me to write a book on match-fixing, based on my experiences with the bookie I had met in the West Indies. The book was called *Not Quite Cricket*, and was published just before the 1999 World Cup in England.

In that World Cup, play was stopped during the India–South Africa match when it was discovered that skipper Cronje was communicating with the coach, Bob Woolmer, through a hidden earpiece. The justification given was that it was enabling interactions between coach and captain without interrupting the game. It was a most audacious experiment, one that didn't fall under the laws of cricket. The umpires asked Cronje to stop doing it.

Many years later, in 2005, Woolmer would meet the police commissioner of Delhi, K.K. Paul, the man under whose watch in 2000 Cronje was caught revealing match information to bookies on the phone. I was the one who arranged that meeting as Woolmer was keen to meet the man who was responsible for 'tarnishing' the image of his favourite cricketer. The meeting had its moments of tension and the earpiece incident was one of the points of discord.

Tendulkar's father passed away during that World Cup. He flew back to India for the funeral but returned for India's match against Kenya at Bristol. For Indian cricket fans at Bristol that day, Tendulkar's return was a highly emotional moment. They were grieving with him and also appreciating his commitment in returning to play. When he raised his bat and looked skywards after completing his century, there were many at the ground with tears in their eyes.

It was around then that my book was released in India. The publishers had sent me a few copies for distribution to the media in England. One of the papers in India published an extract of the book in which Madan Lal, the coach of the Indian team in the West Indies in 1997, was quoted as having told me that though they all knew what was going on, there was no point in doing a story as the establishment would target anyone writing about the player–bookie nexus. Madan was upset with me for having revealed this and told me he would deny having said anything of this nature to me.

I could understand that he was worried about his comments being misconstrued by the establishment. Since match-fixing was yet to be proved, he feared that his admission that it was happening could create problems for him. I still remember his outburst, which took place on the eve of the India–England match. I was a bit rattled, but argued with him, asking what was the point of saying that we wanted Indian cricket to improve if no one was willing to speak the truth in fear of the wrath of the BCCI.

Most reviewers of my book wrote that I had made outrageous allegations without any proof. The book would have generated little interest had not the Hansie Cronje tape come up almost a year later. All of a sudden *Not Quite Cricket* was in the limelight and TV channels wanted to speak to me on the subject. Penguin too realized the marketing potential of the book and immediately ordered a new edition with an updated introduction that included the Cronje episode.

The book's re-release coincided with the hearings of the King Commission, a judicial probe ordered by the South Africans into the match-fixing charges against their captain and some other players made by the Delhi Police. And despite the BCCI's reluctance to accept that this was a serious issue, the Indian government too announced a CBI probe into the scandal. Prime Minister Vajpayee conveyed his decision through the sports minister, Sukhdev Singh Dhindsa, on 27 April 2000.

Because of these developments, as a reporter I was now under tremendous pressure to break exclusive stories for my paper, stories that would detail which matches had been fixed and which players may have been involved. As I had authored a book on the subject, I was suddenly the 'expert'.

Attack on Kapil

In this raging period of match-fixing revelations came another stunning one, this time from I.S. Bindra. On 4 May 2000, just a week after the CBI probe was announced, Bindra alleged in an interview to CNN that the unnamed cricketer who Prabhakar had accused of offering money to fix a match was none other than the legendary Kapil Dev. Ever since that *Outlook* interview in which Prabhakar had made his 'confession', speculations about who that cricketer could be had been rife. No one knew for sure, although it was widely believed that the person being accused was the then Indian captain Azharuddin. Azharuddin's own mysterious defence in Dhaka in 1998 had baffled me, and I had mentioned that private conversation in my book.

Now, the world was being told that the unnamed villain was the Indian cricket hero Kapil Dev! Bindra, who was fighting his own losing battle with the BCCI, had in one stroke driven a sharp knife into the heart of Indian cricket. Having been marginalized in the BCCI after a rift with Dalmiya, Bindra had become one of his most vocal and bitter critics. No one knew the real reason behind this souring of relations between the two former allies. Dalmiya had never accepted that fixing could be a possibility and was against any probe. Bindra was getting back at him through this shattering revelation.

After Kapil's name got dragged in, the pressure on me became worse as everyone knew about our Chandigarh connection. I could sense a feeling in people around me that perhaps I could be hiding some secret to shield my 'friend'. I reached out to a devastated Kapil and found him teetering on the verge of a breakdown. He showed a thick sheaf of papers that had the records of his mobile phone bills with all the numbers he had dialled over the past few years. He said this would provide proof of his innocence.

During the interview he expressed his dismay, said he was emotionally disturbed at what his mother would be thinking about him and that no one could question his loyalty to his country and the team. He was traumatized and I could sense that if I pushed the issue further, he might break down. In fact, shortly after, in an interview with Karan Thapar on TV, Kapil did burst into tears.

I did not believe this was the moment to highlight his misery, and told the edit desk staff not to mix my interview with the report of the TV interview. Yet to my surprise, the next day's page-one interview of Kapil, with my by-line, had been twisted to include his breaking down on TV and rewritten in a manner that presented him as a person who was using tears to hide his guilt. I had no problem with that interpretation but felt upset at it coming across as my opinion and registered my protest. I am sure this must have been construed as my being sympathetic towards him and trying to shield his 'crime'.

Soon articles without any proof or valid sources were declaring that Kapil had amassed a great deal of wealth that he couldn't account for. The income tax department raided his house and offices. Kapil was no longer the great player to be treated with reverence, instead he had become a suspect who was already being pronounced guilty.

The match-fixing saga was getting murkier by the day and finally the CBI report was made public. The whistle-blower Prabhakar was found guilty, along with Mohammed Azharuddin, Ajay Sharma, Ajay Jadeja and Nayan Mongia. Physio Ali Irani had been named as one of the suspects but no proof was found of his involvement. As for Kapil Dev, he was exonerated, with the report stating that no links were found between him and any bookie.

The report also mentioned that some top international cricketers were on the payroll of M.K. Gupta, the Indian bookmaker whose testimony had led to these sensational findings. The names of Brian Lara, Alec Stewart, Dean Jones, Martin Crowe, Aravinda de Silva and Arjuna Ranatunga were on the list. However, as it was hard to prove these charges in a court of law, the report left it to the respective cricket boards of the foreign players to initiate any action or probe further as they deemed proper. The scandal led to the formation of an anti-corruption unit (ACU) by the International Cricket Council (ICC), cricket's apex body.

Ajay Sharma on the CBI Report

One of the intriguing aspects of the CBI report to me was Ajay Sharma's involvement with fixing. I had known Ajay well, having covered his Ranji Trophy batting exploits extensively. I still think he should have played a lot more than the one Test match he played. I had seen him score hundreds on treacherous batting wickets with composure and elan. Ajay's First-Class record is phenomenal, with a career average of over 67—only Donald Bradman, Vijay Merchant and George Headley finished with higher averages.

When I interviewed him for my book *Not Quite Cricket,* he spoke with great candour on the problems of India's domestic cricket and the neglect of the Ranji Trophy. I found it a bit embarrassing and even ironic that my book about match-fixing featured a cricketer who was later pronounced guilty of the same crime. In fact, one of the reviews of the book pointed out that the 'writer's own credibility should be questioned as he quotes two cricketers, Kapil and Ajay, extensively in the book, who themselves are under a cloud'.

But at the time of writing I was not aware Ajay was involved. Since I knew both him and Kapil well and they were willing to speak on these issues on record, I had quoted them. I must admit that Kapil's exoneration was a relief for me, having known him personally. Besides, a taint on him would have left an even greater scar on the Indian cricketing psyche than the one left by Azharuddin's guilty verdict.

The day the CBI report was made public, I met Ajay at his apartment in Delhi with Ajaz Ashraf, a friend and a very insightful journalist. Ajay was curious to know the details of the report as he had not read it. We showed him a copy of the report and spent a few hours with him in order to record his reactions and responses.

We asked him why, if he was innocent, the CBI would give such lengthy details of his involvement with M.K. Gupta, or 'John' as he was known among the betting syndicate and the cricketers involved. Ajay did not deny knowing M.K., who he said was a jeweller, and one of many businessmen who would patronize Delhi cricket. They would encourage budding players and even financially help some of the poorer among them so that they could concentrate on the game. Beyond this, he said, he knew nothing. He insisted that he was being wrongly implicated by the CBI.

As we went through the report, Ajay grew worried that he was being framed. He also felt that some of the others who were named may not have been involved. But he also did not deny he was close to Azharuddin. The CBI report went into great detail of how M.K. was regularly in touch with Ajay, seeking information and paying him money in return.

Ajay recalled his first meeting with M.K. He had scored a hundred, his first, in the DDCA league. After the match, an unknown person put a hundred-rupee note in his pocket and said it was a reward for his performance. Ajay was not from a rich family, and found this friendly gesture very touching. The patron was of course M.K. Gupta. Thus began a relationship that according to Ajay was like any between a fan-patron and a cricketer. There was nothing deceitful about it.

But was M.K. a bookie? Did he really have all these big players on his payroll? Ajay said he couldn't comment on the exact nature of M.K.'s relationship with the others, though, yes, he knew them and was in touch with them. Ajay recalled an incident on the tour to West Indies in 1989. He was in the room of another cricketer when the phone rang. Ajay answered, and the voice at the other end asked to speak to his colleague. Ajay recognized it as M.K.'s voice and was surprised that his teammate knew him as well.

He narrated an interesting story that revealed how widely M.K. was known among the cricketers. Before the CBI report became public, *India Today* had done a cover story on Ajay, alleging that he was one of the kingpins of match-fixing and had now fled to England to escape interrogation. It was a detailed report, its source evidently being someone closely connected to the CBI probe. Ajay says he knew nothing about the report in the magazine, and was happily playing league cricket in England. He insisted that the agreement with the English side had been signed much in advance, therefore his having escaped to avoid the law was all rubbish.

It was one of his Delhi teammates—who later played for India—who called Ajay to tell him about the *India Today* article. What Ajay found very curious and even intriguing was that this player knew that the 'John' referred to in the article was actually M.K., a fact that would be known only to one familiar with the bookie. Ajay said that the player told him that the CBI knows John was in touch with him. When Ajay claimed he didn't know any John, the Delhi player promptly said, 'It's M.K., of course, he is the one called John.'

The conclusions were obvious. All these narrations—and I have no reason to not believe Ajay—only show that M.K. had cast his net far and wide. He was in touch with cricketers who were on the fringe of selection for the Indian team or had the potential to be there in the future, along with some of those who were already playing and had become big names. The modus operandi may have been different depending upon a cricketer's financial status, but they were always groomed to either provide inside information or underperform during a match in return for big financial rewards.

Ajay insisted he was entirely innocent and could not figure out why he was being implicated. Later, along with Azharuddin and Jadeja, he was exonerated by the courts.

I have included this section in the book only after much deliberation. I decided to go ahead as it shows that in the eighties and nineties, the game was deeply infiltrated by the bookmakers right down to the grassroots. Ajay may have been innocent, but the player–bookie nexus was a reality then and, given the developments in the Indian Premier League, it could be a reality even now.

It was a period of great turmoil that shattered the faith of fans and destroyed the myth of cricket being a sport that is played in an ethical, moral framework and instils values of fairplay among the players. The administrative bodies that had all along denied the existence of match-fixing had to resort to firefighting after the damage had been done. Reputations lay in tatters.

7
A World of Uncertainties

My career took several turns following the 1996 tour of England. To the surprise of many in the profession, I finally left *The Indian Express*. Though Shekhar's becoming editor had brought good tidings for me, my two years in near wilderness had left me emotionally and mentally scarred. I felt claustrophobic in the Delhi office, its congested spaces and small cubicles constantly reminding me of my 'humiliation'.

When Chandan Mitra, editor of *The Pioneer*, asked me to consider joining his team as sports editor, the paper he worked for was on the verge of going out of business. Its circulation was dwindling and the finances were a mess. The paper's owner, industrialist Lalit Mohan Thapar, wanted to sell it. I was aware of what I would be getting into, and yet I accepted the offer. I guess I needed to just break my bonds with the newspaper I had worked for ever since I became a sports journalist.

Shekhar tried his best to persuade me not to leave, but I had made up my mind. The day before I was to join *The Pioneer*, the paper closed its Mumbai edition. Shekhar called me late in the night to say that I could still change my mind. I was touched by his concern, but I felt even an uncertain future outside of *The Indian Express* was more acceptable than continuing to stay in a place that evoked unhappy memories.

Shifting Sands

My one-year association with *The Pioneer* was to be a severe test of my patience and man-management skills as I struggled to run the sports department with considerably depleted resources and staff. Since word was out that *The Pioneer* might go out of business at any time and salaries were also not being paid on time, almost everyone on the staff was looking for another job.

Far from the mechanical routine of the *Express*, here every day was fraught with the spectre of an uncertain future. A stage came when I was left with just three people working in the department, two of them rookies, and I was not sure if the sports pages could be even produced for the next day.

I was followed from the *Express* by Siddharth Saxena, who was around fifteen years my junior. His risky decision may have been dictated more by loyalty to me than professional prudence. Siddharth is a fine, sensitive writer, football being his speciality. He had joined the *Express* around the same time that I had been transferred from Chandigarh. We were joined by Kunal Pradhan, a journalism student seeking an apprenticeship. Despite his age and inexperience, he was so good at his work that we made his position full-time but allowed him to complete his studies on the side. Pradhan is now the managing editor of the *Hindustan Times*.

The Pioneer may have been on its last legs, but my brief stint with them was the most productive period of my career. It not only energized me but also gave me a better understanding of the world of journalism. I also forged relationships then that have only grown stronger over the years. Working at *The Pioneer* was an experience that made me a more resilient person; in fact, adversity brought out the best in all those working there even with the appalling financial and working conditions.

Despite abhorring his right-wing politics, most of us considered Chandan Mitra to be a man with a true democratic spirit. He was erudite and had a vast all-round knowledge that included sports as well. He let most of us be. Ajaz Ashraf, who headed the Sunday section called *Agenda*, stood at the opposite ideological pole from Chandan, yet the two got along well. The paper had not yet turned completely saffron, as the Thapars still controlled its financial strings. *Agenda* produced some searing anti-right pieces that Chandan did not spike. He had the capacity to recognize talent and tolerate dissent.

We were told that there was a desperate hunt for a buyer, and Chandan even roped in some of us for help. The design head of the paper, Bindu Sharma, was a close relative of the principal advisor to the Prime Minister at the time. We tried to use that connection to save the paper. Ever since I had moved to Delhi, the impact of political upheavals in the country somehow had got reduced to mere discussions among friends. The pressure of work made me more focused on survival rather than worrying too much about national politics.

The Khalistani movement had almost died down and Punjab was limping back to peace. The reservation system was now widely accepted. And in 1998, India had its first BJP Prime Minister in Atal Bihari Vajpayee, in a coalition government. But Bihar and Uttar Pradesh were controlled by OBC leaders such as Lalu Prasad Yadav, Mulayam Singh Yadav and the Dalit leader Mayawati. They had ridden to political prominence on slogans like '*Tilak, Taraju, aur Talwar, joote maro inko char*'. Tilak is a vermillion mark on the forehead and is a symbol of the Brahmins; taraju is a weighing machine, representing the Baniya caste; and talwar means sword, a symbol of the Rajput caste. It was a revolutionary call to the lower castes to beat with shoes members of the higher castes that had dominated India's power structure for centuries.

Unlike in the south, where the Dravidian movement had led to the shift of power from Brahmins to OBCs much earlier, the north witnessed this change only after Mandal politics played its full course.

After failing to get a buyer for over a year, Thapar decided to close *The Pioneer* operations. He intended to pay a reasonably good severance package to the employees: three months' salary plus all other statutory benefits mandated by law. Chandan did not tell us the owner's intentions, instead announcing that he had negotiated a deal to save the paper. What we were yet to know was that he himself was to be the new owner; presumably the severance money was being redirected to fund the operations. Somehow a few of us found out about this arrangement that Chandan had hidden from the staff.

During a meeting, Chandan announced that he had found a new owner for the paper, but he was not willing to reveal the name of the buyer. But the few of us who knew the truth insisted that he should tell us. Under pressure, he admitted he was the new owner, and that he was forming a corpus from the money intended as the staff severance package, to run the paper. He claimed his intention was to save jobs and since he had not been able to find a buyer, this was the best possible solution.

However, we felt that since this was not his personal money, he should form a trust, including representatives from all sections of the paper, to run the organization. Why should he be declared the owner of *The Pioneer*? We felt it was unethical on his part to run the paper using money that was due to the employees, without their consent. If anyone did not want to be part of this deal, they should be free to take their dues and leave.

Chandan rejected our proposal. In this atmosphere of suspicion, mistrust and insecurity, more than a hundred of us decided to take our dues and quit. Despite knowing that an uncertain future awaited me at the paper, I never imagined the exit would be this dramatic.

Chandan later became a Rajya Sabha member from the BJP, with the paper becoming its mouthpiece. His romance with the right wing lasted almost two decades before he joined the TMC, a political outfit led by Mamata Banerjee. Chandan passed away a few months after TMC fought and won a ferocious battle against the BJP in the West Bengal assembly elections in 2021.

In my brief stint with *The Pioneer*, I made four foreign tours, the most significant being the 1997 tour to the West Indies. But I may never have gone on that tour. The paper didn't have enough funds to keep its promise to send me to the West Indies. Chandan somehow scraped together a budget to cover my travel and stay. However, I needed a laptop to write my stories on tour, but that was too expensive for them. Eventually I bought one myself, raising Rs 30,000 by selling my car. Chandan promised to reimburse me when I was back, and he did.

The company's finances were getting from bad to worse, but that did not prevent me from touring Pakistan, Bangladesh and Sri Lanka. It was because Chandan was desperate to not let the paper's cricket coverage suffer.

I remained jobless for almost a year after leaving *The Pioneer* but as my wife Mukta had a job at the *Financial Express* and she put no pressure on me to take up a job in desperation, I had time to rest, reflect and ponder. What a relief it was to be living without the weight of a job that put huge demands on one's time. Being an editor, I was always worrying about stories rival papers may carry and about mistakes on pages already sent to press. I was finally not tied to any fixed schedule and nor was I accountable to anyone. It was a rejuvenating experience.

Though I was enjoying my freedom, the anxiety of an uncertain future still hummed somewhere in the background. The options were limited as there were no senior positions available. Fortunately for me *India Today* had started its website, one of the first Indian publications to make a foray into the digital world. They had realized its potential to become a strong rival to print media and had started investing a lot of money into the website. I was offered an assignment to help them with their coverage of the 1999 World Cup.

I accepted, and they partially funded my trip to England for the tournament. I was lucky to also be able to rope in many regional papers to publish my reports on the India matches, which meant that I had to write just one opinion piece on each match without having to chase extra stories and scoops. Unlike other reporters who were chained to their computers, I had the luxury of being a tension-free 'tourist'.

One day, Shekhar called me and without any preamble offered me a job. He wanted me to take on the role of cricket editor of *The Indian Express*. The salary he offered matched what I had been earning at *The Pioneer*. I accepted.

But soon disaster struck. In May 2000 came Bindra's accusations against Kapil Dev, which I have written about in the previous chapter. The breaking point in the office came when I was screamed at for not being professional enough. I was accused of making efforts to defend him instead of getting to the bottom of the shady deals he had allegedly made. Distraught and disturbed, I quietly walked back to my cabin, packed up my sundry belongings and walked out of the room, never to return to that office again. A week later I sent in my resignation and was jobless again. My return to the *Express* did not last even a year.

Fortunately, another job materialized only days after my integrity was questioned at the *Express*. The India Today Group was launching an e-paper called *NewspaperToday.com*, the first in the country. Its editor, Anand P. Raman, a business journalist, offered me the sports editor's job. Not aware that I had quit my job, Anand offered me a raise from the salary I was getting at the *Express*. He also promised me the freedom to travel to any part of the world for reporting.

Thus began my new adventure in journalism. Although the promised salary was paid, the travel budget was far from what was described. It was not sufficient to cover travel for domestic games, let alone international tours.

Azhar's Shadow

After the 1999 World Cup, Tendulkar was reinstated as captain in place of Azhar. As he reveals in his autobiography, Tendulkar had felt humiliated when he was removed from the post in 1997. He was not prepared to take it on again. According to protocol, the chief selector had to take the captain's consent before announcing his name. Wadekar was chief selector at the time, but found to his shock that Tendulkar had vanished. They were only able to contact Tendulkar after over a day of trying. Meanwhile, the selection committee went ahead and announced that he would be captain.

I was still with *The Indian Express* at that time, and had talked to Tendulkar a few days before this announcement. On my asking whether he was willing to lead again, he wanted me to write something along the lines of 'Tendulkar has never said that he will not lead again'. From that statement, I presumed that he was not averse to the captainship. There were already rumours that Azharuddin was being sacked, so stating that Tendulkar was to become captain again was a safe bet from my understanding of the situation.

The story appeared on page one. After the drama that followed when the official announcement was eventually made, Tendulkar made it clear that he did not want to lead again and had conveyed this decision to the selectors as well. However, he finally relented and accepted the captaincy. I remained confused: had I misunderstood him and gone horribly wrong with my story?

At the conclusion of the three Tests in Australia, I sought a meeting with him to clarify the matter. I told him that I had written the article only after talking to him, and felt embarrassed to have gotten it wrong. Though his response was polite as always, he did not clarify the misunderstanding. Was Azharuddin a factor in that dramatic game of hide-and-seek played by Tendulkar?

Azhar, through media bites, had made it clear that he was willing to play under Tendulkar, or even Ajay Jadeja, who also was in contention for the leadership role. However, though it has never been expressly stated by anyone, Azharuddin may not have been welcome in Tendulkar's team. Azhar's disinterest in the team's affairs during Tendulkar's previous captaincy stint—and possibly the lengthening shadow of suspicion over his dubious activities—had made Tendulkar wary of him. Or was Tendulkar still sore about the 'heartless' manner in which he had been sacked as captain the first time around? It became clearer when the Indian team under Tendulkar was announced: Azharuddin's name was not on the list.

Tendulkar's second stint started with a brief tour of Sri Lanka. It was followed by a home series against New Zealand before the team embarked on the tour to Australia. Kapil Dev was appointed as the coach. The Tendulkar–Kapil combination, a legend from the past teamed with a present-day superstar, led many to believe that a great future lay ahead.

The home series against New Zealand was a routine win, but a controversial decision to not enforce a follow-on in the third Test at Ahmedabad despite being ahead by 275 runs had been a subject of great scrutiny. Given the general atmosphere of suspicion around the game at the time, there was immediate speculation about outside influence. Much later, when the fixing accusations and the involvement of players proved correct, a probe was ordered into who was responsible for that decision in Ahmedabad. However, it was established after talking to the players and the captain that the decision was unanimous: as the Indian bowlers had been on the field for more than two days in the heat of Ahmedabad, it was decided that the follow-on would not be enforced in order to give them a rest.

The tour to Australia began on a sour note, with a public spat between Kapil and the BCCI secretary, Jaywant Lele. Lele was known for his unbridled tongue, which often made him say things that he had to retract later. This time he had taunted Kapil before the team had left for Australia. When the coach sought more freedom in decision-making, Lele responded that no matter what the coach did, India would lose the series 3–0.

In this series, Australia unleashed Brett Lee, one of the fastest bowlers of all time. India floundered and Lele's damning prediction came true. Tendulkar was the lone exception, mastering the pace and bounce of the Australian pitches with an exceptional display of batting skills. It was the best I have ever seen him bat, bringing his genius into full display. His footwork was precise and perfect and his confidence so high that he would stretch fully forward in defence even to the pace of Lee, as if he was defending against a spinner. While he played with supreme ease and masterly control and scored heavily, the rest just could not cope and India surrendered meekly.

Even players of the calibre of Rahul Dravid failed. I remember him surviving for more than an hour against McGrath's swing and

Lee's searing pace in one of the innings he played. He displayed great technical finesse but the end result was failure. Dravid may have pleased the purists but the scoreboard hardly moved by a few runs. These were learning experiences for him and he would go on to enjoy success on his subsequent tours to Australia.

V.V.S. Laxman was struggling to cement his place in the team at the time. He eventually demonstrated that a counter-attacking approach was the way to tame the Australian attack. In the final Test at Sydney, he launched into a series of ferocious pulls, cuts and hooks on his way to a stunning hundred. But in the end, it made no difference to the eventual 0–3 score line. Tendulkar was the man of the series but it was no consolation as his team had been completely outplayed.

While in the press box, I had overheard something sensational. One of the former Indian greats, who was there as a commentator, mentioned that the Indian selectors were thinking of naming Azharuddin in the One-Day squad. According to him, this had created unease among the team in Australia. Apparently, a message had been sent to the selectors that Azhar was not welcome.

This was a very significant development but before I could write the story, it needed to be verified. I could seek out Kapil but was reluctant to do so as he had been very hesitant to share any dressing room 'gossip' lately. He was now the coach of the team and had to protect its interests. At the end of the day's play, I stood outside India's dressing room wondering whom I could approach.

When I spotted a player I knew well, I approached him and said, 'This question was never asked and this meeting never happened.' Puzzled, the player asked me what I wanted to know. To my surprise, he answered my question candidly: 'Why, the entire team is willing to sign a statement that if Azharuddin is recalled, there will be a revolt.' I had got my confirmation.

The *Express* splashed the story across page one: Azhar's return was being opposed by teammates. The story created disquiet in the press box as most of my colleagues believed it was a leak from the coach to a journalist friend. Kapil was confronted by an angry bunch of newsmen: why this 'leak' to only one person? He very calmly denied having leaked anything of the sort, and went one step further and rubbished the report itself, declaring that Azhar, or anyone the selectors picked, was welcome.

Eventually, Azhar was not selected for the One-Day matches that followed the Test series in Australia. However, once the team returned home to face the South Africans, it became clear that the selectors intended to recall Azharuddin. Indian cricket was headed for another round of turmoil and uncertainty.

This Tendulkar–Azharuddin clash had many dimensions to it. Though at that time Tendulkar's reluctance to accept Azharuddin in the team was being seen merely as an ego clash between the two, in hindsight it becomes clear that many of the players rightly suspected his integrity. That was the main reason why he was not welcome in the dressing room.

After Prabhakar's sensational *Outlook* interview, the BCCI had appointed a one-man panel comprising former chief justice of India Y.Y. Chandrachud to enquire into the allegations. Justice Chandrachud had no judicial power to probe or seek assistance from investigating agencies to corroborate the veracity of any statement made to him. He just had to listen to what people whom he asked to appear before him had to say.

When I appeared before Chandrachud, I felt that the inquiry was likely to become a cover-up job. He gave me the impression of not being too keen to implicate anyone. He did not ask me the name of the bookie who had accosted me on the 1997 West Indies tour nor did he seem interested in knowing if fixing was a possibility and what my thoughts were on it. When I told Chandan what I felt, he told me to do a page-one story stating that the probe was going to be a farce. He took a risk in printing a story that involved direct criticism of a former chief justice of India, not holding back a story from saying that Chandrachud was not interested in finding the truth and was merely playing the Indian cricket establishment's game.

According to Chandrachud's report, Prabhakar had said that he was unclear about the sequence of events in 1994 when he had allegedly been offered money by a teammate to fix a match. He refused to name the player. As for Tendulkar, the report mentions him as saying that he did not suspect any Indian player of throwing his wicket or underperforming deliberately.

The BCCI heaved a sigh of relief that anyone raising doubts over the game's integrity had been effectively silenced.

Tendulkar Demystified

Why had Tendulkar decided to give up the captaincy after his return from Australia? Was it to do with another round of crushing defeats or was it a sign of rebellion against the selectors, who had made up their mind to recall Azharuddin against his wishes?

Everyone connected with Indian cricket has a Tendulkar story to narrate. For the majority of his followers, Tendulkar is not merely a great cricketer but a role model, a saint who can do no wrong. All the great cricketers of the country, the likes of Sunil Gavaskar, Kapil Dev and more recently M.S. Dhoni and Virat Kohli, have all faced extreme media scrutiny and criticism. But it seemed blasphemous to criticize Tendulkar. If ever there has been criticism, it has been muted and the person making such a critical evaluation is almost apologetic about this transgression.

This could be due to a combination of facts: his astonishing achievements, longevity, impeccable public conduct, an untainted career. Perhaps it has also to do with the collective desire of a people steeped in religious 'morality', for their hero to be a paragon of virtue.

When he was still in his teens, Tendulkar was reserved and shy, speaking in his soft, squeaky voice as if he did not want to offend anyone. Most of us in the media were in awe of his talent, and would feel thrilled if he showed any sign of having recognized us at the ground or in a press conference. Except for a very few who had known him from his early days in Mumbai, none of us dared to approach him for fear of being rebuffed.

We would often debate among ourselves on what the real Tendulkar was like. For a person who has lived most of his life being adored by hundreds of millions and being treated like a 'god', is it possible to live a normal life? Did he feel normal human emotions of love, hate, jealously, attachment, anger and indifference? Was there life for him outside the cricket field and, if so, what was it like?

In 2005, Tendulkar passed Gavaskar's record of 34 Test centuries in a match against Sri Lanka in Delhi. I interviewed him after that game and asked him some of those questions. Did everyone treat him with deference and awe? And if so, did he not feel stifled and restricted, finding it difficult to be himself and let his hair down? The inscrutable Tendulkar had an answer.

Yes, it was difficult. That was the reason he spent most of his spare time with his childhood friends, who didn't treat him like a god. They made fun of him, needled him and kept him grounded and sane. Outside the sphere of these old mates and his family, he had no friends. Though he did not say this, it was as if these close people were the ones who kept him from becoming smug and arrogant.

By the time Tendulkar played his last Test match in 2013, I was no longer reporting on matches, having become a columnist with the *Hindustan Times*. I could not attend the match with a press accreditation and regular tickets were hard to get. When I read in the papers that Tendulkar had kept a large number of tickets for his numerous friends and well-wishers to watch his farewell Test, I requested a ticket from him. He obliged, allowing me the opportunity to spend five days at the Wankhede sitting among his family and friends.

Among them was his brother Ajit, with whom I had the chance to converse. Sachin's closeness to Ajit and the guidance, coaching and help his elder brother has provided him throughout his career is widely known even outside of cricketing circles. Ajit has a calm face and a soft voice, and speaks with a degree of clarity and confidence that his brother lacks. I found him to be very humble, articulate and fluent.

What struck me was the complete lack of any trace of self-importance in not just Ajit but also the other members of the Tendulkar family. They were just a normal family, watching a cricket match like anyone else at the ground, not self-conscious about being the family of the great Tendulkar, the man of the moment. Among the family watching the match were his daughter Sara, wife Anjali, and mother-in-law Annabel Mehta.

Tendulkar has never missed an opportunity to acknowledge the debt he owes his late father, Ramesh Tendulkar, who let him pursue his dream. In India, we all tend to overemphasize the greatness of our parents and attribute all our achievements and positive qualities to their upbringing and blessings. Tendulkar is no exception. In those five days I got the sense that Tendulkar's grooming at home must have been a tremendous help in fortifying him to face the challenges of the world and perfect his skill and craft with single-minded concentration and passion.

When Tendulkar nicked a ball from Narsingh Deonarine into Darren Sammy's hands, it signalled the end of a staggering career. The stadium fell silent. In his last innings, Tendulkar finished 26 runs short of what would have been his fifty-second Test hundred. The crowd, after expressing its collective sense of grief through their momentary pause, came back to life, applauding their hero off with tears in their eyes. Ajit was quiet but I could see that his eyes were moist.

Among the many memories that flashed in my mind as he walked back one last time on a cricket field was the one from 2000, of a Kanpur hotel room late in the night after India had played a One-Day match against Zimbabwe. Instead of walking into a luxurious five-star suite of India's biggest icon, I stepped into a room whose only occupants were a mattress spread on the floor, a video recorder and a picture of Satya Sai Baba on the table. It was in these austere settings Tendulkar explained that ever since a career-threatening back injury, he had stopped sleeping on soft-cushioned beds. Sleeping on the floor strengthened his back muscles. For any sportsperson, injuries are part of the journey, and Tendulkar has had more than a fair share of them. How one deals with them determines one's longevity, and Tendulkar was able to handle his injury problems better than most.

It is not that Tendulkar's career was without controversy. His relationship with the controversial agent and businessman Mark Mascarenhas is one which has puzzled many. On the face of it, it was a perfectly legitimate business deal between an agent and a player. Mark signed Tendulkar in 1995 for a figure of around Rs 25 crore, which increased to Rs 100 crore in 2000. It was the biggest deal in cricket then.

Mark, who lived in the USA, ran a company called WorldTel. His company had acquired the broadcast rights for the 1996 World Cup for around Rs 50 crore. However, he was to be later charged with economic fraud. Despite denying the allegations, most of his cricketing ventures came to a stop. Yet, Mark's business relationship with Tendulkar endured. A man widely respected and acclaimed as a true role model stood by another being accused of financial misconduct by the Indian authorities.

Mark was tragically killed in a car accident in 2002 and as a mark of respect, the entire Indian squad wore black bands in a match that was played following that tragic event. Tendulkar's involvement with Mark has never been a subject of any controversy, nor has anyone ever alleged that their dealings were not above board. But to us journalists, there seemed something 'unethical' about Tendulkar continuing to be financially managed by a man accused of financial misconduct.

I only understood Mark's popularity among cricketers across the world when Ian Chappell, who was then writing a column for the *Hindustan Times*, called me from Australia. I was the sports editor of the paper at the time, and Chappell wanted to inform me that he was writing an obituary for Mark but did not want to be paid for it. The obituary showed how much respect Ian had for Mark.

In his autobiography, Tendulkar lavishes high praise on Mark, describing him as a friend who 'understood my cricketing goals and needs and never interfered in my cricket'. It was only on the eve of his 100th Test match at the Oval in England that I finally mustered the courage to ask Tendulkar what defined his relationship with Mark.

I did not think it wise to ask him about Mark in the presence of others, so I waited till I had an opportunity where there was no one else around. He replied that Mark was his agent and nothing else. However, he requested me to not write anything controversial as he did not want anything to distract him from that milestone Test. I respected his request and did not touch upon his relationship with Mark in my article that day.

However, I have been critical of him on other occasions. For example, he did not want to pay taxes on a Ferrari presented to him by Fiat after he equalled Don Bradman's record of twenty-nine Test centuries. Also, he hardly ever attended a session of the Rajya Sabha despite being a nominated member. There are many in the cricketing fraternity who say that he has a long memory and does not forget or forgive anyone who has been critical of him. My experience has been otherwise, as he has never shown any hostility towards me despite the criticism. In fact, in his long career, he has hardly ever responded to any criticism or criticized anyone else.

His most 'controversial' stands have been on the issues of his own captaincy and on team selection. Some of the selectors during his first tenure as captain found him 'unreasonable' at times during the selection committee meetings. Once, he almost was on the verge of tears when the selectors did not agree with one of his choices. 'He was very passionate when it came to the team selection,' recalls a former Indian cricketer who was one of the selectors witness to this incident. 'However, it was shocking to see him almost burst into tears on being denied one of his choices, whom we all felt did not merit selection. We felt terrible to see one of the legends of the game reduced to such a state. However, we stuck to our guns.' It is a reflection of Tendulkar's personality that instead of losing his cool, he almost broke down. I cite this incident not to belittle Tendulkar or the selectors, but to highlight the tensions and pressures that he had to face as a captain when fighting for the team he wanted.

Tendulkar had the desire and ambition to remain captain for as long as he played. His sacking in 1997 after his differences with the selectors may have eroded his confidence, but he was not willing to give up. Yet, captaincy was affecting his mental health. On that tour of the West Indies in 1997, he said that he was so consumed with the game that there were times when he couldn't sleep at night and that sometimes he even went blank while batting. He wondered aloud, 'I wonder how long can this last.'

He may not have been mentally prepared to be reappointed captain, and the embarrassing losses in Australia must have further undermined his resolve. He said that his struggle to be accountable for the performance of others was one of the main reasons for quitting captaincy after the Australian tour. He says in his autobiography that he thought it was better to concentrate on his batting, rather than letting his personal performances dip because of his captaincy struggles. Of course, it is also possible that Azhar's imminent return to the team was behind Sachin's decision to withdraw as captain. I am not privy to any eyewitness account that corroborates this version of events, but it could have played a key role.

From Tendulkar's perspective, Kapil was not of much help. They had played together and had developed a good relationship on the 1992 tour of South Africa, and it was no secret that Tendulkar admired and respected Kapil. That did not, however, translate into a meaningful captain–coach relationship. Tendulkar was not getting the kind of strategic inputs he thought he would, and soon became forlorn, a lonely captain on and off the field. He finally chose peace, preferring to be responsible for his own performance and not have to also answer for his teammates.

When Tendulkar's decision was made public, no explanations were offered either by the player or the Board. The announcement simply stated that Tendulkar would lead in the two Tests against South Africa and then step down. That he would still take on another captaincy assignment was because the new captain needed time to prepare himself.

Sourav Ganguly was announced as captain for the One-Day series that followed the Tests. With Tendulkar no longer captain, rumours abounded that Kapil would also quit in solidarity. However, he decided to carry on, and it did not go down well with Tendulkar fans.

All these dramatic events were soon to appear insignificant, as a catastrophic event turned world cricket upside down. Within a fortnight of that One-Day series against South Africa, Delhi Police lodged an FIR against Hansie Cronje and four other South African cricketers: Herschelle Gibbs, Nicky Boje, Pieter Strydom and Henry Williams. They were charged with being in touch with an Indian bookie called Sanjeev Chawla and agreeing to fix the One-Day series. What was till then in the realm of speculation and rumour had now been dragged into the open.

Cronje named Azhar as the man who had introduced him to the bookmaker M.K. Gupta in 1996, during a Test match in Kanpur. Azharuddin's career came to an abrupt end after 99 Test matches. Injury had forced him to miss the first Test, and the second Test in Mumbai, which would have been his 100th but for that injury, turned out to be his last.

Had Azharuddin's link with M.K. been revealed before the South African series, there is a strong possibility that Tendulkar may have stayed on as the Indian captain. Instead, not only did he quit, but also, because of Bindra's accusations, Kapil resigned as coach. Indian cricket was now rudderless, and an inexperienced Sourav Ganguly was tasked with giving it direction.

8
Enter Sourav Chandidas Ganguly

The crisis that had engulfed Indian cricket was unprecedented in nature. It could be accepted that there are administrators who are corrupt, self-serving and untrustworthy. But the revelations that some of the main stars and role models were guilty of taking money to underperform, cheating their team and spectators alike, was shocking. It seemed to us the fabric of the sport had been torn and it would never again have the popularity and trust it once did.

Miraculously, cricket not only survived but continues to thrive, despite nasty reminders from time to time that fixing may not have been eradicated completely. Fans may have become sceptical about the integrity of players at large, but their unshakeable faith in the sport and in its entertainment value has kept cricket going. Following the scandal and the establishment of the ACU, a number of new rules were implemented for the players. Whether these measures were going to be effective was debatable, as particularly in India bookie infiltration had deep roots going right down to the junior club leagues.

Ambassador of Bengal

India now had a new captain: the elegant left-handed batsman from Bengal, Sourav Ganguly.

Bengal has a unique place in India's history and culture, whether in literature, music or cinema. Icons such as Vivekananda, Rabindranath Tagore, Satyajit Ray and Raja Rammohan Roy are recognized as masters in their fields. Many of these stalwarts were products of what historians call the Renaissance movement in Bengal, which was a result of the British-introduced Western education and the local cultural values combining to produce intellectuals from mainly the elite upper-classes, who were known as *bhadralok*.

Ganguly's time as the Indian captain had a great impact not just on the Indian team and its work ethic, but in his home state as well. They saw in him their cultural ambassador who was reminding other Indians of the glorious contribution of Bengalis in the larger construct of an Indian nation, a contribution which they felt had not been properly recognized. For the outsider, Bengal may be just one of the many states that make India, but for Bengalis it is a country within a country: undermine its significance at your own peril.

I had attempted to write a book about the Ganguly phenomenon, with the player's consent and participation. However, just like the one I tried to do on Tiger Pataudi, this too unfortunately never materialized. Though, my research provided me with a lot of information and anecdotes that throw light on the Ganguly era.

He is an unlikely hero, an arresting figure who shaped a future for Indian cricket unknowingly, maybe even accidentally, not aware himself of the enormity of events taking place while he was leading India. For Bengali cricket fans, Ganguly became a symbol of pride, one of their own who gained international fame from a state with hardly any cricketing legacy. Before him, the best-known cricketer from Bengal was Pankaj Roy, who is celebrated for the 413-run opening partnership, a world record at the time, with Vinoo Mankad against New Zealand in 1956.

Roy, with an average of 32 in the 43 Tests he played, means much more to Bengal than to India. He is seen there as an icon with many myths surrounding his rise and fall, the latter being attributed mainly to the fallacies of the Indian selectors. Every cricketing story in Bengal would have some reference to the greatness of Roy and his genius. This was until Ganguly came along.

Ganguly was captain of India from 2000 to 2005. It was a period in which the Indian team flourished and realized its true potential, both at home and overseas. However, it was not without controversy. Ganguly's relationship with the coach Greg Chappell deteriorated even as he was fighting for his survival as captain and player. There was not one moment of respite while he was at the helm and when he finally played his last Test in 2008 in Nagpur, he failed to score a century by just 15 runs. Had he scored the hundred, he would have joined his adversary Chappell in the small list of players to have scored a hundred both in their first and last Tests.

Another Career Move for Me

Less than a year at *Newspaper Today* was enough to make me desperately look for a new job. This e-venture was turning out to be a failure: it faced a financial crunch and so our travel coverage was restricted. The editor, Anand P. Raman, seemed on edge all the time. I started worrying about my future and feared that the venture would go out of business. It did eventually wind up, but only after I had already quit.

My stay in the India Today group however was not altogether a failure, as I got an opportunity to cover the epochal, transformative India–Australia series of 2001. While there, I also had the opportunity to be interviewed for the position of sports editor for the prestigious *Wisden* cricket magazine. They had decided to launch an Indian edition, and the India Today Group would have been their local partner.

Anand P. Raman recommended my name to India Today Group owner Aroon Purie for the editorship, saying, 'Why look outside when we have the person to do the job already in the organization?' A meeting was set up between the two of us. Anand, with a rather dark, urbane sense of humour, that could sometimes be wicked when dealing with his staff in a bid to make them more disciplined and responsive to their office work, was my well-wisher. While preparing me for the interview, he gave me a few instructions, the foremost being that I should make sure that I look straight into Purie's eyes without blinking while the interview was on. The reason, Anand said, was that Purie once rejected a candidate because he was shifty-eyed and did not look into his eyes while answering his questions.

What I remember the most of that interaction, or grilling, is that not once did I shift my eyes from his piercing gaze, not moving them or blinking for a second, following Raman's instructions to near perfection. If anything, it was Purie, who baulked under my steadfast gaze and dropped his eyes. Whether this stratagem played a role in my finding favour with Purie I am not sure, but I was his chosen man after this meeting. Alas, I was unable to convince the Wisden board that came down to interview me, and did not get the final nod. This time around I had no Raman to instruct me in which direction to look while being interviewed!

Within a year of Ganguly's ascendancy to captaincy, I joined the *Hindustan Times* (HT) as its sports editor. *HT* had a much larger circulation than *The Indian Express*, and therefore the impact of an article was greater. I was given the responsibility of revamping its staid and conservative sports coverage. I had no limitations on my authority.

Playing the Game

My new job at *HT* gave me the opportunity to travel more and I could interact with the players again. Very significantly, Ganguly became our columnist, and this helped me understand the functional dynamics of the Indian cricket team better.

Ganguly is perhaps the most fascinating cricketer I have known. From watching him for the first time in 1991 in that Duleep Trophy match in Guwahati to being present when he scored that debut century at Lord's in 1996, I had seen him evolve from a young player with potential to become one of the mainstays of the Indian batting line-up. He was in tremendous form during the 1999 World Cup, and his innings of 183 at Taunton against Sri Lanka is still vivid in my mind.

I interviewed him for the first time in London after that World Cup. His reputation preceded him: a snooty, temperamental person who had been spoilt by his rich father. This was what people talked about more than his talent. I was determined to find out if this image was accurate, as in my few brief interactions with him until then he had come across as a polite, well-behaved person.

Ganguly has a very disarming, welcoming smile. He may not always arrive for an interview at the promised time or might ditch you altogether, but once he meets you, he is all courtesy and it is difficult not to like him. That day in London, he was at his best behaviour. Ganguly's fist-pumping, aggressive body language on the field which he displayed when he became captain later was not associated with Indian cricket until then. But off the field he was usually a well-mannered and pleasant person. On that day in

England, he was a very satisfied man, having performed well on world cricket's biggest stage.

While I interviewed him in the lobby of the hotel, there were a number of Bengali journalists who were loitering around in the hope of catching his eye and getting a quote from him. For the vibrant regional press and its cricket journalists, Ganguly was growing in status. The man himself was aware of the significance of the Bengali press, and treated them with a familiarity and warmth that one reserves for one's family.

There was a freelance photographer from Bengal who would keep his luggage in Ganguly's room if he could not find a convenient place to stay on tours, and Ganguly sometimes even let him sleep in his room. There were many others who would believe he was their close friend and that he shared his secrets only with them.

As Ganguly grew in stature and began to control and dominate Indian cricket, his relationship with them only strengthened, despite his not having enough time now to indulge them. He knew exactly when to be warm towards them and when to ignore them.

In response to my question about why he did not seem to get annoyed at the constant presence of journalists from Bengal around him, he told me that his home in Behala, Calcutta, was always open to friends and well-wishers, who would come in great numbers to congratulate his parents on their son's achievements. I later discovered his home is a huge mansion with sprawling lawns that could easily host events with hundreds of attendees.

Ganguly understood the needs of the Bengali journalists and the demands their respective newspapers put on them because a local lad was doing so well in the Indian team. 'They need a few quotes and a bit of access,' he said, 'and I am OK with it.' It was hard for me to associate arrogance, conceit or self-absorption with Ganguly after that interview.

That image of arrogance perhaps stemmed from the statements by Ranbir Singh Mahendra, the former manager of the Indian cricket team when Ganguly received his first India call-up in 1992. Ganguly would always shrug at Mahendra's assessment of him, wondering what led him to express such an unwarranted opinion. Perhaps an explanation could be found in the fact that Mahendra was a rival of Jagmohan Dalmiya and saw Ganguly as someone who had been pushed into the team because of Dalmiya's backing, and made him a victim of that perception.

At many points throughout his cricketing career, Ganguly has had to endure scathing criticism that stemmed from his perceived association with India's most powerful official ever, the wily Dalmiya. An insight into the Dalmiya–Ganguly relationship and its significance in the larger perspective can be had from an anecdote from the time Ganguly was made vice-captain in 1999.

According to an official of the Board, when the news was broken to Dalmiya, his reaction was not one of joy or satisfaction. Instead, he said, '*Inhonne mere gale mein saanp ki rassi daal di hai* (They have put a rope around my neck).' Dalmiya was a Marwari businessman thriving in the state, and was in no position to oppose a real native of Bengal. The fear of being ostracized in Bengal was a driving force greater than any fondness he may have had for Ganguly. He knew now that Ganguly had been made the vice-captain, his path to the captaincy was paved. Dalmiya could not afford to be seen as being a hindrance to Ganguly's career and whatever he demanded from him. Thus, as long as Dalmiya ruled Indian cricket, Ganguly enjoyed unbridled power.

The benefit from Indian cricket's perspective is that Ganguly shrewdly used this equation to make sweeping changes in the way the team was being run, whether in training methods or the coaching staff. His inputs benefited the team immensely. As one senior player once put it to me, 'To give credit to Ganguly, we would put many demands that we felt were needed for the betterment of the team, and he would get them approved by Dalmiya.'

Ganguly, it should not be forgotten, was made captain of a team that had other strong candidates for the post, including his senior, Kumble. In fact, Kumble perhaps had reason to believe that he was the logical choice, and Dravid may have felt he was in with an outside chance.

I remember interviewing Dravid in England after India had won the Headingley Test at Leeds on the 2002 tour. Ganguly had made a statement of positive intent by choosing to bat first in overcast, seaming conditions, and India saw out hostile seam and swing bowling to rack up a huge first innings score. The innings rode on the technical brilliance of Dravid and Sanjay Bangar, the openers who set a great platform for Tendulkar and Ganguly to take them to victory.

In the interview, I asked Dravid whether he nursed captaincy ambitions and would at some time in the future want to lead the team. He replied in the affirmative, saying that he, like most players, did wish to captain the national team someday. It was an innocuous and honest answer. In fact, Dravid commanded tremendous respect for the dignified manner he handled himself in public. He always chose his words with great care, not wanting to say anything that could create a controversy.

Later, when I was writing the article, Dravid came to me and said, 'Pradeep, please drop that captaincy question.' I understood his dilemma and agreed to his request. While there was nothing wrong in what he had said and in no way was he trying to create any discord in the team, he did not want his answer to be misconstrued as being a challenge to Ganguly's throne.

By that time, Ganguly had cemented his place as captain. However, he had had his challenges at the beginning. The problems came not from within the team but from the internecine battles that plague the BCCI. The most vocal critic of Ganguly was Raj Singh Dungarpur, a fierce adversary of Dalmiya at that time. Dalmiya's friend was a foe, and Dungarpur lost no opportunity to run Ganguly down and had even tried to get Kumble appointed vice-captain before the selectors decided on Ganguly.

So unabashedly strident was Dungarpur's opposition to Ganguly that on India's tour to Sri Lanka in 2001, he told Dravid to prepare to lead while ensuring that most of the junior members of the team were within earshot. These and many such comments were widely reported in the media as Dungarpur made his opposition to Ganguly public through newspaper columns and by speaking to the press. In an article published by *The Times of India* in December 2001, he wrote, 'In my view Ganguly was never captaincy material. One, he is self-possessed [presumably he meant self-centred], two, he is not a good student of the game, and three, he sets a bad example on the field, because he is our worst fielder.'

However, Dungarpur was to change loyalties a few years later, seeking Dalmiya's support to become the Board president. He even came to admire Ganguly and the changes he brought to Indian cricket. This just goes to show that, just as in politics, there are no permanent friends or foes in Indian cricket administration.

Ganguly did not let all this negativity affect his resolve. He was a remarkable character, able to take a lot of flak and handle all the criticism he was getting. He genuinely wanted to overcome his shortcomings and above all was desperate to make his team improve and win, especially outside India.

Prince of Kolkata

To understand Ganguly better, we need to delve a bit into his background. His father's booming printing press business had made their family among the richest in Kolkata. Chandidas Ganguly was not only a member of the Cricket Association of Bengal, he was at one time a very close associate of Dalmiya. His influence in the cricket circles of Kolkata meant that his two sons (the elder of whom, Snehasish, was also a promising player) could have received favourable treatment when it came to team selection, though no one doubted their talent. Ganguly made his First-Class debut for Bengal before he turned seventeen, in the Ranji Trophy final against Delhi. Ironically, his selection had been at the expense of his own brother, who was dropped. Sambaran Bannerjee, a former Bengal cricketer, was the local selector responsible for this decision. An interesting coincidence is that Sambaran was one of the five national selectors in 1996 and played a prominent role in Ganguly's recall to the Indian team.

Ganguly, like most Bengalis, loved playing football in school, even though his brother and father preferred cricket. However, he showed great talent and promise as a cricketer. He was a powerful batsman despite his frail frame. Shortly after choosing to play cricket full-time, he was picked to play for India on the tour to Australia in 1992.

However, after the incidents on that tour, he was unceremoniously dropped and remained in the wilderness for four years. He played for his state team with average results, not accomplishing anything outstanding that would have merited a recall. However, he was picked for the England tour in 1996. The Indian team hadn't changed much since 1992, and he would have seen familiar faces in the dressing room—including the captain, Azharuddin. I am not sure what the team thought of his return, but the press certainly did not believe that he deserved to be there.

The sniggering around his selection was brought to an end by his century at Lord's. He still had many detractors, who doubted whether he could maintain his performances, but Bengal was euphoric. They now had a hero outside of football, in a sport which is deeply entrenched in the pan-Indian psyche.

Ganguly's success as a batsman and a captain owes a lot to his fierce ambition and desire to constantly learn and improve. He tried to eliminate his batting flaws, including his weakness on the leg side. Soon he became better at the pull shot and could handle being targeted on his weaker side. He also improved his fitness and running between the wickets. He was mentally strong and when slighted, he had the strength to fight back, as he did to make an unlikely comeback after being dropped from the Indian team in 2005.

He once told me that he wished to be remembered as a selfless captain who did not favour anyone. He wanted to earn his team's respect. Whether all his teammates thought that or not is hard to say, but two players eternally grateful to Ganguly were Virender Sehwag and Yuvraj Singh. Both were explosive talents who needed to be backed in their early days when they were still struggling to find their feet. Sehwag has paid glorious tributes to him many a time. He once told me that but for Ganguly's backing, he and Yuvraj may have been dropped before their careers had really taken off. 'Our future appeared bleak as we were not making any runs,' he recalled. 'But Ganguly reassured us and said that we would be given ample chances to prove ourselves. We need not worry about our next innings.'

This was one of the unique qualities of Ganguly: he recognized talent that was not in any conventional mould. He never showed favouritism towards any particular region, class or religion. Apart from Sehwag and Yuvraj, Zaheer Khan, Harbhajan Singh and Ashish Nehra are among those eventual superstars who may not have fulfilled their potential under a captain with a more conservative outlook to the game. They would probably never have been given the kind of protection from failure as they had from Ganguly. He had this uncanny ability to identify match-winners and would ignore their failures, indiscipline and other shortcomings.

Nehra and Zaheer were confrontational characters, but Ganguly was patient with them. He acted more like a friend than a leader. These individuals responded to their captain's faith and the team performed better. Ganguly may have fallen out of favour with some of them in the latter part of his captaincy, when lack of form and Chappell's harsh scrutiny was making him feel insecure and lonely, but for most of his tenure he was their mentor and hero.

A more difficult job for Ganguly could have been how he handled senior players of the likes of Tendulkar, Dravid, Kumble and Laxman. Indian cricket captains in the past have suffered when they were unable to manage the egos of the senior, or more talented, members of their team. But this group was different. They all took great pride in their performance and were fiercely competitive. They wanted their team to do well, and were not willing to let egos and petty grievances come in the way of team performance. Ganguly was fortunate that these senior players, whatever reservations they may have had about him as a person and as a captain, were willing to give their best to him and the team.

As the world moved into the twenty-first century, Indian cricket was truly blessed to have this core of players who were not only supremely talented but selfless as well. What followed was a gradual transformation of the Indian team as they started performing exceptionally well not just in their comfort zone of home but also in places like England, Australia and even South Africa. They may not have won a series in Australia or South Africa, but they won Test matches and competed well. The Indian team was now a formidable force, no longer one to be scoffed at and rolled over.

One of the key decisions that played a major role in this transformation was the choice of coach. Until then, India had chosen home-grown coaching talent, and the likes of Bedi, Patil, Anshuman Gaekwad and Madan Lal had performed the role. However, Ganguly wanted a more neutral, professional coach. After consulting with Dravid and other senior players, he zeroed in on the former New Zealand opener John Wright.

Wright was then the coach of Kent in England, and Dravid had played under him during his stint as an overseas player. He had been very impressed by Wright and Ganguly went with his suggestion. The no-nonsense Wright turned out to be an inspirational choice. He was the right man to build a professional work ethos in the Indian team, free of the regional biases that the players felt an Indian coach might be susceptible to.

A Coach for All Seasons

Wright is a tall man with piercing eyes. He generally kept to himself, especially when it came to interacting with journalists. However, with a glass of beer in hand, he would be more warm and friendly, and liberal with his opinions. Yet, even after having spent the previous evening drinking with you, he would sometimes not acknowledge you at the ground the next morning. He could be abrupt, even appearing rude.

He was a committed professional, working in chaotic conditions where proper planning, training schedules and discipline were terribly lacking. In India, cricket stars could be hard to manage and, to succeed, a coach had to keep his star players happy. Once, Wright revealed one of the more creative methods he employed to get the players to follow his inputs without ruffling their pride. 'I know they are huge stars with big egos,' he said. 'I have to be careful as they don't like to be given instructions. You don't point out mistakes to people who are like rock stars. I work very subtly on their mind. Plant an idea slowly, till a stage is reached that they come to me and say themselves, "Hey John, I have decided to do this", and it is the very thing I had wanted them to do in the first place. The difference is that now they believe that it was their own idea and I had nothing to do with it. I didn't mind that, as I had achieved my aim.'

Wright had understood Indian superstar culture well, unlike Greg Chappell, who would famously fail a few years later. Wright had a very perceptive mind, very wary of the distractions that are a part of Indian cricketers' lives. He worked around these carefully and silently, putting in place a system that could instil a more professional outlook and a sense of pride in playing for the country.

Sharda Ugra, one of India's most independent journalists (there are not many left today), was working with *India Today* during Wright's tenure as India coach, and co-authored a book with him about that period titled *John Wright's Indian Summers*. She told me about a tactic used by Wright that tells us a lot about his way of functioning.

Wright was struck by the game's huge popularity in India, and amazed by the way people worshipped cricketers. It was on a scale he had never seen anywhere else in the world. He decided to use it to help him with his aims. In one of his first interactions with the team, he organized a lecture by the television commentator Harsha Bhogle. Bhogle spoke to the players about the god-like status they enjoy in the country and how let down their millions of fans feel when they do not perform well. He helped them understand what it meant to be worshipped so blindly, and how devastating it was for the fans when India lost. Conversely, a victory was like a dream fulfilled, especially when it came against a stronger team.

Wright's aim was to make the players realize that they owed it to themselves as well as their fans to work hard and achieve victory. It was a clever way of playing on their egos to inspire them to set a higher team goal. Instead of a straightforward lecture on values of discipline, team ethics and hard work, which they may have not really processed, he was making them feel important and in the process subtly reminding them of their responsibility.

Wright was never too comfortable with an overly demonstrative, sentimental approach to cricket. He was a very private person and remained an outsider who preferred the solitude of his hotel room. Perhaps he found it hard to connect with an alien culture where hierarchies, whether in the team or dealing with officials, mattered more than individual worth.

Yet, he succeeded. He may not have transformed India into a world-beating team but he did help the team shed its insecurities. He put systems in place to instil a team culture that emphasized a collective work ethic over personal goals.

During Wright's tenure, Ganguly's role as captain is significant. It is said that Wright would have preferred to work with someone like Dravid or Kumble as his captain. Of all the members of the Indian team, Dravid perhaps was closest to Wright in his thinking and would have best understood Wright's impatience at the slow and at times even indifferent responses to his demands. Yet, what worked better for the team was the synergy between two contrasting personalities and viewpoints. Wright was a stickler for processes, while for the laidback Ganguly, results, no matter how they were achieved, were all that mattered. Despite the two being so different in their approaches, their overall goals were in sync and they never let their differences disrupt team harmony.

I have seen Wright fretting and fuming over Ganguly doing exactly the opposite of the dressing-room strategy out on the field. In the hotel bar after the day's play, Wright would be cursing the captain for not listening to him. But he never let his frustration spill over and destabilize the team. He was, unlike Greg Chappell, neither insecure nor a control freak. Wright may have disagreed with Ganguly on many occasions, but he let the captain be the ultimate boss of the team.

Wright's tenure ended in 2005, and two years later, he was working as a commentator during the 2007 World Cup in the West Indies. When I spoke to him then, he acknowledged that 'Ganguly was a great captain'. On the field, an Indian team that was no longer united suffered a shock exit at the preliminary stages of the World Cup. Perhaps, after having had the time to reflect, Wright had realized how difficult it was to manage a team with bloated egos and interfering officials. That had helped him arrive at the conclusion that Ganguly was indeed the best person to have led the team during his time as coach.

A lot of the credit for maintaining a healthy balance in the relationship between the coach and the captain and players should go to Ganguly as well. He knew when to stand by his demands and when to give in. Speaking about his later differences with Greg Chappell, Ganguly said, 'There were times when Wright would be so upset with me that he wouldn't even talk to me for days.' During these periods, Ganguly too would remain quiet and not precipitate matters. Eventually things would return to normal, and 'we both would move on'.

Ganguly's First-Class debut in the 1989–90 Ranji Trophy final had seen him come up against a Delhi team that was foul-mouthed and abusive. They incessantly sledged the Bengal players. In that Delhi team were Kirti Azad, the late Raman Lamba, Manoj Prabhakar, Atul Wassan and Maninder Singh, while the Bengal side included the likes of Arun Lal, Ashok Malhotra and Pranab Roy. Due to a combination of bad light and excruciatingly slow batting by both batting sides, neither team could bat a second time. Ganguly scored a crucial 22 and saw some of the best-known players of his time at their worst behaviour. However, Delhi's intimidating tactics failed, and Bengal won that match. They were crowned Ranji champions for only the second time ever.

Right from that first match, Ganguly had been exposed to the on-field tactics that didn't appear in coaching manuals, and over the years he developed an understanding about what worked and didn't work tactically. He did not always keep faith in strategies drawn up in dressing rooms; his responses on the ground were dictated by his intuitive reading of the moment.

For instance, Harbhajan was proving ineffective during a Test match, and during a session break the coach and captain decided to give the ball to someone else when play resumed. However, just before they went back to the field, Ganguly spotted Harbhajan bowling with great rhythm on the side of the ground. 'When the match resumed, I handed the ball to Harbhajan, going against the plan,' recalled Ganguly. 'He immediately got us wickets.' But he accepted that there would be times when his gut feeling would not work. 'The coach may then justifiably be upset,' he said. 'What matters in the end is your intention, the result is not always in your hands.' Ganguly said this while his personal battle with Greg Chappell was going on, trying to put the coach–captain relationship in perspective.

The Ganguly–Wright combination was in charge during the 2003 Adelaide Test where India chased 230 runs for a historic win. I have three very contrasting anecdotes that are revealing about the different emotions that play out in the minds of those in the centre of these high-voltage situations.

At the end of the fourth day, India still needed another 193 for victory. Dravid came to my room at the hotel that evening, probably to take his mind off the pressures of the match. He started a light-hearted conversation but the journalist in me tried to move the talk towards the match. Dravid quickly made it clear that he didn't want to talk or think about the match.

During India's chase, Sehwag played a wild heave against Stuart McGill and was out for 47, putting the Indian team under pressure. India managed to win the Test on the back of Dravid's unbeaten 72.

Ganguly contributed only 12 in a torturous forty-one minutes at the crease.

After the victory, the Indian captain was excited, thrilled and in a joyous mood. When I asked how he had soaked in the pressure, he was frank enough to confess, 'When I was batting, I was so nervous that I could hardly see the ball.' The restless Ganguly had spoken to Dravid during his innings and explained his state of mind. He was grateful to his deputy for taking India to victory.

The third incident occurred later that night, and illustrates Wright's all-consuming passion to see his team follow the processes set in place. If a player deviated from the norm, the coach would be extremely unhappy, even if the end result was a happy one, as it was on that day. Wright was in the bar with trainer Andrew Leipus. I congratulated them and joined the celebrations.

Though very pleased with the victory, he was very upset about the manner of Sehwag's dismissal. For Wright it was an unpardonable act to throw away your wicket in attempting such an outrageous shot, that too in a situation where India was on the cusp of a historic win. 'What the hell was he thinking,' Wright muttered in a string of expletives. I could understand his frustration at the pressure that dismissal had put on the team.

Wright was like that. He would prefer to err on the side of caution. For him, process and discipline was everything. The team had to adhere to a proper fitness regimen and not deviate from plans.

A Fighter and a Rebel

Ganguly believed that his bowlers, particularly the pacers, bowled better with an aggressive approach. A few hostile words mouthed at the batsmen helped this strategy. His core bowling team of Zaheer, Nehra and Harbhajan were never afraid to hover at the edge of unsporting behaviour, and may have been even encouraged to do so by their captain.

In the home series against Australia in 2001, Ganguly was late for the toss for the first Test played in Mumbai. It is considered extremely disrespectful for the captain of one team to make the other wait at the toss. Ganguly claimed that this was a genuine mistake, not something he had done intentionally. But when he realized that it had upset and irritated the opposition captain Steve Waugh, the same act became a strategy. The second time he deliberately arrived late, as 'it made Waugh lose his cool and affected his game', Ganguly told me years later. He had sensed an opportunity, and used it without bothering about the conventions of the game or about being seen as unethical and discourteous. As far as he was concerned it worked in his team's favour and he was breaking no rule. There is no penalty for a captain who does not walk out to toss with his rival captain or even makes him wait for a couple of minutes.

Ganguly's aggressive persona on the field won him many admirers, who saw in it a reflection of an India that was growing in self-confidence and could fight fire with fire. Unlike his on-field image, Ganguly in real life is more circumspect and restrained. Those close to him were surprised at his transformation while playing a match. His wife, Dona—a classical dancer who was his childhood friend—told me that the family always wonders where the trademark Ganguly gesture—fists raised and scowling—came from.

Ganguly's rebellious streak and single-minded obsession to pursue his goals was again apparent when he went against the wishes of his parents and secretly married Dona in 1997. In fact, his parents heard about the marriage only through the papers when they published his marriage certificate. Ganguly was touring Sri Lanka with the Indian team at the time. His defiance shows his strong character and the ability to withstand pressure and do what he believes is good for him, whatever the costs may be.

During the 2002 tour of England, Tendulkar, Dravid and Kumble realized that they were contracted with companies that were rivals of the official sponsors of the World Cup scheduled for the following year. The ICC had banned players from doing any advertising during the World Cup period for companies that were rivals of the tournament's sponsors. Many of the Indian players would suffer financially because of this clause.

There was resistance to this from players of other countries as well but none of them would be as affected as the Indian players. Among the Indians, the captain was the least affected by this clause as most of his endorsements were not breaching the World Cup sponsor regulations. However, he decided to stand up for his colleagues.

While still in England, the Indian team decided to rebel, issuing a threat to boycott the World Cup if this clause restricting sponsorship was not scrapped or modified. A committee was formed and Dravid and Kumble were asked to draft the team's concerns and convey these to the BCCI. However, Dalmiya knew that overturning the conflicting clause was going to be difficult, if not downright impossible.

He would have normally put his foot down and forced the players to agree, but he had to first take on Ganguly, who had openly stated that if the clause was not withdrawn, his team would not play in the World Cup. It was an unprecedented situation, and I suspect that had anyone other than Ganguly been at the helm, Dalmiya would not have budged. It went back to his reluctance to be seen as going against Bengal's biggest icon, as his flourishing business enterprise in the state could suffer.

The headlines were devoted to this issue and not the good cricket India was playing in England. I remember most of us journalists chasing this story rather than focusing on the matches. Ravi Shastri was in England doing television commentary, and found himself appointed the players' representative to negotiate with the Board. Ravi rose to the occasion, challenging the Board to a debate on the issue while being extremely critical of Dalmiya.

During this period, Ganguly was writing a column for us in *HT*. Prior to approaching the paper for the column, he had syndicated it through an agency that had various newspapers across the country carrying it regularly. He made a direct approach to us, guaranteeing exclusivity at a reasonable rate. We agreed and he began writing the column himself. A neatly handwritten piece would be faxed to us, and each time he would make an interesting point or two.

After some time, he began emailing the column to me, and I would forward it to the office. Ganguly did not always meet the deadline and often he would neither answer the phone nor call back. Once I got so frustrated that I sent a terse message about this lack of courtesy. He responded immediately, calling me and apologizing, resulting in our relationship becoming a bit more informal than it had been till then.

Before the historic tour to Pakistan in 2004, one of Ganguly's agents called me to say that if we wished to retain his column during the tour the fee would be over four times what we were paying then. If we didn't agree, he would shift the column to *The Times of India*, *HT*'s main rival in Delhi. I called him to convey my displeasure at the steep increase in rate and the threat to withdraw the column. His response was, 'Don't worry. The agent may have seen in this an opportunity to make money, but I am committed to write for you and won't increase the rate at all.' He kept his word.

Back on that England tour in 2002, Ganguly's defiance had become a headache for Dalmiya. My roommate in London at that time happened to be a journalist from a leading Bengali newspaper. One night he got a phone call from his editor in Kolkata enquiring about Ganguly's whereabouts, as Dalmiya was unable to contact him. He was not answering his phone nor responding to messages. Dalmiya had to resort to seeking help from the paper to track Ganguly down in London and request him to call back. The reporter did manage to find Ganguly and conveyed Dalmiya's frantic message. The Indian captain feigned ignorance and said maybe the phone signal was bad in the area where he was staying.

I overheard the entire conversation and immediately wrote a story about how Ganguly was avoiding Dalmiya and not responding to his calls while this conflict between the players and the Board was raging. The report appeared on page one the next day, and soon the editor of the Bengali paper was seeking an explanation from my roommate as to how HT got hold of this information, which only the two of them had been privy to. Dalmiya must have been embarrassed at being painted as powerless.

The ugly confrontation was eventually resolved with both the players and the ICC reaching a compromise. However, when the team returned home from England, they formed a players' union. Tiger Pataudi was made president and Arun Lal the secretary, but the union soon became defunct. That gave the impression that the union was more about safeguarding the financial interests of the main stars and less to do with the larger issues affecting Indian cricketers as a whole.

It is often said that most journalists were afraid to be critical of Dalmiya. There were even allegations that he had 'control' over their opinions. However, I was often critical of his actions and that made our relationship an uneasy one. Given that I had been the target of the Board's ire ever since my story on the bookie–player nexus in 1997, his attitude towards me was frosty.

When the match-fixing scandal was finally exposed, I wanted to talk to Dalmiya for a story for *The Indian Express*. I don't think I had talked to him in a long time. I called him from the office landline and he answered. What followed was a lengthy diatribe, the gist of which was that he blamed me for causing serious damage to Indian cricket through my malicious writings. One line from that castigation still resounds in my ears: '*Aapne to Hindustan cricket ke kapde tak utarva diye. Ab khush hain aap?*' Loosely translated it meant: 'You have stripped Indian cricket naked. Are you happy now?'

However, this conversation, if it could be called that, may have had a cathartic effect on him, as from that day onwards, we were back on friendly talking terms. Our professional relationship was restored without any past ill will remaining.

When the West Indies were to play a Test match at the Eden Gardens, Dalmiya invited me to be his guest. His secretary called me to convey that this would be an all-expenses-paid trip. I had heard stories of how Dalmiya would 'please' journalists with many 'offerings'. I politely declined. This was followed by another invitation, to pay the expenses of my flight and I turned that one down too. Then Ganguly invited me to the launch of the players' association, to happen at the same venue and time as the Test. This to me was an important development and I made an official trip for it.

Dalmiya looked stumped to see me in the press box. 'I thought you weren't coming?' he sheepishly asked. When he understood the reason for my presence, he immediately knew that I was backing Ganguly, a man who was a huge headache for him as a cricket administrator. The BCCI has constantly resisted any threat to its monopoly, especially from the players, whom they have always treated as employees who have to be obedient.

While the Indian cricketers resolved their issues with the ICC before the 2003 World Cup, the team had been distracted and was completely outplayed on a tour to New Zealand prior to the global event. For Wright, being thrashed in his home country was an unpleasant experience. However, he had a better memory from the previous overseas tour to England.

In the final of a One-Day tournament, India took on England at Lord's and chased down a target of 325 from an impossible position. The game is remembered for the heroics of young guns Yuvraj Singh and Mohammed Kaif, but also for Ganguly breaking the code of behaviour at the ground that is considered the home of cricket. Standing on the players' balcony, he stripped off his shirt, baring his chest, and waved to the crowd in vigorous celebration. Ganguly's irreverent act at the most revered of English grounds, soaked in 'noble' traditions, was for many Indians a symbol of the new India which had shaken off any colonial hangover, a purification ceremony that all television channels dutifully air whenever India play England now.

An English cricket writer was to realize this change a few years later, while covering England's tour of India. On the eve of the Wankhede Test, that was also to be Dravid's 100th, he was, like most reporters, pushed and shoved around by the stifling security and the jostling crowd at the ground. This was not what he had experienced in his earlier visits. As he said, 'My white skin was like a password for me to get preferential treatment here. But India has changed, now I fear I may even get lynched because of the colour of my skin.'

9
The 2003 World Cup and After

The 2003 World Cup was held in Africa, co-hosted by South Africa, Zimbabwe and Kenya. It was soon clear that the tournament had political overtones to it. England refused to play in Zimbabwe because of President Mugabe's divisive, dictatorial policies while New Zealand refused to travel to Kenya due to security issues.

I spent a few days in Harare, the capital of Zimbabwe, and was shocked by the horrendous inflation and the scarcity of fuel and food. There was a sense of misery all round and extreme levels of distrust among its people. If I remember correctly, we exchanged $100 for around 100,000 Zimbabwean dollars. Tips of at least a few thousand in the local currency were expected by the waiters, and in the hotel where we were staying, women driven by poverty would be soliciting in the reception area without any fear or inhibition. I am still haunted by the female voices that would desperately call out, 'I want to come to your room', hoping to make a few bucks by tempting the dollar-flushed tourists.

We were advised not to travel at night, not to move around alone and to avoid lonely spots even in a group. Even for an Indian belonging to a society and a country divided by caste conflict and gross inequality, the Harare experience was numbing. Fear and the threat of violence hung in the air, affecting every moment.

The Indian team was soon putting on embarrassing displays, first just about managing to win against rookies Netherlands and then being mauled by Australia. The harsh media coverage led to Mohammed Kaif's home being attacked by irate mobs. The news unnerved the team. In a most unusual move, Sachin Tendulkar spoke in front of the media on the eve of their third match, to be played against Zimbabwe in Harare. The revered cricketing figure appealed to the Indian public to have faith in their team, as the tournament had just begun. The next day he played one of the many brilliant innings he would play in that World Cup, and India won the match by 83 runs. After that turnaround, India kept winning and progressed all the way to the final.

There had been a controversy with the team selection for the World Cup, as V.V.S. Laxman had been omitted, much to the shock and anger of the player himself. The reason offered for this decision was that he was a slow runner between the wickets, and from Wright's point of view that made him unsuitable for the number 6 position where he batted. Laxman made his displeasure public, and even when back in the Test squad he did not talk to Wright for months.

The team was in no way affected by this minor controversy and notched up resounding victories over England and Pakistan before being given a scare by minnows Kenya. After a top-order collapse, Ganguly's century ensured India's victory. New Zealand had refused to play Kenya on the grounds of security, and the walkover allowed them to qualify for the semi-finals, where they met India again. The

Indian skipper promptly scored another hundred as India brushed them aside yet again.

However, Kenya reaching the semi-finals was a remarkable achievement. They were being coached by Sandeep Patil during the tournament. But the team could not build on that performance, while Patil quit after the tournament as a major rift among the players erupted. No one was sure of the reason, but soon a key member of the Kenyan squad, Maurice Odumbe, was banned for five years by the ICC for his involvement with Indian bookmakers. Since then, disciplinary issues, lack of money and a host of other administrative problems have plagued the team. At present Kenya is on the margins of international cricket, a fate also suffered by their neighbours Zimbabwe.

I had interviewed Ganguly midway through the tournament, and he had told me that the team felt bad when the media and public turned against them, but expressed confidence that they would do well. He displayed a mature, almost statesmanlike manner in talking about his team. He was aware that some sections of the media wanted to create the impression that there was a rift between him and Rahul Dravid. He was disappointed that some of the reporters from his own region were part of this mischief, but his faith and confidence in Dravid was unshakeable and they both trusted each other immensely. I had not attached much significance to the rumours, as I saw no possibility of Dravid opposing his captain.

Ganguly stated that Dravid was one of the most important members of his team; Ganguly had fought for his position in the One-Day squad. For Dravid to be retained, Ganguly said he had given the 'wicketkeeper's slot to him so that he is not dropped'. The selection committee viewed Dravid's batting as slow and not suited for One-Day cricket, but Ganguly persuaded them to retain him by making him double up as a wicketkeeper. Dravid shouldered this responsibility as a challenge, and also started changing his batting style to became more adventurous in One-Day cricket.

India fancied their chances against the formidable Australians in the final, played at Johannesburg's Wanderers stadium. Ganguly exuded tremendous confidence on the eve of the final, even promising me a grand dinner once they won. However, I sensed a certain amount of tension among the Indian players that evening. Was it a sign of nervousness? They were unusually quiet and did not seem to be enjoying their training routines. Was it the pressure of a World Cup final and the expectations of the fans that were reflected on their faces, or was it just my imagination?

The sky was layered with clouds on the morning of the big game. It even drizzled for a while, though by the time the match started the sky was blue and the sun was shining once again. India won the toss and chose to bowl first, worried about the clouds and Glenn McGrath's skills with the new ball. It did not seem to have been a unanimous decision, as there were reports that the captain and the coach differed on what to do if they won the toss.

The decision backfired on them as opposition captain Ricky Ponting played one of the great One-Day innings. It was evident that a grave error had been made in dropping Kumble for Dinesh Mongia in the final. Australia's huge score of 359 sealed India's fate even before they got a chance to bat.

Memories of South Africa

My visit to South Africa had memorable moments outside of the cricket field as well, the most significant being my visit to the Phoenix settlement that Gandhi had founded near Durban. South Africa was the country where Gandhi began his transformation from a Gujarati Baniya lawyer into a great visionary leader of the masses. The transformative journey is believed to have begun on a railway platform in a small town called Pietermaritzburg, where he was thrown out of a train because he was travelling in a first-class compartment not meant for Blacks and 'coolies'.

India had a game against Namibia scheduled at Pietermaritzburg, and the local administration arranged a visit to that infamous station. There was even a short train journey played out for the players and the media—we rode in an exact replica of the train that Gandhi was travelling in when the incident took place. The area where Gandhi is supposed to have been dumped from the train has been marked, and for his followers it is now a pilgrimage spot. The whole recreation of the incident was like a dream for me as I sat in the replica train and tried to imagine what it might have been like for Gandhi back in 1893.

When I was a college student in Amritsar, I had devoured every bit of information I could find on Gandhi. But I could never have imagined that one day I would be standing in faraway South Africa on the same platform, at the same spot where his journey of change had begun. At that spot, there is a plaque that reads: 'In the vicinity of this plaque M.K. Gandhi was evicted from the first class compartment on the night of 7 June 1893. This incident changed the course of his life. He took up the fight against racial oppression. His active non-violence started from that date.'

However, though Gandhi fought for racial equality and dignity for the thousands of Indians in the Kwazulu-Natal area, I was to discover he was not revered by Black South Africans. In fact there was palpable tension between Blacks and Indians, who saw each other as rivals on the economic and social ladder.

When in Durban for the India–England match—in which Ashish Nehra produced a hostile spell of swing bowling to demolish England—I was keen to visit the Gandhi farm. To my disbelief, no one seemed to have heard of the place, be it the Indians or the

Blacks. Finally, one Black taxi driver said he had an idea of where the place could be, but warned us not to go there as it was right in the midst of a 'notorious' Black area and we could be mugged on our way there. He said we needed a police escort for our visit. I was determined to make the trip no matter what, and visited the police station to arrange an escort. The cops agreed to send a jeep to escort our taxi.

The drive to the Phoenix Ashram took about an hour, winding through a desolate area. The final stretch was a narrow road that ended at the premises. There was one tourist bus parked outside. Apparently, the place was not as unknown as it had appeared to be. Inside, instead of the old structure I was expecting, there was a new building in place.

I learnt that the original was burnt down by a Black mob in 1985, in anger against a large section of Indians in South Africa who they felt had sided with the Whites and shunned Blacks. Mandela's government had it rebuilt after the 1994 elections. The new structure had been built as similar as possible to the original.

The caretaker was a Black man. He greeted us and showed us around, pointing out the rooms where Kasturba and Mohandas Gandhi had lived and worked. I asked the caretaker why there was tension between the Blacks and the Indians. His terse response was, 'Indians think they are too clever.'

In my interaction with the two communities, I could sense their mutual mistrust. The Indians felt they were 'culturally' superior to the Blacks, and in the elections that followed the abolition of apartheid in 1994, the majority of the Indians were believed to have voted against Mandela. The Indians felt that the Blacks were too aggressive and unfairly favoured, even though the affirmative action laws that were introduced post Apartheid included both Blacks and Indians as its beneficiaries.

South Africa, like India, was struggling with the problem of 'reservations', and in their case it extended to sports. The row has often threatened to derail South African cricket. Predominantly a sport played by White people, the cricket board introduced a law that mandates that every team at the domestic level should have six 'players of colour' (non-White players), and three of them must be Black. At the national level too the same rule applies, with a requirement of two instead of three Black players.

Players like Makhaya Ntini and Kagiso Rabada, both fast bowlers of outstanding merit, are a result of this policy. However, it is a reflection of class divisions within the game of cricket that there has been hardly any Black batsman of repute to have emerged from the country. During the time of the British empire, the working-class people were condemned to the menial tasks of bowling and fielding, while the nobility enjoyed batting. South African Blacks alleged that they are advised to become bowlers when they start playing as children, as if 'our race is born to only bowl and not bat'.

This was not my first visit to South Africa, having been there in 2001 to cover India's highly controversial tour that year. After the second Test of the series, played at the St George's Park in Port Elizabeth, match referee Mike Denness infamously charged Sachin Tendulkar with ball tampering. He also punished Virender Sehwag, Harbhajan Singh, Shiv Sunder Das and Deep Dasgupta for excessive appealing and skipper Ganguly for being unable to control his players. Each player was banned for one match.

Denness, the former English cricketer who had toured India as deputy to Tony Lewis in 1972 and had scored centuries against India in 1974 at Lord's and Edgbaston, was suddenly labelled as racist for banning half of the Indian team 'unfairly'. The punishments no doubt were harsh, and had left the players and a large section of the accompanying Indian media stunned. It did not help matters that Denness maintained complete silence while being bombarded with questions at a press conference. What was the point of his attending the press conference, if he would not say exactly what had happened to make him hand out these punishments?

The most outrageous accusation as far as the Indian media and public was concerned, was that Tendulkar had tampered with the ball. He denied the charge and the BCCI immediately challenged all the bans, refusing to comply with them. India threatened to withdraw from the third and final Test of the series—which was to be played at SuperSport Park, Centurion—as the ICC insisted that Sehwag could not play that Test. His ban was effective immediately, unlike the others, who were given suspended bans.

Finally, the match was played as scheduled, when the South African Board supported the BCCI on their stance. Mike Denness was removed as match referee as per India's demands, and the Indians then agreed to sit Sehwag out. Denness's forced removal was in complete defiance of the ICC. The governing body did not take kindly to its authority being undermined, and declared the Centurion match to be an 'unofficial' game. Even though it was won by South Africa by an innings, the match is not counted as a Test and neither the result nor the players' performances are included in official statistics.

The clouds of uncertainty moved over to Mohali, which was the venue of the first Test of England's tour of India that followed the South African tour. India, ignoring the unofficial status of the Centurion match, insisted that Sehwag had served his one-match suspension by sitting out of that game, and would play at Mohali.

Sensing the public mood and using the support from the media, which wanted swift revenge for all past wrongs, perceived or real, Dalmiya used the 'Denness affair' to make a display of India's power. While India insisted that Sehwag would play, the ICC could also not be seen as succumbing to 'blackmail'. Finally, after much public posturing, the BCCI withdrew Sehwag from the Mohali Test but claimed a major victory as Tendulkar was absolved of the charges of ball-tampering. In the Indian public's perception, Dalmiya had scored a major victory for India by forcing the ICC to acknowledge that it was a mistake on the part of Mike Denness to have accused India's greatest cricketer and icon of cheating.

Of course, it was mere coincidence that this massive ruckus—more political than sporting in nature—about discrimination in cricket had erupted in South Africa, Gandhi's first battleground, where he had launched his satyagraha movement in 1906 against the discriminatory laws of the White government. In all his struggles for justice Gandhi put a lot of emphasis on the ethical framework under which protests had to take place. Yet, in the twenty-first century that ethical framework does not matter or even exist, with commercial interests being the raison d'etre of most battles, cricketing or otherwise.

During the BCCI–ICC standoff in 2001, the South African Board became an Indian ally only to prevent their own losses had the third match at Centurion been called off. Also, with good reason, there was a growing fear of India's economic might in cricket and repercussions for those who opposed the BCCI. Today India is considered to be world cricket's biggest bully and anyone questioning the BCCI finds themselves isolated.

In South Africa, much as it is in India, cricket, politics and race are closely intertwined, though expressed in different ways. The large Indian community, whose forebears had migrated to South Africa in the nineteenth century, follow cricket keenly and support the Indian team. The ushering in of democracy in 1994 has given them a greater voice within the system, though some of them still feel resentment against the more marginalized Black natives.

Today the fate of Blacks may have improved but I could see a majority of them still leading impoverished lives. One could see their settlements of small sheds with tin roofs while travelling around the countryside and in the city suburbs. Taxi drivers warned tourists not to visit some of the Black-dominated areas such as Soweto, in the main city of Johannesburg. I requested a taxi driver to show me the real South Africa. He first took me to a posh, White-dominated area, which had large sprawling mansions. Then he took me to Soweto, a large township, warning me against getting out of the taxi for fear of getting mugged or even killed.

Driving through the streets of Soweto, I saw shabby, dilapidated surroundings that reflected neglect and poverty. Then we visited an area that was supposed to be a hotspot of drugs and addicts, where the crime rate was high. What a striking contrast it made to the grand homes I had seen in the posh neighbourhoods. However, as an Indian, I was used to such extreme inequalities, even worse, in my own country.

During the 2001 visit, I was in the city of East London to cover a tour game the Indian team was playing against a local side during an interlude between the Tests. After the day's play, I had gone with a colleague to a shopping area a few kilometres from the hotel. We enjoyed a drink at a restaurant and stayed out a little late. While on our way back, we could not find a taxi and were forced to walk. As we were making our way along a pavement, we suddenly felt hostile eyes on us. There were scores of young Black men, shabbily dressed and eyeing us greedily. A few of them started following us. It was scary and both of us panicked.

We were sure we were going to get mugged, but miraculously, a car stopped alongside. Someone shouted from inside, opening a door, 'Get in, get in!' Providence, in the shape of two Indian South Africans, had saved us. They were shocked that we were on the road at that time of the night in an area where people are routinely mugged and even killed. Their own friend had been badly beaten up a couple of days back and was still in hospital, lucky to have survived with a few broken bones.

Before that incident, we were in Bloemfontein, the home city of former South African captain Hansie Cronje. India was playing the first Test in this city of wide roads and beautiful parks. We could hardly spot a Black face anywhere, as the area we lived in and the venue of the Test were 'all-White areas'. It was here that Virender Sehwag made his debut, scoring an outstanding century and sharing a 220-run partnership with Sachin Tendulkar after India was in trouble at 68 for four.

It was one of the most enjoyable afternoons of my life, watching a young Sehwag match his idol Tendulkar hit for hit. Though the Indians lost that Test, the Sehwag–Tendulkar partnership lingers in the memory.

Enter Greg Chappell

India was to begin a tour of Australia in the November of 2003. Ganguly, always looking for an opportunity that could help him and his team raise the bar, had quietly flown to Australia for a recce of his own much before the start of the series.

Among the many people he met there was the former Australian great Greg Chappell. Those who have met Greg will tell you what a brilliant speaker he is, always cogent and rational in his arguments, and his technical knowledge and tactical understanding of cricket are difficult to match. Ganguly's interaction with Greg in Australia left an indelible mark on the former.

Ganguly, always struggling to play the short ball, was offered a solution by Greg: he was advised to keep a squash ball inside his left glove when batting. This would help him keep the ball down and lend greater control to his pull shots. The trick worked. In the first Test at Brisbane, India was in trouble at 62 for 3 in reply to Australia's score of 323. Instead of becoming a sitting duck for the bouncing ball, as we all expected in the press box, Ganguly unleashed a flurry of strokes. He pulled the short balls and drove the length balls on his way to a spectacular hundred, one I rate as his best. This not only saved the Test for India but set up the four-match series as a contest between equals.

This result raised Ganguly's admiration and respect for Chappell immensely. As the series progressed, India won at Adelaide and could have even won the final Test in Sydney. They had delayed their declaration in the second innings and ended up not having enough time to dismiss the Australians. The hosts were set 443 to win and ended up with 357 for 6.

The series ended in a 1–1 draw, a terrific accomplishment for India. No one had expected them to have matched the strong Aussies in their own den. Among the moments to cherish was Tendulkar's double hundred and Laxman's century, and of course the audacious 195 made by Sehwag in the Melbourne Test which India lost. Sehwag had attempted reach his double hundred with a six, only to be caught in the deep.

Sehwag batted at only one rate, regardless of his score or the match situation: at a galloping pace. Some people don't allow themselves to be confined by already defined boundaries. In their defiance of the conventional, they stretch the limits to create something new. While 'experts' in the press box would endlessly debate his shortcomings as a batsman—from not using his feet, to being too indiscriminate—and predict his demise, he would continue to entertain and score runs.

It was not as if Sehwag was untutored and only hit the ball without a plan. He had failed on his One-Day debut, unable to handle the speed of Shoaib Akhtar. In response, he spent hours and months in the nets with his coach, A.N. Sharma, facing bowlers from half the length of the pitch to improve his reflexes. And to get his leg and foot movements right, his coach would tie a rope around his feet that restrained him from stretching them out more than required. This helped him maintain the right body balance. A lot of effort, thinking and hard work was behind Sehwag's relaxed, almost nonchalant figure at the crease and his remarkable 'lack' of batting technique.

India had now developed a formidable batting nucleus that made them serious contenders for the title of world's best Test team. They officially acquired that status in the ICC Test Rankings for the first time ever in 2009, under the captaincy of Mahendra Singh Dhoni. Ganguly had already retired from international cricket the previous year. But no one would deny that the foundations for that achievement were laid by the team that was led by Ganguly.

Ganguly always fought for his team, even if it meant annoying the selectors. For the 2003–4 Australian tour, the selectors wanted to drop Kumble from the squad altogether, citing his poor overseas record. Ganguly disagreed and, according to him, it was around 2 a.m. when he finally managed to persuade the selectors to retain Kumble in the squad. While Harbhajan played ahead of Kumble in the first Test, the next three Tests saw Kumble taking 24 wickets, playing a major role in that drawn series.

Ganguly didn't always get his way. For instance, he would have preferred someone with the hitting ability and fearless mindset of Sadagoppan Ramesh to open with Sehwag in Australia. The two had similar styles of batting, and because Ramesh was a left-hander, it would have made the combination even better.

Ramesh, who was a terrific timer of the ball and had earned his spurs against the likes of Wasim Akram in the 1999 series against Pakistan with his devil-may-care attacking batting, was part of the squad in Australia. He scored runs in the tour games leading up to the Test. But something transpired in the evening before the match that forced Ganguly to accept Aakash Chopra as Sehwag's partner, instead of his preferred Ramesh.

It would appear that it was Wright who had the final say on that matter. The coach was averse to risk-taking and thus not too comfortable with having two batsmen lacking in 'proper technique' opening the innings against a side like Australia and that too on their own bouncy tracks. So it was Chopra, Sehwag's Delhi teammate, who opened with him in that series, and displayed a remarkable appetite for remaining scoreless for hours together. The only thing he did was to either defend or leave the ball, letting Sehwag do all the scoring.

The exasperated Australian bowlers found a wall in front of them, which would neither break quickly nor hurt them at all. But his obduracy ensured reasonably decent starts for India, which was what Wright wanted.

This was the tour which may have convinced Ganguly that the team needed a change in its coaching staff. On the one hand was Greg, the master communicator and at the other extreme was Wright, taciturn yet stern, edgy but accommodating, someone who had ushered in a positive change but somehow lacked the sophistication of Greg.

Greg Chappell must have sensed his opportunity, because throughout the tour he appeared keen to impress us, the Indian media, with his oration. He would have friendly interactions with us and even gave us a power-point presentation detailing his coaching philosophy. I could not attend that session, but I heard all around me gushing praise for the man and his understanding of the game.

Greg's silken batting skills are as famous as his notorious act of making his brother, Trevor, bowl the final ball of a One-Day international under-arm. It was in a match against New Zealand in 1981. Greg was the Australian captain at the time, and he did this unthinkable act, though legal at that time, to ensure that the New Zealand batsman would not be able to hit the six runs required to win. As Greg's younger brother rolled the ball on the wicket, his elder brother Ian was commentating on television and was heard saying, 'No, brother, no, you can't do this.' Following widespread outrage, under-arm bowling was banned by the ICC.

Greg's legacy is scarred by this unsporting act that showed that he could go to any lengths to win a match, even if that meant exploiting loopholes in the rules. This was the man whom Ganguly and a large section of the Indian media would root for as a replacement for Wright. The following year, Greg Chappell was indeed appointed the Indian coach on the strong recommendation of the Indian captain, but not before other contenders—including the likes of Dav Whatmore, John Emburey, Tom Moody, Mohinder Amarnath and Desmond Haynes—were given the opportunity to present their respective cases.

Parleys in Pakistan

But before Chappell made his foray into Indian cricket, India played three more series, two against Pakistan, which included the historic series in 2004 and one against Australia at home. Before that tour, India had last played a Test series on their neighbour's turf in 1989–90, and had only visited one other time, in 1997, to play a three-match One-Day series. Of course, both teams had played against each other at neutral venues and in World Cups. There had also been a Test series in India. But the 2004 tour had more political significance than ever.

In 2004, India had a right-wing government firmly established at the centre. Atal Bihari Vajpayee from the BJP had been prime minister for five years. After winning the election in 1999, he had undertaken a bus journey to Lahore as a prelude to the resumption of the Lahore–Delhi–Lahore bus service. This service continued even during the Kargil conflict that followed. Despite Kargil and the 2001 attack on the Indian Parliament (both of which India blamed on Pakistan), Vajpayee looked favourably upon the BCCI proposal for an Indian cricket tour of Pakistan in 2004.

Reports in the media suggested that his deputy, Lal Krishna Advani, was opposed to the tour, and that there was even a rift in the government on the matter. Dalmiya was pushing for it as the BCCI was keen on the resumption of money-making matches between the two sides, as the series would command huge television audiences.

Security teams were sent to Pakistan in advance to assess risks and to ensure that arrangements were in place for fool-proof security. Pakistani president General Pervez Musharraf was equally keen on the tour, and finally a go-ahead came from the Indian government. I did not cover that three-Test series, but I did go to watch, making a bus journey for the Lahore Test

Before the Test series there were five thrilling One-Day matches, and India edged that series 3–2. However, the Tests were staid and maybe even boring. The results were one-sided, lacking in competitive edge and excitement. India won the first Test by an innings, Pakistan the second by nine wickets, and India the series decider once again by an innings, thereby winning their first ever Test series in Pakistan.

Given the strained relationship between the two countries, the victory was of immense satisfaction to the people of India. Ganguly and his men were feted and praised. However, the Indian captain, if he was alive to the situation around him, may have noticed warning signals that all was not well within the team. Ganguly injured his back and was fit only for the final Test, watching the first from the dressing room and the second from India, where he returned for treatment.

India's performance in the first Test, played at Multan, was dominant. However, a messy drama unfolded at India's declaration at 675 for 5 on the second afternoon of the Test. The timing of the declaration meant Sachin Tendulkar was left stranded on 194, one shot away from a double hundred. Despite Sehwag scoring over 300, it was this incident that reverberated across India, with Sachin making his displeasure known to everyone.

He devoted a lot of space about this incident in his autobiography, *Playing It My Way*. Given the restraint he always exercised over the years, never being too critical of anyone, his writing at length on this incident reveals how angry, upset and hurt he had been with that decision. The declaration had left him shocked. He was aware that the declaration was going to come but with three days left in the match, it did appear harsh and unfair that he was denied his double century.

The question arose of who was responsible for that decision. Though Ganguly was not playing the Test, he was in the dressing room at that moment. However, he denies having any role to play in the decision-making. Wright too did not accept responsibility, so it fell on Dravid, the stand-in skipper. From a cricketing perspective it was a bold decision, sending a message that in the interests of the team even the statistical interests of the great Tendulkar were of no consequence.

What is very interesting is that Tendulkar also writes in detail about the Sydney Test in January of the same year, where India delayed their declaration in the second innings after having taken a 231-run lead in the first innings. Tendulkar and Dravid were both batting well when the overall lead went past 400. Tendulkar writes that Ganguly sent a few messages to them, wanting to know when should they declare:[6] 'Rahul was the vice-captain of the team and I said to him that it was his decision as much as Sourav's. I was ready to go whenever they wanted. Rahul was keen to bat on a little longer and we finally declared just after he was hit on the head by a Brett Lee bouncer when he was on 91 and I was 60 not out.' He goes on to add: 'In hindsight, I must say we delayed the declaration too long. The ball was turning and bouncing, and we should have given Anil and the bowlers a few more overs on the fourth evening than the four they eventually bowled.'

It is clear what Tendulkar is hinting at: Dravid, nearing his hundred in Sydney, wanted to play on though India should not have waited; whereas in Multan, he declared though Tendulkar was nearing his double hundred and, unlike in Sydney, time was not a key element there.

Amrit Mathur was the media manager of the Indian team on that Pakistan tour. He recalls that the moment Tendulkar came back into the dressing room, everyone could clearly see that he was furious. Mathur later accompanied Tendulkar to the press conference that he was to address. Realizing that the media was bound to raise the declaration issue, the only advice he gave Tendulkar was to be careful with his replies. An angry, disgruntled Tendulkar in the team would have been a sure recipe for disaster. However, according to media reports, Dravid and Tendulkar had a one-on-one chat back at the hotel, and buried the hatchet.

As the media still made wild speculations, Ganguly returned to India for treatment, stepping away from the storm momentarily. He returned for the final Test to find that his place in the final XI could only come at the expense of dropping the in-form Yuvraj, who had made a hundred in the Lahore Test that India had lost by nine wickets. The Indian captain's place in the team had become a matter of debate.

Finally, Aakash Chopra was dropped as an opener, and wicketkeeper Parthiv Patel pushed up to open in order to make place in the middle order for Ganguly. India won the final Test in Rawalpindi by an innings, with Dravid scoring a double hundred and Ganguly scoring 77. Yet, there were early hints that cracks might be developing in the team. For the captain to exercise his command he has to be at the top of his game and his own position in the playing XI should remain unchallenged. Ganguly's subsequent batting failures put a huge question mark over his future.

In hindsight, the Dravid–Tendulkar differences on the declaration issue was the start of a long chapter of discord in the Indian team that peaked under Greg Chappell and led to an upheaval that was to finally culminate in India's inglorious exit at the group stage in the 2007 World Cup.

A Team in Turmoil

Following the tour of Pakistan, India hosted Australia for a Test series. In the first Test, played at Bangalore, India lost by 217 runs. Australia had a new batting star in Michael Clarke, a lean, wiry, daring stroke-maker with nimble footwork neutralizing India's spin threat with ease. After a rain-affected drawn second Test at Chennai, the real drama took place in Nagpur. It was the hometown of Shashank Manohar, who at that time was a sharp critic of the BCCI regime led by Dalmiya.

The Test was played at the old Vidarbha Cricket Association ground, situated in the heart of the city. The Indian team arrived at the venue trailing in the series, needing a win to have any chance of claiming the series. They would have wanted to play on a spinning track, that would play to their strengths. To their utter shock and horror they found instead the wicket covered with grass. Such a pitch would give a massive advantage to the visitors.

Ganguly immediately requested the groundsman to shave off the grass, but he refused. He had his instructions and could do nothing against the wishes of the president of the local association, Manohar. Ganguly found it impossible to get Manohar on board, who simply pointed to the BCCI diktat that matches should be played on firm, green wickets.

What he was referring to was the Board advisory on domestic wicket preparation that had asked that they be firm and green in order to allow domestic Indian batsmen gain experience on the kind of wickets they encountered when playing away from home. This was meant for Ranji Trophy matches, and no one expected an Indian ground to provide a green top for an international game, especially not a Test against Australia, known for their lethal pace attack.

The Australian captain, Adam Gilchrist, who was standing in for the injured Ricky Ponting, expressed his surprise and delight at the track during the pre-match press conference. He said it resembled an Australian pitch, but to me the wicket in Nagpur actually had more grass than I had ever seen on any Test pitch in Australia!

I had a lengthy chat on the eve of the Test with Ganguly, and he was a worried man, tense and at a loss for words. He seemed completely baffled at the kind of wicket provided for the match. On the morning of the Test, we were all startled to see Dravid walk out with Gilchrist for the toss. The official message was that the Indian captain had a hip injury and was unfit to play. But tongues had started wagging. Was the injury for real or had the sulking Indian captain withdrawn from the Test? According to reports, Dravid was informed that he was to lead on the morning of the Test, leaving him no time to prepare for the job.

As expected, the Indian team was outplayed. They failed to cross 200 in either innings and lost the Test by a whopping margin of 342 runs. The rout, the drama surrounding the wicket and Ganguly's abrupt withdrawal at the last minute were to have its impact on relationships within Indian cricket.

The Indian captain's credibility as a responsible leader was now being questioned, and his slide probably started from that match. His withdrawal became the cause of much disquiet and his own teammates had started doubting his motives. The man who had built a new Indian team, encouraging his young teammates, backing them and making them feel secure, seemed now to be assailed with self-doubt and was even being accused by the same teammates of being selfish.

I happened to become privy to certain facts that can shed light on a very traumatic series of events that did no credit to Indian cricket. I am sure all those involved would agree that things could have been handled with far greater maturity to avoid the suspicions and divisions that finally culminated in the embarrassing ouster from the World Cup in 2007.

A day after the Nagpur defeat, I was at a bar with Kunal Pradhan. Anand Vasu, cricket writer with the website Cricinfo, joined us and in the course of the conversation whose focus was India's defeat, Vasu revealed that there was a feeling within the Indian team that Ganguly had chickened out after seeing the green top and that his injury had been feigned. Sometimes we journalists love to gossip and can be guilty of creating imaginary issues and made-up stories. Was Vasu speaking the truth or was this just another rumour that had no basis in reality? I sensed a story and I wanted to somehow verify its authenticity.

I knew Ganguly well, better than any other cricketer. My relationship with Dravid was not bad either, but more formal in nature, and like most journalists I had immense respect for his integrity and professional conduct. After digesting what Vasu had said, on an impulse I walked out of the bar, found a secluded spot and called Dravid.

I knew Dravid was a very private person who hated gossip and would never speak about team issues with any journalist. Yet, I thought there was no harm in seeking clarification on these rumours. At worst, I thought, he would refuse to take the call or simply not comment.

10

More Discord

Dravid answered. As there was a break of a few days before the final Test in Mumbai, some of the team had flown back to their hometowns. Dravid was one of them, and he was in Bangalore when I called. I don't remember how I broached the topic with him as the matter, to my mind, was very sensitive. To my surprise, Dravid's response was polite and frank. He was worried and said that there were indeed players in the team who felt that Ganguly may have feigned injury to avoid playing on the green Nagpur track. He made it clear that these were not his own thoughts.

Vasu's information had been correct and had opened a window for me to probe further. As a well-wisher of the Indian team, I was concerned that this trust deficit meant serious trouble, a throwback to the squabbling past that this team used to suffer so much from. This was not good news.

My next step was to send a text message to the Indian captain, enquiring about his injury status as well as his team's response to his withdrawing from the Test. This was late at night, but Ganguly replied, curious to know what had prompted me to ask about the feelings of his team members. I conveyed to him that there was a strong possibility that some of the players in his team might have doubts about his credibility. He did not believe me when I told him this was my hunch and not based on any proof. It was too late in the night to carry on the conversation and he said that he would be in Mumbai the next day and we could talk face-to-face then.

The next day, I happened to meet Dravid outside the hotel gymnasium in Mumbai and asked him again about this issue. Dravid himself was now confused, not sure what to believe. He said that he had huge respect for Ganguly, who had done so much for the team. Dravid admired the manner in which Ganguly had addressed the needs of the team by becoming a bridge between them and the Board and getting the authorities to act in ways they may not have otherwise. Ganguly had stood by the players, especially the newcomers, providing them protection and security that helped them find their feet in a highly competitive atmosphere.

Dravid was worried that those questioning Ganguly's motives were 'some of his own trusted players'. There were even doubts being raised over his back injury in Pakistan. Dravid said he did not believe all these stories, but there was little doubt in my mind that he was a disturbed man. I had my sympathies with Dravid and was grateful that he had trusted me by sharing his concerns. He meant well.

The next day Ganguly invited me for breakfast in his room. He was keen to know why I thought that the team suspected him of feigning injury. He appeared to have aggravated the much-doubted injury, as he was not able to walk without using a stick for support. I refused to divulge my sources, hinting obliquely at rumours emanating from my media friends. He did not buy my pitch, because he was sure that I would not have broached this subject with him unless I was privy to something that was more tangible and authentic.

I liked Ganguly and my intention was to make him realize that he had a serious problem at hand and needed to address it immediately. It was not just his captaincy but the larger interests of Indian cricket that were at stake. I was not comfortable with what I was doing as throughout my career I have tried my best not to become close to a player. Bias creeps in and it can affect one's judgement.

After Kapil had denied making the comment about his players in the interview with me in 1983, I had felt so let down that for years I had maintained a healthy distance from all players. Yet, here I was, telling the Indian captain that his players might have unflattering things to say about him.

He insisted I reveal my source so that he could decide whether what I was telling him was true or not. I was caught in a bind. If I revealed the name, it might create a major rift. Besides, I would be betraying Dravid's trust in me. But I also felt it was my responsibility to convince the Indian captain that I was speaking the truth. Finally, I gave in, but not before a long preamble where I spoke glowingly of the person who had informed me of this development. I made sure Ganguly understood that the source himself did not believe what others were saying as he had immense respect for the captain.

Ganguly was rattled when he heard who it was. Whether he realized the gravity of the situation, I can't say. I remember telling him that it was not important to know the identity of the players who suspected him; more important was to remove their misgivings for the sake of cohesiveness and team harmony. I told him he should not harbour any ill will towards Dravid as he meant well. To ease my own guilty conscience at having revealed the name, I extracted a promise from Ganguly—for whatever it was worth—to not let anyone know what I had told him. From my point of view, it was now up to him to do whatever he deemed necessary to correct the perceptions of his teammates.

After having unburdened myself, believing that I had done the right thing—except for revealing the name of my source—I had a professional decision to make. This was too major a story to be not told to the readers. Imagine the headlines—*Teammates suspect Indian captain of feigning injury*—and the impact it would have. More importantly, if as a journalist I was privy to something major brewing, I would be shirking my responsibility by not writing about it.

At the same time, I did not want to reveal my source or write in a manner that would create a sensation and more suspicion in the team. I discussed this dilemma with my roommate and friend, Kunal and we debated arguments both for and against doing the story. Eventually, I decided to do two stories.

The first, that appeared on page one in *HT*, was about how there seemed to be mistrust developing in the team as some of the players suspected that Ganguly may have feigned injury to avoid playing on the Nagpur green top. It was a matter-of-fact story, without any interpretation or blaming any side, and not revealing the source of the news. The next day I wrote a longish piece, more analysis than news, on why it was unfair to blame Ganguly: it is difficult to be a leader of a team without ruffling a few feathers.

In that second article I also put in a bit of advice for Dravid, who was to lead in the Mumbai Test as well because Ganguly's injury had not healed. I wrote that Dravid would realize himself that it was not possible to please everyone in the team and there would always be some players dissatisfied and even disgruntled with the captain. The readers may not have understood, but I was appealing directly to Dravid to not make the mistake of believing all that he was told. In short, the piece appealed for team harmony and was written in defence of an Indian captain and not an individual.

Ganguly returned home and Dravid led India to its only win of the series in Mumbai. The track there seemed to overcompensate for the green top in Nagpur. It was orange-brown in colour, badly underprepared and was turning square from the first ball, with uneven bounce thrown in. It may have made batting a nightmare but the contest was riveting and ridden with uncertain twists and turns that made for fascinating viewing.

Batting first, India was shot out for 104, and Australia secured a 99-run first innings lead. On a track like that it seemed insurmountable. But India recovered in the second innings, with Laxman playing another of his heroic knocks, scoring 69, and Tendulkar chipping in with a half century to help them set a target of 107. The diabolical nature of the track could be gauged from the bowling figures of Michael Clarke, who rarely bowls. His efforts at bowling left-arm spin were rewarded with astounding figures of 6 for 9. One just had to toss the ball in the air, land it on length and leave the rest to the wicket: the ball would turn, jump or keep low, and sometimes go straight through. Incredibly, Australia was dismissed for 93 and fell short by 13 runs. The match did not last more than two and a half days.

Despite the win, India had lost the series on home ground to a team that had last won a series in India in 1969. For a side aspiring to become the world's best, this loss was as much a setback as it was embarrassing. It was not just the players, even Wright now appeared more distant and unhappy. There were reports that he was not interested in extending his tenure; that he would have quit after the high of a series win in Pakistan but had stayed back for this important series.

During the series another controversy had erupted that had directly affected Wright: Sunil Gavaskar had been appointed India's batting consultant. At one of the Test venues, Gavaskar showed up at the nets and I remember Wright saying that he had not been aware of this appointment. Despite his impassive face, I could sense his hurt at not being consulted for this important decision.

Conflicting versions on Gavaskar's appointment appeared in the media. Some said that even Ganguly was not aware of it, even though Gavaskar had made a public statement that it was the Indian captain who had requested him to help the team. Whatever the facts, it was becoming increasingly clear that Wright was on his way out.

Ganguly returned from his injury to lead India to a 1–0 win at home against South Africa and then a 2–0 win away at Bangladesh. Despite these wins, it was obvious that the Indian team now lacked the intensity that had made them hungry for more wins. Wright's last assignment as Indian coach was a home series against Pakistan.

It was a series that raised fresh doubts about Ganguly's form and leadership. Pakistan drew the three-match series 1–1, losing in Kolkata but making a strong comeback in Bangalore to square the series. This was not the result the Indian public wanted. To make it worse for the Indian captain, he had completely lost his batting form, looking out of his depth and appearing a forlorn figure on the field. Ganguly would have realized that he was getting isolated in the team he had built with care and acumen, and that one of the reasons for his authority getting undermined was his own lack of form.

Ironically, the players whom he had backed in the Indian team—giving them a long rope because he trusted their potential and explosive talent—were now his competitors for a slot in the middle order. The prime example was the dashing left-hander Yuvraj Singh, who, despite his One-Day heroics, was yet to secure a permanent place in the Test team. In a team loaded with some of the all-time greats of Indian cricket, Yuvraj usually found himself sitting on the bench—not because he was not good enough but because others were better than him.

Yuvraj had seized his opportunity in Pakistan when Ganguly was out injured in 2004. He had scored a Test hundred, but his place in the middle order disappeared once the captain returned. Much to his dismay, he was made to open against Australia, and not surprisingly, failed. Unlike Sehwag, he did not have the ability to adapt his game to different positions, and failed to capitalize on the opportunity created for him to retain his place in the side. Even though he was grateful to Ganguly for having nurtured him in the team, one could understand if a certain amount of resentment had started to brew.

There were others too, such as Mohammed Kaif, who was a player close to Wright's heart: hard-working, disciplined, brilliant in the field and committed to the team cause. But there was simply no room for even such talented young players in a batting line-up where a player of Laxman's class was batting so far down the order.

Therefore, given the talent waiting in the wings, it was imperative for Ganguly to consistently score runs to justify his place as a batsman in the playing XI. If he didn't, his captaincy could be viewed as an 'unfair' privilege that guaranteed him his place in the side at the expense of more deserving players eyeing his spot.

A Battle for Survival

Ganguly was now a vulnerable man, and it was at this crucial stage of his career that Greg Chappell replaced Wright as the Indian coach. Having been instrumental in putting Chappell at the helm, the Indian captain must have expected his coach's complete backing. Unfortunately, while pushing for his appointment, Ganguly had been so taken in by Greg's oratorical skills and coaching tips that he may not have thought of checking out his track record as a coach.

Greg had coached the South Australian team in the domestic Pura Cup from 1999 to 2002–03. The team had not moved up the ladder, finishing fourth among six teams. More significantly, he had not left a good impression on the players, many of whom had gone on record criticizing his team-management skills. Paul Wilson, who played for South Australia during that period, was quoted as saying, 'Greg Chappell is a fantastic individual skills and batting coach but he was a poor coach when it came to looking after a group of people' in a report in Cricinfo in 2005, by which time Chappell had already been appointed the Indian coach.

In the report, written just when the rift between Chappell and Ganguly surfaced, Wilson said, 'No real batting talent came through and I don't think he looked hard enough within his own squad or within the state for the players that could have improved.' Wilson then made an ominous statement, saying that many players coached by Chappell were 'surprised that he was appointed India's coach'. No one heeded the warning in India at that time; most of us in the media had become Chappell fans, bowled over by his cricketing stature and logical statements.

After he took over as the Indian coach, Chappell gave lengthy interviews, not just to influential sports journalists but also to editors of newspapers. One of his interviewers was the editor-in-chief of *The Hindu*, N. Ram. From the interviews given, it was obvious that he was on a PR drive, cultivating the press to create a favourable impression of himself. He had done the same when India had toured Australia in 2003–4. The contrast between his predecessor Wright's understated, quiet ways and Chappell's assertive methods was stark. It was clear that Chappell was completely taking over the team and would be first among equals.

I must confess that before his appointment I had no opinion for or against Greg Chappell. I was neither a fan nor a critic. I was in the neutral zone when Greg arrived in India in July 2005 to hold a conditioning camp before the tour to Sri Lanka for a One-Day tri-series. Ganguly could not play the first few matches of the

Sri Lankan series as he was serving a six-match ban for maintaining a slow over rate. He had sat out the last two matches in the previous series against Pakistan and still had four matches to serve. Thus, fate ensured that Ganguly would not be leading the side on Greg's first assignment as Indian coach.

Ganguly planned to miss the camp as he was playing for the English county side Glamorgan at that time. However, Chappell had other ideas. One of his first acts as coach was to warn the players directly and through the media that he was beginning with a clean slate and no player, veteran or youngster, should take him for granted. He wanted Ganguly to be present at the camp, despite it being only for five days. Ganguly was forced to change his plans and fly over to attend the last two days of the camp. Greg was making it clear that there would be no prima donnas in Indian cricket during his tenure.

There was appreciation all around for the new coach's strict disciplinarian approach and his stock had immediately risen in the public imagination. Events at the camp itself would shape Greg's mind and his opinion of Ganguly. I wasn't aware of it then, but stumbled on this bit of information while doing research for my proposed biography of Ganguly.

One of the many trainers who were present at the National Cricket Academy during that period was Chinmoy Roy, incidentally from Ganguly's home state of Bengal. He was to become Bengal's Ranji Trophy physical conditioning coach later, and even worked on Ganguly's fitness during his period of exile from the Indian team post his row with Chappell.

According to Chinmoy, Greg was very keen on improving the fitness levels of the players and had issued instructions that the schedules he had made were to be followed strictly. Instead, the new coach found that some of the players were not too keen to follow his guidelines despite his repeated instructions. He quickly learned that these players were Ganguly's favourite boys and because of that they were taking the coach's commands lightly. That infuriated him. From that moment onwards, those players were marked men, including the very man who had facilitated his appointment as coach. If this eyewitness account is to be believed, Greg, the control freak, may have made up his mind to get rid of the Indian captain within a few days of his arriving in India.

Ganguly joined the team under Dravid for their later matches against Sri Lanka and the West Indies, scoring a half century before missing out on another match due to an injury. He did not get a big score in the other matches he played, and India lost to Sri Lanka in the final of the tri-series. The rumour mills were already churning with reports that some of Ganguly's favourites— the likes of Harbhajan, Zaheer, Nehra and even Sehwag—were in for some 'special treatment' from the new coach. Ganguly was at the top of the list of players that Greg wanted to 'discipline'.

Struggling with his form and being out of favour, Ganguly could no longer bank upon Dalmiya's support in the Board as Ranbir Singh Mahendra—the man who in 1992 had branded Ganguly a pampered, undisciplined kid—had become the Board president. He was appointed after a high-stakes, no-holds-barred election in which he defeated the heavyweight Sharad Pawar. They had both tied at fifteen votes each, and it was the casting vote from outgoing president Dalmiya that sealed victory for Mahendra. It was obvious that the Board was split down the middle and Pawar, despite his political clout, had been checkmated. However, Pawar would get his own back a year later and sweep the Board elections by twenty votes to eleven in December 2005.

The five-member selection committee headed by former Indian wicketkeeper Kiran More kept its faith in Ganguly and he remained captain for the tour to Zimbabwe in August–September 2005. This was probably his last opportunity, putting to rest speculations that Dravid, who had led in Sri Lanka, would be retained as captain. I did not cover the Zimbabwe tour, so my account of the ugly public display of hostilities between Chappell and Ganguly that transpired there is pieced together from various sources who were present at the scene.

On the eve of the first Test at Bulawayo, it was reported that the two protagonists had a confrontation at the ground on team selection, though no one was sure about the exact details. Anand Vasu once again became my news source. According to him, Greg had told Ganguly that he did not deserve to be in the team as his inclusion blocked either Yuvraj or Kaif's place in the playing XI. I needed to confirm this story and luckily managed to reach the Indian team manager, Amitabh Choudhary, on the phone in his Harare hotel. He confirmed the story but did not want to go on record.

My story was carried on page one of the *Hindustan Times* and gave details about what had transpired between the captain and the coach, the gist being that when Ganguly had asked Greg which of the two—Yuvraj or Kaif—should be picked for the playing XI, the coach had responded that both of them deserved to play and that the captain himself should sit out.

In the Test match that followed, the captain played with a composure that gave no inkling of the turmoil and uncertainty prevailing in the team and his mind. In a painstaking six-hour century, perhaps his slowest ever, Ganguly and the dominant Laxman, the other centurion of the match, led India to a huge first innings score that resulted in an innings win for India.

Zimbabwe was not expected to stretch India and the win itself may have had more statistical value than any great cricketing merit, but in the backdrop of what was taking place in the dressing room, it meant a lot to Ganguly. A more significant development took place in the post-match press conference. Ganguly, in response to a pointed question regarding his place in the team being questioned replied, 'I was asked to step down from captaincy before the Test began.' The answer created a sensation back home. Though Ganguly did not mention the person who had asked him to do so, the inference was obvious. Only the coach of the team could have had the courage to tell the captain that he should quit, that too the day before a Test match.

Greg Chappell, not to be fazed, was determined to see this fight to the finish. Soon an email that he had written to the Board was leaked to the media. In this correspondence, over 2000 words long, Greg levelled a series of serious accusations that portrayed Ganguly as a scheming, plotting individual who was destroying the team fabric. The full text is widely available on the net but it is worth mentioning a few points here.

Chappell claimed that at no stage had he asked Ganguly to step down from captaincy, or threatened to resign as coach. By his account Ganguly had himself asked for his honest opinion on where he stood as a player. Greg wrote: 'I told him that I thought he was struggling as a player and that it was affecting his ability to lead the team effectively and that the pressure of captaincy was affecting his ability to play to his potential. I also told him that his state of mind was fragile and it showed in the way that he made decisions on and off the field in relation to the team, especially team selection.'

Then, quoting a series of incidents from the tour, Chappell painted a picture of a man destroying team morale and damaging the mental state of the players by making last-minute changes in the team. He claimed that the captain's nervousness and being prone to panic in pressure situations was affecting the team. On the matter of selection for the first Test, Greg stated that he asked Ganguly where he thought he should bat, and he said 'number 5'. Greg then told him that he might like to consider opening, as the middle order was going to be a tight battle with Kaif and Yuvraj demanding selection.

Greg further accused Ganguly of not wanting to face the new ball and feigning injury to rest in the dressing room till the ball became old. He claimed he spoke with a number of players about this and they recounted a list of times when Ganguly had suffered from mysterious injuries that usually disappeared as quickly as they had appeared. So, he added, 'I was so concerned about the effect that Sourav's actions were having on the team that I decided I could not wait until the selection meeting that evening to inform him that I had serious doubts about picking him for the first Test.'

Then comes the vital part of Greg's side of the story on the captaincy issue: 'Sourav asked me whether I thought he should be captain of the team. I said that I had serious doubts that he was in the right frame of mind to do it. He asked me if I thought he should step down. I said that it was not my decision to make, that only he could make that decision, but if he did make that decision, he had to do it in the right manner or it would have even more detrimental effects than if he didn't stand down.'

The letter stated that a short time later Amitabh Choudhary (the team manager) informed Greg that Ganguly had told him Greg did not want him as captain. Ganguly wanted to leave Zimbabwe immediately if he wasn't playing. Greg and Choudhary then met Rahul Dravid in the dressing room, where they agreed that this was not the outcome anyone wanted and that the ramifications would be against the interests of the team.

They had a long talk with Ganguly and eventually convinced him that he should stay on as captain for the two Tests and then consider his future. Greg said, 'In my view it was not an ideal solution but it was better than the alternative of him leaving on a bad note. I believe he has earned the right to leave in a fitting manner. We all agreed that this was a matter that should stay between us and should not, under any circumstances, be discussed with the media.'

The rest of the letter makes many accusations against Ganguly: inciting players against the coach, playing favourites, breaking team discipline, creating an atmosphere of mistrust, a lack of interest in fitness regimens. The letter goes so far as to say, 'This team has been made to be fearful and distrusting by the rumour mongering and deceit that is Sourav's modus operandi of divide and rule.'

The letter ends, 'I can assure you of my best intentions. Yours sincerely, Greg Chappell MBE.' In adding his honorary title, awarded by the British monarchy for the services rendered to the 'Empire', Chappell was perhaps flaunting his credentials as a man of impeccable integrity and conduct.

Around the same time as this official letter, Greg had emailed a journalist who had asked him about the rumoured rift:

> Things are better but until Sourav is excised from the group we will not go forward. He is manipulative, corrupted and past his sell-by date in all ways. Nehra did pull out because he does not want to work hard and wants to save himself for ODIs. It is a disgrace; he is a disgrace and that is why I sent him off. He should never play for India again. Zaheer is the same and Harbhajan has to change even more if he wishes to survive. If we cut these cancers out of the group we will move forward quickly. If the BCCI/powerbrokers don't support this there is no point me being here. I have worked out a group of fifteen or so with whom I can work and this is what I will put to the special committee, if they survive the election, once I get home. If they support my view, it will be exciting to see what we can achieve. Any support you can give will be greatly appreciated.

The language used by Greg in this email shows the visceral hatred he had developed for the Indian captain. There was no hope for Ganguly from that point onwards. If he had to survive, Greg had to go, and the possibility of that appeared remote given the changing power structure of the Board. It seemed that Ganguly's exit from the Indian team both as captain and player was simply a matter of time.

A temporary peace treaty was formalized by a handshake between the two main protagonists during the Zimbabwe tour, and a photo of the moment was splashed in the newspapers. The BCCI set up a four-member review committee to investigate Chappell's allegations. Subsequently, a hearing was held in Mumbai and both Ganguly and Greg were asked to appear.

I booked myself into the Taj, where the meeting was to take place, knowing that it was my only chance to catch Ganguly and other members of the probe committee alone in order to learn what had transpired. Ganguly had prepared a rejoinder of more than 5000 words to Greg's letter. This listed some astonishingly serious charges against the coach, which were not taken seriously by the review committee. Had they done so, the coach, if not sacked immediately, would have at least faced a further probe to confirm the veracity of the captain's allegations. But Ganguly's diminished clout was clearly demonstrated by the fact that the committee, the Board and even the media ignored his statement.

I have a copy of the letter, typed tightly on an A-3 sheet. Ganguly had handed over a copy to each of the review committee members, one of whom was Sunil Gavaskar. The committee, probably fearing that one among them might leak the letter, returned every copy to Ganguly after reading it. One of those copies ended up with me. Ganguly had requested me to not publish or quote from it, as the committee would know who had leaked it, and he feared that he would be targeted more severely if the leak was traced to him. From a defiant person who had challenged the establishment many a time, he had become lonely, insecure and worried about his future.

I will now quote some relevant portions from Ganguly's letter verbatim:

Mr Chappell and I met in Mutare on the first day evening on the side game where I asked Mr Chappell what does he think will help me become a better player and make the team into a better one. He said that I have not been in the best of forms and that I should give up captaincy which should help me concentrate on my cricket because he feels at the present moment I am spending too much of my energy to sort out the teammates and trying to get them play better. He was aware I had spoken to Zaheer Khan that evening before trying to tell him what the coach expects of him and he should follow his training ways and if require get up in the middle of the night and bowl in the nets if the coach wants him to. I had a similar chat to Harbhajan on these lines because these were the issues raised by the coach in the selection committee. The coach said about his own instances how he felt mentally tired after captaining 47 Test matches and when he gave up how mentally free he felt and played good cricket for the next one and a half years. I listened to him because at the end of the day it was his opinion and I also knew that he had helped me in the year 2003 with my batting in Sydney. I told him that I will give it a thought after the two Test matches are over because these two Test matches were very important for me. Any thought now will take away my focus in the next two games. We then discussed about various other issues in world cricket and the conversation finished there.

Ganguly goes on to refute Greg's accusation that he had feigned injury to avoid playing the new ball. He cites team physio John Gloster's report as evidence of his elbow injury and the treatment he was given in the absence of any MRI machine being available at the venue of the match. Then Ganguly criticized Greg for questioning individual players about what they thought about Ganguly's injury. This, he said, showed Greg's 'mental make [up] of complete distrust on everything and coming to a conclusion abruptly'.

The most important point of dispute was addressed next: the matter of Ganguly stating in the press conference that he was asked to quit, and Greg's denial of that allegation. Ganguly reported that the coach told him 'that he wanted Yuvraj and Kaif to play Test matches consistently from now on and that I should step down from the captaincy and allow them to play'. Ganguly said that he was shocked and upset, but after some arguments, 'I told him that if he wants I will do it. He told me you think about it and let me know.'

Ganguly stated that he told Rahul Dravid what the coach had said, and Dravid said he would speak to Chappell about it. The final decision was that Ganguly should play two Tests as captain and then a decision would be taken. From Ganguly's account, he was present in the dressing room when Dravid and the manager had spoken to Greg and that 'there were a few guys taking treatment on the table and I am sure they must have heard the conversation. I would also request this should be clarified with the manager of the Indian cricket team and Rahul if possible.'

Ganguly then described certain acts of the coach that, if true, not only show him in poor light but as a man given to eccentricities, mistrusting the players he was dealing with and desiring complete control over the team and the captain. One example, probably unheard of in international cricket, is that the coach went out to the toss in a practice game at Mutare without the knowledge of the captain. Ganguly didn't make an issue of it, but said, 'It showed complete lack of faith in the captain and an indirect way to insult.'

In conclusion, Ganguly listed nine points that according to him sum up Chappell's 'autocratic, vindictive' attitude:

1. He has repeatedly told me he wants to be the boss of the team.
2. He talks something on your face and something at the back. His press statement before the day of the second test match and his report to the board president proves my point.
3. In team meetings he never makes strategy. All he talks about is the selection. He agrees before a game to the points you say and if the game is lost the next day he uses it against you.
4. He sleeps in the dressing room when the game is on. It has happened both in Sri Lanka and Zimbabwe and there by fails to send messages in the right time of the game and it's no point discussing it after the match is over.
5. Most of the players are scared to go and tell him their problems because he uses them as [proof] that [they are] not good enough instead of trying to help them out to become better players.
6. I also want to bring to your notice that everything which is discussed in private is out in the media. [Ganguly gave examples of such leaks.]
7. He has passed a statement on my elbow injury without even knowing the facts. [Here Ganguly also describes an incident when the coach misrepresented him to others as being selfish when he was batting on 97 with a clear plan in mind.]
8. The coach has spoken of my lack of mental fitness. I would just want to ask one thing that somebody who has been asked to step down the day before turns up and gets a hundred that day after. Isn't it enough proof of his mental

strength provided the person concerned has a free mind to accept things.

9. Lastly I want to say when Chappell was appointed coach I was probably one of the few supporters of him. Now does it make any sense on my behalf not to cooperate with and break a team which I have led for five years.

The letter ends with the sentiment: 'I also have best intentions of Indian cricket in mind.'

Ganguly may have had the best intentions of Indian cricket in mind, but the immediate battle was to save his career and his reputation. In hindsight it seems strange that so little note was taken of the points he made in his letter. The Chappell aura held sway in the Board and in the media, and Ganguly's own form, despite his century against Zimbabwe, was being cited as one of the reasons why he should not play again, let alone lead the side.

When the Sri Lankan team toured India, an injury kept Ganguly out of the first four One-Day matches, all of which India won under Dravid. When the team was reviewed for the remaining matches, there was no place for Ganguly in it. For a brief while, he retained his place in the Test squad as a useful 'all-rounder'—a term used by chief selector Kiran More while announcing the Test squad for Sri Lanka. But the new 'all-rounder' of the Indian team was finally axed from the Test side after playing against Sri Lanka at Delhi's Kotla without contributing anything substantial. Not only had he lost his captaincy, he was no longer part of the Indian team.

Had Ganguly's career ended there, he would not be the larger-than-life figure in Indian cricket he is today. Though under his leadership the Indian team had risen from the lows of match-fixing to become a formidable outfit with a professional outlook, Ganguly would have been remembered more for Greg Chappell's accusations of being 'petty' and 'selfish'.

'Excised' from the team, as Greg had wanted him to be, a humiliated Ganguly was stuck with accusations of being a disruptor and an impediment to the team's growth. The stigma could have stuck to him for life had he not chosen to fight back and not give up.

In a remarkable feat of grit and determination, Ganguly used his humiliation as a tool to motivate himself and made a comeback that could well be an inspiring story for the ages.

11
Great Comeback, Great Fall

Kolkata is a city where the past, present and future seem to seamlessly coexist. It can leave an outsider confused and exhausted in mind and body. It is a sea of humanity that floods the streets and maidans of the city, dripping with sweat, yet moving with an energy and purpose that seems oblivious to its harsh struggle for survival.

On a Test match day, the whole city seems to head for Eden Gardens. The crowds line up outside the stadium, serpentine queues stretching for long distances. How such a large number of people manage to enter the stadium without any major accident or riot is a miracle. The cops, firm and even aggressive while screaming and shouting in Bengali, manage to enforce order in these unruly conditions, showing remarkable resolve and tact to guide the swelling numbers into the stadium. What seems an impossible task is completed with admirable efficiency.

My first encounter with Kolkata was in 1991, the year Haryana won its only Ranji Trophy. They played against Bengal in the semi-final, and I was given the opportunity to report on the game by *The Indian Express* because my 'home' state was playing. Despite initially finding the city to be daunting, almost intimidating, I soon discovered a hidden tenderness. Once I shed my own fears and inhibitions, I fell in love with the city and its people.

In many ways, I found parallels here with my Kashmiri ethos. The Bengali pride in their cuisine, the love and care with which they cooked and the passion with which they ate were traits familiar to me. You could sense the Bengali's innate belief, not without reason, that nothing in the world is comparable to their rich culture of festivals, language, music, cinema, arts, aesthetics and literature. I realized that for them, just as it was for us in the Kashmir of my childhood days, to be a Bengali was more than just being an Indian. Here was another community fiercely loyal to its own cultural past and somehow stricken by a feeling that they had not got their due in the pan-Indian imagination.

Outsiders were very welcome as long as they respected their individuality and identity. Probably the Left Front—the political party that remained in power for almost thirty-five consecutive years from 1977—was not just an expression of their ideological frame of mind, but may have also fulfilled their craving for a distinct identity.

This was the Kolkata that I, rightly or wrongly, related to. Sourav Ganguly may not have been a representative of that collective Bengali psyche, but he sure was a living embodiment of what they were capable of achieving in the cricketing arena, where their accomplishments were fewer than in other spheres.

Down and Out

But the Indian captain from Bengal, who had redefined India's gameplay and given new respect to the country in the cricketing world, was now an outcast, dumped and humiliated by the BCCI. Even those in Bengal who never identified with Ganguly as one of their own—because they saw him as a representative of the rich upper class—felt outraged. The anger spilled over when India played South Africa at Eden Gardens in November 2005, immediately after Ganguly was dropped. Thousands screamed 'Sourav, Sourav' from the stands.

When they heckled Greg, he showed them the middle finger, adding fuel to an already raging fire. After severe criticism and pressure, Chappell claimed that he had not been insulting the crowd but attending to his injured finger, an entirely ridiculous explanation of his childish reaction that left no one convinced.

India was to tour Pakistan a month after the Sri Lankan series, and speculation was rife whether Ganguly would find a place in the team. The tense drama was playing out in the media, with protests being organized in Kolkata over the 'wrong' done to Ganguly. The issue acquired political overtones when the chief minister of Bengal, Buddhadeb Bhattacharjee, voiced his support for his state's most popular figure. The Left Front, which was an ally of the ruling Congress Party at the Centre, even raised the issue in Parliament, accusing the BCCI of discrimination against Bengal.

However, Sharad Pawar, who had by then become the Board president, was also an influential member of the United Progressive Alliance (UPA), which had defeated the Bharatiya Janata Party in the general elections in 2004. Pawar had a friendly relationship with the left and Buddhadeb could not be seen as being critical of him.

It was around that time *HT* planned a cover story on Ganguly for its weekly magazine, *Brunch*. I visited Kolkata to meet the former captain at his home and profile his life beyond cricket. In contrast to the general sense of anger and hurt among the people, Ganguly appeared calm, smiling, courteous and welcoming when I visited his home. He took me through a huge hall on the ground floor where his trophies and awards were displayed to the upper floor, where the bedrooms, kitchen and living room were.

His mother, Nirupama, served an exquisite Bengali meal. What touched me was the attention and care with which the lady served the meals herself, ensuring we ate properly.

When the team to tour Pakistan in 2006 was announced, Ganguly's name was on the list. After a very brief period of hiatus, he was back in the team. It was difficult to predict how things would pan out and whether he would find a place in the playing XI.

The first Test was to be played in a chilly Lahore in the middle of January. On the eve of the match, there was a dramatic conversation at the centre of the Gadaffi Stadium between Ganguly, Greg and Dravid. It was witnessed by those present at the ground, and even broadcast on television in India. We were out of earshot but clearly it was a heated argument, with both Ganguly and Greg being quite demonstrative with their gestures. What was going on?

Indian reporters covering the tour were under tremendous pressure from their editors to find out the exact details of what had transpired. An advantage of working for one of the bigger papers was that we could afford to stay in the same hotels as the team. This meant that we could sometimes approach the players privately and have a better chance than most to get a few inside details. Lahore was no different, as I soon bumped into Ganguly himself in the lift. He said there was no tiff, just that he was insisting that they let him open the innings. This was probably his way of making sure of being included in the playing XI, as Greg had said there was no place for Ganguly in the middle order. However, Dravid was not in favour of Ganguly opening.

Once in my room, I called Dravid for his reaction. He had been appointed the full-time captain for the tour. His response was equally forthcoming, confirming what Ganguly had told me.

In what to me seemed a remarkable gesture, Dravid, to the surprise of many, opened in the Test, letting Ganguly bat in the middle order. I remember what Dravid told me in the evening on the first day of the Test: 'I couldn't sleep the whole night, thinking over it. I couldn't do this to Daadi (Ganguly is fondly called Daadi by his teammates).'

On a wicket that in cricketing parlance is called a 'sleeping beauty', runs could be scored with freedom and impunity. Only eight wickets fell over the course of five days, although the third day saw only fifteen overs played due to bad weather. Pakistan scored more than 600 runs before declaring, while India lost just one wicket in making over 400 runs. Virender Sehwag played an entertaining knock that saw him record the second-fastest double hundred in Test history, while Dravid scored an unbeaten hundred.

Ganguly never got a chance to bat before being dropped from the second Test, replaced by fast bowler R.P. Singh. The reason offered for the change was that the bowling needed strengthening. The second match was at Faisalabad, where another 'dead' track resulted in another drawn run-feast.

The third and final Test provided the only real contest. On a green-top in Karachi, Irfan Pathan stunned Pakistan with a hat-trick in the very first over of the Test. Ganguly was back in the XI, replacing Harbhajan. He scored 34 and 37 in the two innings and did not seem out of form or rusty. Both innings promised more but did not turn into big scores.

India lost the match by a whopping 341 runs. The series defeat did not go down well with Indian fans and the team was distraught.

Away from the action, another story was unfolding at the centre of which was Raj Singh Dungarpur. The former Board president had accompanied the team as its manager because his diplomatic skills were important on a tour to a country where tact and political nous were often required. Unfortunately, the towering figure of Rajbhai, as he was popularly known, was not really himself anymore, struggling with growing signs of what was later diagnosed as Alzheimer's disease.

In the middle of the tour an interview of his was published in a Bengali daily, in which he was critical of Greg and his coaching methods. However, after the interview appeared, Dungarpur denied having talked to any journalist. His denial of an interview he had given had made journalists wary of him as they had realized that it was no longer wise to quote him in their articles. Soon, Dungarpur was being shunned by the journalists on the tour.

That was when he started confiding in me on many team issues he was uncomfortable with. He would seek me out at the venue or in the hotel lobby and immediately break into incoherent monologues. He said there was no communication between the coach and the manager, which was hurting him the most.

In my previous interactions with him over the years, I had been awed by his oration, impeccable diction and ability to recount interesting cricketing anecdotes that held his audiences spellbound. Dungarpur had spent all his life living and breathing cricket, advising, guiding, criticising, praising and drawing up strategies, and had even served as national selector for two terms. It won't be wrong to say that he had been one of the more influential figures in Indian cricket of his time.

But the Rajbhai we saw on that tour was a tragic figure, someone who should have been resting at home. He was already seventy, frail in mind but still enthusiastic. He would try his best to assert his authority, though it was obvious that he was no longer being taken seriously by the coach or the players. He had become a pariah among the very people who had once respected and even feared him.

Dungarpur was extremely critical of Greg's methods, saying that the coach had no tactical nous. Ganguly had mentioned in his letter to the Board that Chappell would fall asleep in the dressing room while a match was in progress, and Dungarpur verified that this statement was indeed true. To my surprise, given how critical he had been of Ganguly in the past, Dungarpur was full of praise for him now. 'I have never seen a more disciplined, courteous cricketer and can't figure out why Greg is targeting him,' he said after the Test series. Ganguly had been dropped for the One-Day series that was to follow, a decision that, according to Dungarpur, was Chappell's alone.

I am not sure how much of Dungarpur's anger and criticism of the coach stemmed from a hurt ego at not getting the respect that the veteran administrator felt he deserved.

Dravid's Dilemma

On that Pakistan tour was Siddhartha Vaidyanathan (Sidvee), a young spirited, knowledgeable cricket writer from the website Cricinfo, who after the Test defeat was being briefed by the Indian coach. In this off-the-record conversation (meaning whatever was said was not to be ascribed to the person) Greg was conveying to the reporter his assessment of what went wrong and what he thought needed to be done to raise a team that could be a strong contender for the 2007 World Cup.

To Sidvee's horror and shock, the coach was telling him that Tendulkar, Sehwag, Laxman were not good enough to be playing the 2007 World Cup and should be dropped and a new set of players groomed in their place. Greg wanted Sidvee to do a story that would present this as the reporter's own assessment of the best way forward for India. This opinion would be expressed as Sidvee's without any reference to Greg.

Sidvee was on his first major cricketing assignment and was left too rattled to make any sense of this. He immediately sought me out as a friend, and we had a lengthy discussion on what this meant for Indian cricket. What was disquieting was not that Greg felt the way he did about the best Indian batsmen, but that he had sought out a reporter, one he did not even know well, to plant this idea in in the media. Perhaps he had chosen Sidvee because he preferred the story to be on the internet (Cricinfo is a website), or because he thought this young journalist would do his bidding.

If Greg could talk so openly to someone he did not even know personally, he surely must have been saying similar things to others as well. Imagine Tendulkar and the others learning that their coach was criticising them behind their backs and that too to the media, and wanted them out of the team! We knew that such a thing would create havoc.

The young journalist and I both decided that it was our responsibility to prevent such an eventuality from taking place. The first step would be to inform the Indian captain that the coach was making statements that could divide the team. Sidvee did not want to be identified as the journalist in whom Greg had placed his 'trust' to do this story, but otherwise didn't mind the whole conversation to be conveyed to Dravid.

The urgency in my voice when I called him in his room made Dravid agree immediately to meet me. I was a bit nervous as, much like my conversation with Ganguly in 2004, this too was about internal team bickering and I was the outsider telling tales. I rushed into the details without much preamble, emphasizing that if this got out, as was likely, it would create a rift that could spell trouble for him and his team. I admitted that as a news reporter this was a sensational story, but as a well-wisher of the team I wouldn't want to publish it. However, it was very important for him to know what his coach was up to.

Dravid appeared disturbed after hearing me out. He asked me about the credibility of the journalist from whom I had heard the story. Despite me trying to assure him that had the source not been trustworthy, I would not have been alarmed enough to contact him, Dravid did not look convinced. He said that it was important for him to know the identity of that reporter. I had no option but to convince Sidvee to identify himself even if he did not want to talk to the Indian captain directly.

The young journalist was new to the world of cricketing intrigues and worried that he may be in breach of 'professional ethics', but he eventually agreed. Once Dravid realized it was Sidvee, whom he knew, had read and believed to be a well-meaning, honest person, the reality must have sunk in. He appeared upset and like us did feel that this 'loose talk' should not go out in the public domain. We did not know who else, apart from Sidvee, Greg had talked to, but on my own part I promised to keep quiet about it. To his credit, Sidvee has since never even referred to what could have been a sensational scoop for him.

I don't know what went through Dravid's mind after he heard me and I had no clue what his relationship with Greg was. As a captain his responsibilities and accountability had to be far greater than those of the coach, and to be worrying and dealing with the fall-out of his coach's indiscretions was the last thing he would have wanted.

It is always hard to get Dravid to talk about people and controversial issues. On India's tour of the West Indies in 1997, when he was just a year into his international career, he had expressed his annoyance at journalists focusing on controversies rather than on cricket. His views on this subject even now would probably not be any different.

Leading a cricket team means much more than marshalling your resources and displaying strategic acumen on the cricket field. With captaincy comes a whole range of issues where the team leader has to be responsive to the needs and problems of his teammates. He has to take everyone's views on board, even those from people he may not like or understand. All these concerns have to be dealt with extreme care and sensitivity for the sake of team harmony. This is not an easy job, especially for someone who is happy to be left to himself.

Dravid understood the game's nuances and its technical aspects as well as anyone. What he may have lacked was the patience and intent to go out of his way to establish a personal rapport with each of his players and assuage their fears and insecurities. Unfortunately, he was saddled with a coach who was driving a wedge between his own players. The Indian team needed a coach with a better understanding of how to keep a team united despite its diversity in terms of social background, religion and language. What Dravid had to deal with, instead, was a person whom Tendulkar describes in his autobiography as the 'ringmaster', a man who only cared about his own opinions. Greg had accused Ganguly of 'divide and rule', but this accusation could apply perfectly back to the coach himself.

The only way for Dravid to sort out the mess was by forcing a showdown and getting Chappell removed as coach. That possibility was remote as Dravid neither had the ears of the BCCI nor was he the sort to confront knotty issues head on. Dravid's choices were limited. He had to deal with what seemed a fait accompli. This may have made him let things drift, which compounded the team's and his own problems.

I met Dravid one more time on that Pakistan tour, at the conclusion of the One-Day series which India had swept 4–1. The resounding victory must have buoyed his spirits and he agreed to an interview with me. Indeed, he appeared peppier and more confident when we met.

I did not dwell too much on the Greg issue, but Ganguly's omission was a topic that I wanted to explore. His answer was interesting: 'If Anil (Kumble) can be dropped, India's greatest match winner, why can't anyone else?' He probably was referring to a period when Ganguly had preferred Harbhajan to Kumble in the XI. Kumble had won more matches for India than anyone else, including Tendulkar. Dravid was indirectly saying that if such a player could sit out, why was there so much fuss about dropping a batsman who was struggling with his form?

Throughout that thirty-minute interview, I sensed a feeling of unease underneath Dravid's cheerful demeanour. Both of us knew that we were simply going around the more uncomfortable topic of the coach's actions without touching it, but it remained an issue the captain had to deal with.

Pressures of the Job

When reporting from Pakistan, I was quite critical of Greg Chappell in my stories. I did not expect that it would lead to problems at my workplace. I was told that I was being biased and unduly harsh on Greg, and that the chairperson of *HT*, Shobhana Bhartia, wanted me to dilute my criticism of the coach. This upset me no end.

I called my editor, Vir Sanghvi, who had given our department complete freedom to write what we believed was correct. He responded that he was not in India and would sort this out once he was back in the office. However, he assured me of his complete backing, saying, 'You are my sports editor and I have full trust in you and your judgement. Write what you think is right.' Despite these reassuring words those in the office, perhaps under pressure, didn't relent.

At the end of the series, I was told to get an interview with Greg and also write a piece eulogizing his splendid contribution to the

Indian team. These instructions came from the head of the desk, the person responsible for overseeing and coordinating stories that appeared in the morning edition. I responded that I would write what I thought and believed in. I still remember the words from the other end of the line: 'All I am doing is trying to save your job, as Mrs Bhartia is upset at your writings that are critical of Greg.'

I couldn't take it anymore and lost my cool. My irritated response was: 'I am not beholden to anyone for the job and won't write anything about which I am not convinced. Get someone else to do this job. If you insist on my writing a piece, I will do it, but it will still be critical of Greg's methods. My own integrity is more important to me than my job.'

Did I really mean what I said, though? I was nearly fifty years old and had been the sports editor of *HT* for almost five years. It was a job that had taken its toll on my mind and body.

A newspaper office is a lively, throbbing place with many shades of opinions, but facts are facts, and reports based on credible sources need to be published without fear of anyone, howsoever powerful that person may be. A basic tenet of journalism is to be highly sceptical—believe nothing and doubt everything till proven true. This is the advice that is given to young reporters, bubbling with ideas and idealism, when they join the profession.

Over the years, the pulls and pressures of various stakeholders—the editors, the marketing department, the owners, the powerbrokers or the ones about whom we write—can turn the best of us into wrecks. Mental peace is the first casualty. Retaining one's self-esteem becomes difficult. A sort of neurosis sets in that can make a person go insane.

I have gone through my share of these problems, battling the increasing influence of commerce on editorial content, the business and political interests of the owners, and even doubts whether my own personal likes and dislikes were colouring my judgement.

And when one is, like I was, heading a department, one has to deal with fragile egos of the staff who, if not given their preferred assignment, start suspecting one's integrity. Life can become irritatingly demanding.

After being pressured to praise Greg Chappell in my articles, I felt that I did not want to keep working for *HT*, despite the decent salary and perks. I was to fly back to India the next day and in my hotel room in Pakistan I took a long look at myself and where I was heading. Once home, I had a lengthy discussion with my wife Mukta and we decided the circumstances had made it not worthwhile to continue in my job. I drafted a resignation letter which referred briefly to work pressures and finally mentioned the Greg issue as the main reason for my deciding to quit. I remember writing: 'If the owner of the paper does not trust you and questions your integrity, it is time to quit.'

I handed over my resignation letter to Vir Sanghvi on my first day back in the Delhi office. Vir is a man of few words. He read the letter in my presence and just said, 'You are going nowhere.' He asked me to wait and left the room.

After an hour or so, he came into my cabin and said that he had had a talk with Mrs Bhartia and she was not going to accept my resignation. He also assured me that she had no intention of influencing my writings and was 'apologetic' if I thought otherwise. 'You work for me and not for her,' said Vir, and handed my resignation letter back to me.

Quitting my job would of course have meant a loss of earnings as I had no alternate offer in hand. I knew that job opportunities become fewer the higher you rise, so I was not too unhappy with the outcome. I had made my stand and, from my point of view, the organization had retreated. But it was never going to be the same again.

I was on borrowed time, not because I feared any retaliation from the top but because I realized that my heart was no longer in the work and my energy was sapped. From idealism to cynicism and even despair, my journey as a journalist had reached a breaking point.

I was to last for another year and a half in my job, with my last assignment being the 2007 World Cup in the West Indies. I had not planned to cover the tournament myself, assigning it to my prolific and talented colleague Kadambari Murali. However, she pulled out at the last moment due to personal reasons, and I had to travel to the Caribbean. After India's inglorious exit, I returned and put in my papers.

No amount of persuasion could make me change my mind this time, though on the organization's request I continued my association with *HT* in the capacity of a consultant. Kadambari was promoted and replaced me as the paper's national sports editor, becoming probably the first woman to head the sports section of a major newspaper in the country.

Ganguly's Return

The time between the 2006 Pakistan tour and the 2007 World Cup was another tumultuous one for Indian cricket, with Ganguly's continued exclusion dominating public imagination. Greg's quixotic methods—which included having no fixed batting order and multiple team combinations—were now proving to be the duds many of us thought they would be.

The England team toured India in March 2006. To the shock of critics and fans alike, they managed to draw the series 1–1. It was the first time since 1985 that an England side did not lose a Test series in India. The result was even more galling as England was not at full strength—injuries to skipper Michael Vaughan, pacer Simon Jones and left-arm spinner Ashley Giles had weakened them considerably. Their problems were compounded by the mysterious departure of opening batsman Marcus Trescothick midway through the series. Despite these setbacks, they managed to get the upper hand in the first Test at Nagpur, though it ended in a draw. They lost the second at Mohali and were not expected to put up a fight in the third and final Test at the Wankhede in Mumbai.

The Mumbai Test was to be Dravid's hundredth. Given the milestone, I had decided to cover it and also interview Dravid. In the interview, Dravid reminisced about his debut at Lord's, saying he had been like a kid in a candy shop. He expressed his gratitude to the game and attributed his success to discipline, hard work and luck.

The Test itself did not prove lucky for him. The first mistake was deciding to bowl first. The wicket was bare and conditions were good for batting, but the pitch was expected to assist spinners as the game progressed, making scoring runs more challenging in the fourth innings. Yet, England was given the best conditions on a platter. They made the most of India's generosity, posting a total of 400 and taking a grip on the game that they would not release. Little-known off-spinner Shaun Udal took 4 for 14 in the fourth innings to dismiss India for a mere 100, which meant England won by 212 runs.

During the post-match ceremonies, even while Dravid was on stage, the stadium was drowned in chants of 'Ganguly, Ganguly'. This was not Kolkata's Eden Gardens clamouring for their hometown hero, but Mumbai's Wankhede expressing who they sided with in the Chappell–Ganguly saga. That decision to bowl first reflected Greg's bizarre love for experimentation just for the sake of doing something different, even if it made little sense.

Yes, he was trying to build a young team, but was doing it by humiliating the seniors. Among his growing array of confounding words and actions included describing then-teenager Suresh Raina as the most outstanding talent in the world and pushing fast bowler Irfan Pathan to open the innings. This kind of randomness created great insecurities among the players and had a negative impact on the team's fortunes. The seniors were left insecure and those very young players he was encouraging were caught in the cross fire that may have impacted negatively on their own game too.

Following the poor result against England, India then failed to qualify for the final of a tri-series in Malaysia, where Australia beat West Indies in the final. This failure now created apprehensions even among those who had spoken glowingly about Greg and his 'bold' methods. Worse was to follow in the Champions Trophy that was held in India, as the home team did not even make the semi-finals. Greg's star was on the wane.

Next up was a tour to South Africa, which was seen as Greg's last chance for redemption. But the team performed miserably again, losing the five-match One-Day series 4–0, blown away in four consecutive matches after rain forced the first match to be abandoned. Indian cricket fans were now no longer enamoured of the coach and there were rumours that even Tendulkar was unhappy with him. Greg's writ was no longer the law in Indian cricket. The Greg–Dravid combine was now being seen as blundering along even as they prepared for the Test series that was to follow. And there was a surprise in store when the squad for that series was announced.

Comebacks in international cricket are not rare or unusual, but Ganguly's return to the Indian team was a miracle of sorts. When he was axed from the team in Pakistan, his career appeared as good as over. People laughed at the temerity of an ad filmmaker who made a clip of Ganguly endorsing a product and saying he would soon be back in the Indian team.

Much like his first comeback in 1996, luck may have played a big role in Ganguly's third coming. BCCI president Sharad Pawar also served as a minister in the central government, a government that was being backed by the Left Front from Bengal. He may have thought it wise to please these allies now that Greg was no longer seen as panacea for all the ills plaguing Indian cricket.

When the squad for the Tests in South Africa was announced, Ganguly's name was on the list. This time there was unanimity both in the public and the media that Ganguly had been treated badly and deserved another chance. The joke was now on those who had backed Greg and scoffed at Ganguly.

However, despite agreeing on Ganguly's inclusion, the media was divided on Greg's term as the Indian coach. In my memory, I had never seen the Indian media split into two factions like this. The pro-Greg lobby even accused those in the other camp who were always critical of Greg of 'sabotaging' Indian interests.

Ganguly had remained far removed from these games in the media and had instead focused on preparing for his comeback. His efforts paid off, and in his remarkable return in South Africa, he scored a half century and played a pivotal role in India's first-ever Test win in the country. Soon he was again one of the mainstays of the Indian batting line-up, being as successful as he had been when at his peak.

Ganguly had kept in mind the support some of us in the media had lent him while he was fighting his battles with Greg. After his successful Test return, he sent me a text message saying, 'I will never forget the support you gave me.'

When Ganguly was on a tour of England with the Indian team, I spent a few days in his home town listening to stories about his strong-willed character and grit, and the efforts he put in to better himself and prove his detractors wrong. I visited his home again and his mother showed me the same affection as before. The purpose of my visit was to collect material for his biography I intended to write, for which he had promised me full access for my research.

I heard from his parents how, at a time when the world believed his time was up, their son had whipped himself up into a frenzied schedule that had left them bewildered and worried. His father, Chandidas Ganguly said, 'One night I heard some loud sounds and discovered him practising his shots in his room.' The parents wanted him to relax and not react in such an illogical manner to his being dropped from the Indian team, but Ganguly didn't pay them any heed, continuing with his 'insane' training. He would spend the entire day working on either his batting technique with his coach or his fitness in the gym.

The Bengal team trainer, Chinmoy Roy, was helping Ganguly train. He told me that initially Ganguly did not believe a skill-based sport like cricket needed the kind of fitness regimen needed in other sports such as football and athletics: 'He said that even Sachin did not do much fitness training.' Roy remembers Ganguly's performances on the Beep test, which measured one's cardiovascular endurance, was quite ordinary. 'He would run out of breath too quickly,' said the trainer.

Ganguly's attitude to his training changed after three months out of the Indian side. Then began the real training that transformed Ganguly from a laidback cricketer into a lean, strong athlete. Roy says he convinced him that the most glaring shortcoming he had was lack of speed and agility, especially turning speed, because of which he could not convert singles into twos while running between the wickets. It also led to his low-energy displays in the outfield as well.

Roy recounted two incidents that showed how much Ganguly missed not being part of the Indian team and his determination to make a comeback. 'We had a TV in the gym,' he said. 'India was playing Sri Lanka at home in 2005. I could sense the disappointment in his eyes as Irfan Pathan walked in to bat at number 3. Disagreeing with the decision, he turned his back to the TV and increased his workout intensity.'

The second anecdote is about the time India announced its One-Day team to South Africa. Ganguly believed that he would be chosen. On finding his name missing, 'anger and disappointment was written large on his face', recalled Roy. 'I thought he was in no mood to train. But he trained as if his life depended on it.' At one point a drained Ganguly lay on the ground, close to throwing up from the exertion. When Roy suggested they pack up, he heard an expletive from the former captain for the first time: 'F...k no, I will do more. I have to come back. They can't keep me out.'

When the call finally came, he was mentally and physically ready, and motivated to give his best. While the world was focused on what reception he would get from the coach, Ganguly instead had his sights set on not letting this one last opportunity slip from his grasp.

The one trait I found most common among successful sportspersons is self-confidence. Ganguly displayed this characteristic in abundance. In the meetings I had with him during his period of exile from the team, he talked about his comeback as if it was an inevitability no one could prevent. Not only was he sure of his return, he equally sure that he would make big runs once again.

A Team on Edge

Ganguly's successful comeback may have done wonders for his own self-esteem and career, but the Indian team as a whole was now a dispirited collection of individuals—uncertain, edgy and consistently looking over their shoulders. This was the condition in which they flew to the Caribbean for the 2007 World Cup.

India was in Group B of the first stage of the World Cup, along with Sri Lanka, Bangladesh and Bermuda. The top two teams from each group would qualify for another round of league matches called the Super Eight. A team needed to win two matches in their group to ensure their progress into the next round.

The Group B games would be played in Trinidad, and thousands of Indian fans from across the globe arrived to support their team. Most also had tickets for the later stages of the tournament, as they were convinced India would go far if not till the very end. They were oblivious to the fact that the team they were backing was a collection of insecure individuals, especially the seniors who were more like schoolchildren in a sulk and resentful of a coach whom they neither respected nor wanted to listen to any longer.

As for the man himself, the coach who had thought of going to the World Cup without Sehwag, Tendulkar and Ganguly was now 'saddled' with all three. The troika were all claimants for the opening slots, with Tendulkar naturally being the leading contender. Sehwag's case was a curious one. According to reports in the media, he was not in contention for selection, being out of form and favour, and that it was only on skipper Dravid's insistence he was included in the team.

In a press conference on the eve of the tournament's opening ceremony, Dravid was asked if Sehwag's selection in the squad was justified. To the shock and surprise of all of us present in the room, Dravid lost his cool. I had never seen him react with such irritation. I don't remember the exact words but he did say that Sehwag was no 'Ramu kaka', which could be roughly translated to the English 'Tom, Dick or Harry', meaning an average person or a nobody.

Another victim of the uncertainty prevailing in the team was Irfan Pathan. Greg had experimented so much with this talented player, even making him bat at number 3, that it had probably made his bowling suffer. In a practice match, Irfan bowled a series of wide balls that reflected his state of mind. To be seen as Greg's favourite in the Indian team was now fraught with danger.

India's first match of the tournament was against Bangladesh. The coach decided to push Tendulkar down to number four from his preferred opening position. Ganguly and Sehwag opened. The batting floundered. Despite being the only batsman to pass 50, Ganguly was accused of batting too slowly. He ended up with 66 runs off 129 balls as India was bowled out for a paltry score of 191.

There were Indians in the press box who still believed that this was a good enough total, because the opponents were only Bangladesh. Even after opener Tamim Iqbal launched a fearless assault on the Indian bowlers, the possibility of India losing to their neighbours was not accepted as reality. As Bangladesh inched closer and closer to the Indian total, the Indian faces in the press box grew more and more sullen. An agency reporter, sucking at his cigarette with all his nervous energy, started muttering, 'No, this is not possible, India can't lose.' But lose they did. The reactions of disbelief in sections of the Indian media reflected both the faith they still had in Greg's coaching methods and their failure to see the deep cracks in the team.

A resounding win against minnows Bermuda followed, but they were a collection of part-time cricketers and the performance held little significance. Of more significance was the fact that India had juggled its batting order once again, with Sehwag dropping down to number three and Tendulkar dropped further from four to six. Experiments were being made even in the midst of a global tournament, with little care about what effect it may have on the confidence of the players.

India's only hope now lay in winning their final league encounter against Sri Lanka. I remember wondering what must be going through Dravid's mind. Even though he was captain, Greg had become the face of the team. On an impulse, I called him from the hotel lobby to wish him well and tell him not to brood too much over what had already happened. I have rarely, if ever, indulged in calling a player, especially a captain, on the eve of a match. I think I was feeling sorry for Dravid and concerned for his state of mind after all that he had endured because of the coach.

In the match against Sri Lanka, India restricted their opponents to a modest score of 254, raising hopes of a win. However, their batting let them down once again. As wickets started to fall and the result became inevitable, the predominantly Indian crowd started booing the batting team. Dravid stuck around for a while but was dismissed for 60, which would end up being the highest Indian score. With his wicket, it was just a matter of time, and India eventually lost by 69 runs. They were knocked out of the World Cup.

I remember the hostile reception Chappell got from the Indian media in the post-match press conference. The questions were direct, some of them even rude. Greg, being Greg, was as stone-faced as ever. He clearly did not accept his own crucial role in this failure. To a question on what went wrong with his 'processes'—a Chappell pet phrase—he responded, 'This is an inflammatory question.' Then he began apportioning blame to long-term structural problems in Indian cricket, saying, 'Well, I don't think India has won a tournament overseas since 1985. There is a bit of history to it. There are obviously some reasons for it.' Defiant and obdurate, Greg was being himself that day. For a man who believed that the only way was his way, with him having complete control of the team, it was a bit strange to see him take cover behind 'collective responsibility'.

India exiting a World Cup at the first stage was a catastrophic result, not just for the country, but also for the tournament. With no Indian involvement at the later stages, television viewership plummeted and there was a huge drop in interest in the coverage of cricket's premier tournament.

The first fortnight of March 2007 was a stressful period for me. While reporting on the World Cup, the demands from the office were becoming unmanageable. I was by now a reluctant journalist, not enjoying my job, and had more or less made up my mind to quit once I was back in Delhi.

What sealed my decision to quit was the pressure being put on me by the new editor, Chaitanya Kalbag. He was a very hard taskmaster who would treat his staff harshly. He would scream and shout at people while pointing out their mistakes or if they did not follow his command. He had made it clear that he was unhappy with my work. Like most newly appointed editors, he wanted his own trusted people in key positions, and was on a recruitment drive.

India's unexpected early exit provided me with an opportunity to leave too.

12

Life as a Columnist, Television Journalism and the IPL

When I quit *HT*, I was fifty-one years old. When my resignation letter reached Mrs Bhartia she immediately called me to her office. She urged me not to leave and assured me that they would sort out any problems I may be facing with the editor. But I did not change my mind.

I was then made a second offer to work as a consultant, a role that would allow me to write whenever I wanted to but without being accountable for the day-to-day running of the paper. More importantly, I could take up any other work that was not in conflict with my writing. This alleviated my financial worries and I accepted this generous deal.

From 2007 until 2017, when my contract was terminated, I regularly wrote a column called 'The Big Picture' without fearing any sort of censorship. I have many reasons to be grateful to the owner who, on several occasions when it came to a confrontation, chose to take a step back instead of exercising her authority.

My *HT* exit coincided with an offer from Vir Sanghvi, who was in the process of setting up a new television channel owned by the husband–wife duo of Peter and Indrani Mukherjea. Peter was a well-known name in television, having successfully run the Star entertainment channel. Indrani would be the managing editor of the new channel. I accepted Vir's offer.

I worked for six months to set up the sports department for the channel, named NewsX, before quitting after differences arose with the management. During this preparatory period before its launch, I realized that television was not the medium for me, even in the role of an advisor. Though NewsX had a stated goal to not succumb to sensationalism, something both Vir and Peter would repeatedly emphasize, I somehow was not comfortable with the situation I had got into. The channel was hoping to free television from the monstrous hold TRP ratings had, but I could see how difficult it would be to follow that path.

I grew sceptical of the vision that Vir had for the channel even as the differences between Vir and the management were growing. Shortly after he quit, I, too, resigned. Despite a huge dip in my monthly income, quitting NewsX brought me a sense of relief. After all the ups and downs I had faced in my jobs, I had developed an aversion of sorts for any role that chained me to an organization.

In the meantime, the seismic effects of India's World Cup exit were being felt all over the country. Greg Chappell's term was coming to an end and there was no way his tenure would be extended. On the day Tendulkar, who rarely said anything controversial or negative, went public in his criticism of Greg, the Indian coach announced he had decided not to renegotiate his contract with the BCCI. All of a sudden, players found their voices and were now airing their anger against their coach. Once it was clear he was on his way out, even those journalists who had backed his style of functioning were now finding faults with Greg Chappell.

The Rise of T20

The Greg Chappell storm had raged long enough and died down with his ouster, but Indian cricket landed in fresh turmoil for entirely different reasons. The new nemesis was television czar Subhash Chandra, the owner of the Zee TV network, who launched a city-based T20 tournament without permission from the BCCI.

Chandra had failed in his bid to acquire the television broadcasting rights for Indian cricket, and was so upset with the BCCI that he decided to establish his own cricket league. He began hiring cricketers from around the world, including a number of Indian ex-cricketers and uncapped players. It was not dissimilar to Kerry Packer's venture in the late seventies, when he created the rebel World Series of Cricket, hiring the best Test cricketers across the world to play a series of matches in Australia that would be televised live by his TV station, Channel Nine.

Chandra had backed Sharad Pawar's campaign to defeat Jagmohan Dalmiya in the Board president elections. However, despite this, BCCI rejected Chandra's bid for exclusive TV rights. In the last round of bidding in February 2006, the rights were awarded to Nimbus instead. Chandra watched the rival bidder walk away with the rights till 2011 for a sum of $613 million; his own bid ended up being $100 million short. Furious, he decided to create original cricket content for his channel and challenge the hegemony of the BCCI over cricket in the country.

Chandra made Kapil Dev the face of this rebel cricket venture, named the Indian Cricket League (ICL). Cricketers across the world began signing contracts to play. However, the ICC refused to grant the ICL official status, and under BCCI pressure, threatened to ban all who joined it from playing official international and First-Class cricket.

Since the operations of the ICL were opaque, no one knows for sure what kind of money was offered to players to defy the official ban. However, several big names—including New Zealand stars Shane Bond and Chris Cairns, and former Pakistani captain, Inzamam-ul-Haq—had sufficient incentive to break away from their respective national teams.

Being semi-retired by then, I had no first-hand experience of how the league was managed, though information trickling in from the venues was not very positive. Denied proper, established venues by the BCCI, the new tournament was held at grounds that lacked proper infrastructure. The crowd response was encouraging at some places and lukewarm at others.

Whatever the financial consequences the ICL may have had for Subhash Chandra, it did play a major role in making administrators and broadcasters realize the commercial potential of T20 league cricket. It would not be wrong to say that, just as Packer had changed cricket forever, Chandra's ICL had a revolutionary impact on world cricket too.

Although the T20 format was attracting crowds and there were many who backed this new concept of short-form cricket, the BCCI was not a fan. When the ICC decided to go ahead with a T20 World Cup, India was a strong opponent and initially refused to participate. The BCCI perhaps believed that there was no space for one more format in the congested cricket calendar. Had Chandra not conceptualized the ICL and India not suffered a shocking premature exit from the World Cup, it is possible that India would not have changed its stand. An Indian team was sent to the inaugural T20 World Cup in 2007, played in South Africa.

The Indian team at this new World Cup was shorn of many of its stalwarts, who had been replaced by rookies. It was led by a new captain, M.S. Dhoni. Perhaps to their own surprise, India emerged from this first-ever T20 World Cup as champions. They defeated arch-rivals Pakistan in a nail-biting final, and the new format was suddenly all the rage.

There is an image of Dhoni after the final that has stayed with me. Away from the frenzied celebrations of his teammates, he took off his shirt and handed it over to a teenage fan at the ground. I was so impressed by his handling of the team and how he didn't let pressure affect his calm demeanour that in my column after the final I wrote that Dhoni would be the new Ganguly of Indian cricket.

I had heard of Dhoni from Ganguly back in 2004. That was the period when Indian cricket was desperately searching for a wicketkeeper-batsman. Ganguly had told me about a youngster from Ranchi who was one of the finest hitters of the ball he had ever seen. He was sure that lad would soon be playing for India.

That prophecy came true and Dhoni soon established himself in the team with his unbelievable hitting power. In fact, he was one of the favourites of Greg Chappell, who would always talk about him in glowing terms. Dhoni also displayed a strategic understanding of the game that was valued by his teammates. It came as no surprise that the BCCI decided to try out the dynamic youngster in a leadership position in a new format.

After that surprise World Cup victory, the BCCI decided to create its own city-based league on the pattern of the ICL. The driving force behind this radical step was a little-known man with a surname famous in the corporate world: Lalit Modi.

Board Games and Politics

Lalit Modi was born into one of the most well-known business families of India. His father, Krishan Kumar, was the son of Raj Bahadur Gujarmal, the founder of the Modi group. In 1933,

Gujarmal had set up one of the first sugar factories in India, and expanded his business empire into other industries, most successfully in textiles. A popular version of his story was that Gujarmal had left his village for the city with a *lota* (mug) as his sole possession, and had made his fortune through sheer hard work.

Lalit went to study in America, where he was charged with conspiracy to traffic cocaine, assault and second-degree kidnapping in 1985. Following a plea bargain, he was given a suspended two-year prison sentence, placed under a five-year probation and ordered to do 100 hours of community service. A year later, citing bad health, he sought permission to return to India, which the court granted.

Modi then established the Modi Entertainment Network in the 1990s, which failed to take off. He then tried his hand at cricket administration in Himachal Pradesh, becoming one of the local cricket association's office-bearers in 1999. Failing to make any inroads there, he later became the vice-president of the Punjab Cricket Association.

Modi had been harbouring an idea of a city-based, franchise-driven league on the pattern of the NBA in America. Modi's initial plan in 1994 was to have a league that would have matches in the 50-overs format. The concept proved too revolutionary for the Board to entertain. It was a time when the BCCI was just beginning to fight the state stranglehold on cricket broadcasting. Modi's idea was ahead of its time and the Board, involved in its own commercial battles and power games, rejected it outright. The rejection could also have been due to Modi's insistence on running the league without the Board's involvement, except for revenue sharing.

The ambitious Modi, then only thirty-one, had a gambler's streak combined with strong resolve and irrepressible energy. He bided his time for over a decade to finally become the fulcrum of a new league that would change cricket forever: the Indian Premier League (IPL).

Back in 1994, Modi had consulted professionals to execute his grand project and give it a practical shape. Among those he spoke to was Amrit Mathur, who later became the CEO of the IPL team Delhi Daredevils. Mathur said that those who believe that the IPL was patterned on the ICL, and that Modi had just copied the model, do him an injustice.

To understand the IPL's commercial reach, its professional success and the nepotism and corruption within its administrative structure, one needs to decipher Board politics. There were increasingly high-profile interventions trying to influence the BCCI elections, as the winner would have control over its bulging coffers and exploit its popularity to spread their own personal businesses or political clout. Mathur is the best person to take us through that journey, as he has closely watched and even been involved with BCCI election and administrative procedures since the nineties.

This was the period when the Board president was a Bengali businessman, Biswanath Dutt, who also had a long tenure as the head of Bengal's cricket association. It was during Dutt's tenure that Jagmohan Dalmiya was baptized into cricket politics. At that time, the cricket administration was controlled by businessmen, government administrators, bureaucrats and not many high-profile politicians would venture into its set-up. Among the rare politicians in its administrative set-up was Congress Party stalwart N.K.P. Salve, credited with having played a major role in India–Pakistan jointly hosting the 1987 World Cup.

Madhavrao Scindia, the son of the last Maharaja of Gwalior, besides being an influential member of the Congress Party, was a keen cricket follower. Scindia had an interesting political profile, having won his first election at the age of twenty-six from Guna constituency in Gwalior. He was the candidate from the right-wing Jan Sangh, which later morphed into the BJP as we know it today. He later shifted loyalties and joined the Congress, and in the 1984

Life as a Columnist, Television Journalism and the IPL

Lok Sabha elections defeated the popular BJP stalwart Atal Bihari Vajpayee.

When Scindia became railway minister in 1986, he took a liking for Mathur, a junior secretary in his department. Despite being twelve years younger than the minister, Mathur's understanding of and fondness for cricket allowed him to create a special bond with Scindia. Soon, Mathur was made the head of the Railways Sports Board, causing heartburn among the seniors who were passed over. Scindia backed the young bureaucrat in all the major policy decisions he took concerning Railways sports.

The Railways are the biggest patrons of sport in the country, having more than 1000 sportspersons on their payrolls. They participate in all major sporting disciplines played in the country and provide jobs and support to many of the country's athletes. According to Mathur, Scindia relied on him in matters of cricket, even when it came to the Board. As head of the Madhya Pradesh Cricket Association, Scindia was an important member of the BCCI.

In 1990, Scindia decided to take on the ruling establishment of the BCCI by contesting the presidential elections against Dutt. Scindia needed a majority of the twenty-seven votes from its affiliate members to win. He could count on the votes of the three central government-backed units of the Board—the Universities, the Services and the Railways. Indications were that it was going to be a very close contest, where even one vote could tilt the scales.

Mathur was still heading the Railways Sports Board, and was all set to vote for his former boss and mentor. However, a directive arrived from the then railway minister, the firebrand trade union leader George Fernandes, to vote for Dutt. Mathur was in a predicament: as a government servant, he could not defy the minister's orders. Scindia then contacted Prime Minister V.P. Singh, who, as a former Congressman himself, was on friendly terms with Scindia. The Indian Prime Minister's office (PMO) persuaded Fernandes to change his stand, and also ensured that the Universities and Services voted for Singh's former party colleague.

When the final results were announced, Scindia had won by the solitary vote. For the first time in the Board's election history, or perhaps in any sporting body election, the Prime Minister had played a significant role in deciding the winner. The Board had seen many high-profile presidents since its inception, including politicians, maharajas and businessmen, but had never before witnessed such a powerful intervention from the very top in its elections.

Until then the Board, despite all its intrigues, was closed to outside influences. Mathur feels that the events of that election saw the use of money, power and political clout to influence outcomes become the norm. The significance of that political intervention in Scindia's win became apparent when the election for the post of secretary was held, going (again by one vote) to his opponent's man, Dalmiya. The Board was now being governed by a powerful politician and a businessman.

As an aside, I have my own little story to narrate on how the Board elections became more vicious and manipulative in nature, with some candidates even resorting to direct coercion and abductions. The story is from 2001, by when Dalmiya and Bindra had become arch enemies. Dalmiya was no longer the supremo he used to be. A businessman from Chennai by the name of A.C. Muthiah had dethroned a Dalmiya-backed candidate a year earlier. Dalmiya wanted to stage a comeback and take on Muthiah again. Dalmiya had the backing of Arun Jaitley of the BJP, while Muthiah was backed by Pawar.

A couple of days before the election, I was on a flight to Chennai to report on the event for *HT*. On the same flight was Sunil Dev, a former Delhi wicketkeeper who later became a Board official and also served as the manager of the Indian team on the 1996–97 South

African tour. He was now a vocal opponent of the Dalmiya–Jaitley combine. I noticed him in conversation with a fidgety, nervous man, who Dev introduced to me as one of the Board members.

When we landed at Chennai, Dev offered me a ride. The cagey behaviour of his companion had aroused my curiosity and I welcomed the offer. I accompanied the two to Dev's hotel room, where the nature of their relationship and the reason for that person's nervous behaviour became clear. Strangely, Dev was himself forthcoming in revealing what was going on, saying that the man was there to 'vote for us'.

His fidgety friend, who spoke in broken Hindi laced with a few English sentences, kept mumbling, '*Unko pata lag jayega aur main phas jaoonga* (They will come to know and I'll be in great trouble).' It was obvious he was not with Dev of his own free will, but some outside pressure was keeping him there. Dev revealed that this person was the secretary of the Assam Cricket Association, and a powerful official of a political party had pressured him to shift his loyalties from Dalmiya to Muthiah.

From what I could gather, he feared his job would be in danger if he did not vote for Muthiah, although the brief from his association was to vote for Dalmiya. To ensure that he did not get cold feet or spill the beans, he had been 'placed under observation', with Dev appointed as his chaperone.

According to calculations, every vote was crucial and the Assam vote could have been decisive. Dev was confident that with the trump card under his watch, Dalmiya was going to lose. The next morning we were sitting in the hotel lobby, minutes from the start of the election, when suddenly his face went pale. His eyes were on someone who had just entered the lobby. The man was Prafulla Kumar Mahanta, the former chief minister of Assam and then president of the Assam Cricket Association.

His arrival meant that it was he and not the man 'abducted' by Dev who would represent the association in the election. The Assam vote would go to Dalmiya. Dev was just minutes from pulling off a heist, and he was understandably devastated to see his plans in tatters. But what had transpired overnight to put Mahanta on the early morning flight to Chennai to cast his vote personally, when his secretary had already been assigned that job?

I learnt the answer from Mathur. He told me that the day before the elections, Scindia got a call from Dalmiya, who had found out about the Assam board secretary's 'defection'. Scindia was then siding with Dalmiya against the Pawar lobby, and agreed to help. Dalmiya requested him to persuade Mahanta to rush to Chennai early the next morning to foil the opposition plan. Mathur was asked to meet Mahanta, who happened to be in Delhi, and persuade him to board the first morning flight to Chennai.

Mahanta duly flew to Chennai and voted for Dalmiya, ensuring he won the election by seventeen votes to thirteen. Had two votes moved to the rival camp it would have been a tie, and in that case Muthiah's casting vote would have led to Dalmiya's defeat.

This thrilling story of abduction, coercion, use of political power, alliances and last-minute strategic phone calls could be the plot for a thriller movie, but it was played out in real life. This was how the BCCI elections were managed and manipulated.

As time passed, an increasing number of high-profile, ambitious people wanted to see the end of Dalmiya's control of the Board. Sharad Pawar had joined the Bindra lobby along with a major industrialist from Chennai, N. Srinivasan, who owned India Cements. Srinivasan had been a rival of Muthiah in Tamil Nadu cricket politics as they fought for control of the state cricket board. With Lalit Modi already a Bindra loyalist, this lobby finally tasted success in 2005.

The fall-out of this bitter struggle for control of the BCCI was that Dalmiya was expelled from the Board on charges of embezzlement in 2005. He was subsequently exonerated by the courts. Incredibly, after several years in exile, he was appointed interim Board president in 2013 after the Supreme Court ordered N. Srinivasan to step down in the wake of the IPL fixing scandal. Dalmiya was once again elected BCCI president in 2015, but lasted only six months before he passed away.

Dalmiya's final hurrah shows that the Board felt he was the only man who could take them through a difficult period during which the Supreme Court was intervening in its functioning and even threatening its very existence.

Modi's Manipulations

Despite the IPL soon establishing itself as one of the most popular sporting leagues in the world, it was riven with nepotism and scandals. *The Indian Express* labelled it the 'Indian Parivar (family) League'. For example, Modi's brother-in-law owned the Rajasthan team while his son-in-law was part-owner of the Punjab team.

Srinivasan, who was Board treasurer when Pawar took over as president, had forced an amendment in the Board constitution that allowed him to own an IPL team. Until then, Board members were specifically barred from having any business links with any company or entity that had dealings with the Board. Since Srinivasan wanted his company, India Cements, to have a team in the IPL, this clause was done away with, clearing the way for a Board official's team to play in the tournament. Even for a Board that survived on give and take among its members and was never shy of using political and money power to garner votes in its elections, this was a new low that was to destabilize its functioning within five years.

Before all the cricketing action began in the IPL, there was the 'player auction', where international and Indian cricketers were put on sale and the team owners bid for them. The first auction was held on 20 February 2008, a grand ceremony held in Mumbai.

I quote from the column I wrote in *HT* at the time:

Is all this for real? Or was one watching owners of fat cheque-books sitting in a casino and massaging their egos by throwing mindboggling sums at star cricketers? Shahrukh Khan, the owner of the Kolkata team, found the whole bidding process so thrilling that he said he was getting 'addicted' to it. IS Bindra, a BCCI official, and a former Indian Administrative Service officer, had never seen a day like this in his life 'ever' ...

Has cricket in India entered the age of sponsored gambling where its stake-holders are abdicating their responsibility and letting the 'free-market' forces take control of the sport?

What took place in Mumbai on February 20, 2008, could well be a watershed in the affairs of this sport and no one can foresee what direction it is headed for. Is the IPL a fantasy created by the Indian Board, which has enticed the moneyed elite so much that they think by investing thousands of crores into a 44-day inter-city T20 league, they are inventing a goose that will lay golden eggs for them one day?

Even more importantly for the sport's future, are these massive sums being doled out so that direct control of the game swaps hands? And, will what today is the Indian Board tomorrow become a defunct body at the complete mercy of the very corporates who presided over the auctioning of the players and bought them at fancy prices? ...

There is too much money riding on this IPL now and that is why every effort, muscle and money, will be used to make it popular. If it succeeds, corporates will demand their pound of flesh ...

Money and the popularity of this format could mean the end of the way cricket is structured internationally. What today is addictive for King Khan could become the opium of the masses. Who benefits and who loses is irrelevant to those for whom what finally matters is the flow of cash.

Ironically, Lalit Modi, the man who propelled this cricketing revolution is today absconding from the Indian authorities, hiding somewhere in Europe. Despite cases of fraud and embezzlement filed against him, the Indian government has so far been unable to have him extradited. How it all enfolded is well documented.

N. Srinivasan had gradually risen in the power hierarchy to become the all-powerful BCCI president, whose writ became law in running the cricketing establishment. With Srinivasan in control of the Board, Modi ran the glitzy and glamourous event as he wished. Such was his aura that Ravi Shastri called him the 'Moses of cricket'.

To understand Modi's rise, we need to look at his proximity to the BJP leader Vasundhara Raje Scindia (sister of Madhavrao), who was chief minister of Rajasthan in 2005. She helped Modi force his way into the Rajasthan Cricket Association, become its president, and then wrest control of the state body.

Until then, the Rajasthan Cricket Association had been under the control of the Rungta family for decades. Purushottam Rungta had been BCCI president in the seventies, and his brother Kishen and son Kishore became important functionaries of the national body. Similar to the presence of Ranbir Singh Mahendra in neighbouring Haryana, it seemed impossible to dislodge them from the state body.

Apart from thirty-two district bodies that constituted the Rajasthan association, there were also sixty-eight individual members whose votes decided who would get elected to the governing body. If reports are to be believed, most of these sixty-eight were on the personal staff of the Rungta clan, some of them even their peons, and they all voted for their masters.

Vasundhara became the chief minister of Rajasthan in 2003, and two years later, she passed the Rajasthan Sports Act that disenfranchised these individual members loyal to the Rungtas. That left only the district associations as voting members of the body. Modi registered as a member from Nagore district, and with the state government backing him, he became president of the state association in 2005.

In 1990, the prime minister had helped a politician defeat a businessman to become the national Board president; fifteen years later, that politician's sister as a chief minister had helped a businessman to become a state board president. To complete the odd connection, Modi won by one vote, just like Madhavrao Scindia had.

Modi was now a rightful member of the BCCI, and embarked on his ambitious journey in national cricket politics. After playing a significant role in helping Sharad Pawar defeat Jagmohan Dalmiya in the 2005 Board elections, he began to be known as the 'super chief minister' of Rajasthan.

Modi's arrogance only grew after the successful launch of the IPL. He began treating even top bureaucrats and police officers with disdain. There was an incident when he tore up the ticket of an IAS officer Mahendra Singh Surana and refused to let him enter the stadium to watch an IPL match. The reason behind this much-publicized spat was reported to be that Surana was a supporter of the Rungtas. Modi's temper and power were becoming feared and hated. Another incident during an IPL match, in which he slapped a constable who had entered his private box, led to a protest by the entire Jaipur constabulary.

The BCCI soon realized they were dealing with a man whose methods and manners were creating problems for them. Right from the day Modi was appointed the Board vice-president and IPL governing council chairman, an ego battle began between him and Srinivasan. The two would clash on many issues at Board meetings, and within two years of the IPL launch, Modi had become completely isolated in the Board.

There had been allegations that the bids for ownership of the eight founding IPL teams in 2007 had been rigged, and that Modi had ensured that his favourites had won the bids. So when the IPL decided to accept fresh bids for two additional teams to be added to the roster, the process was being closely followed and scrutinized by the media.

To the surprise of many, two new clauses were introduced for the bidding process that ensured that only mega corporations could apply: one of the new clauses stated that the bidder should have a net worth of $1 billion, and the other stated that bidders must provide a bank guarantee of $100 million. Modi's detractors were up in arms and accused him of rigging the bid in favour of certain industrial groups from Gujarat.

When only two bids were received, the minimum net worth requirement was waived and the bank guarantee was reduced to $10 million. Modi was very unhappy that he had been vetoed and his two clauses had been dropped or modified, and began to pick apart any bids that came in. When a consortium of investors led by Rendezvous Sports World (RSW) won the bid for a Kerala-based franchise, Modi immediately wanted to know the identity of the bidders and all those who owned sweat equity in the consortium.

It was revealed that the Congress leader Shashi Tharoor—who was also the external affairs minister in the UPA government at the time—had played a role in putting the consortium together from his home state of Kerala. Modi alleged that the replies from the consortium were evasive and that he was told by Tharoor not to probe the identities of the stakeholders. More dirt was thrown around when Modi revealed that one of the sweat equity holders was Sunanda Pushkar, who was engaged to marry Tharoor. Modi alleged that the shares in the name of Sunanda were 'hidden gifts' for Tharoor.

A massive political controversy erupted, which culminated in Tharoor's resignation from the Union Cabinet. Cricket had claimed a political victim in the country for the first time. Modi, who was seen as being close to the BJP because of his relationship with Vasundhara Raje, had played a significant role in this turn of events. Retribution was inevitable.

Board politics, as we have seen, is a many-layered game where convenient compromises are made to gain power. The IPL—with its massive infusion of money and involvement of major corporations and high-profile politicians—had made everything more complex. The stakes were now much higher and affected even the highest corridors of power in the country. The power nexus had grown to such an extent that the lines between the Board and the Indian government started to become blurry.

Immediately after the IPL final in 2010, Modi was suspended after being charged with corruption and nepotism by the Indian government. The Enforcement Directorate (ED) launched investigations into him as well as the BCCI on various charges related to misuse of funds in contravention of statutory rules. Modi now had both the Board and the Indian government against him. Soon after his suspension, he fled to London.

I participated in a few televised debates on the Modi issue at the time. Often, Modi himself would join as a guest from London, fiercely defending himself and castigating the Board as well as the Indian government. He would argue that he was not responsible for collective BCCI decisions. In one of these debates, when I raised the point about his promoting his own friends and relatives in the IPL by favouring them for ownership, he lost his cool, screaming and accusing his detractors of vendetta.

Modi began accusing his main rival in the Board, N. Srinivasan, of plotting his ouster. He refused to come back to India, claiming that his life was in danger from the underworld as he had refused to pay extortion money to them. The Mumbai Police endorsed his claim, stating that Dawood Ibrahim and his associate Chhota Shakeel had sent hit men to kill Modi and his family when they were on vacation in Thailand.

Meanwhile, fears had been raised that bookies had infiltrated the porous structure of the IPL. Officially sanctioned late-night parties were perfect opportunities for shady characters to access the players. Even the team owners were not believed to be above board. G.S. Virk, a former CBI officer, served as the ACU functionary in the Indian region. Virk had prohibited Shah Rukh Khan, the Bollywood star who owns the Kolkata Knight Riders team, from sitting in the players' dug-out as it was against rules. Khan had taken serious umbrage to this 'insult' despite Virk's actions being in line with the rules of the ICC anti-corruption manual.

In 2013, Modi was found guilty of eight charges, including rigging bids during the 2010 franchise auction, blackmailing the Kerala franchise, selling media and internet rights without proper authorization and plotting to create a rebel T20 league in England. The BCCI committee which was formed to probe charges against Modi comprised two high-profile politicians from the two major political parties of the country, Arun Jaitley from the BJP and Jyotiraditya Scindia, Madhavrao's son, from the Congress. Modi was suspended from the BCCI.

All the accusations which the ED had levelled against him are yet to be proven as Modi is still a fugitive from the law. With the

BJP government coming to power in 2014, not much has been heard of the status of these charges against him or what efforts are being made to extradite him from whichever country he has sought refuge in.

However, if the Board believed that by putting all the blame on Modi they were rid of their own guilt, they were far from the truth. The charges against him showed the extent of wrongdoings in the cricket establishment. And even if a fraction of what was alleged was true, there were dangerous levels of mismanagement and corruption within the Board itself.

It just needed another spark to ignite media and public outrage against the BCCI's functioning, and that happened when Delhi Police arrested Test cricketer S. Sreesanth, and two Ranji Trophy players, Ajith Chandila and Ankeet Chavan, on charges of spot fixing in the 2013 IPL.

13
A Board in Need of Fixing

Despite the sensational police case against an active Indian cricketer, the BCCI president Srinivasan did not seem too perturbed. Even when Mumbai Police revealed that his son-in-law, Gurunath Meiyappan—who was managing Srinivasan's Chennai Super Kings (CSK) team—was in touch with bookies and betting on his own team, Srinivasan's reaction was to dismiss the reports. Under the IPL rules, CSK could have been banned from participating in the IPL.

Mumbai Police had stated on record that they had taped conversations between Meiyappan and a small-time TV and film actor called Vindu Dara Singh placing bets on IPL matches, including ones involving CSK. The police even knew that Meiyappan had kept on changing his bets as the match situation changed. But Srinivasan, despite proof to the contrary, declared that Meiyappan had nothing to do with the team and was merely a 'cricket enthusiast'.

To douse the growing clamour within and outside the Board, Srinivasan set up a three-member probe committee, including two judges from Tamil Nadu. The committee promptly absolved Meiyappan of any wrongdoing, its verdict in line with the owner's claim: that Meiyappan had nothing to do with the CSK team. Srinivasan, the owner of a huge business empire and head of the richest and most powerful cricket body in the world, had used all his power and influence to manipulate the situation and save his team's and his family's reputation.

Even though it was standard practice for the BCCI to be brazenly obtuse in reacting to any charge of wrongdoing against them, Srinivasan's stonewalling was a bit too much for some members to digest. The Board secretary at the time was Sanjay Jagdale, the genial, soft-spoken former Madhya Pradesh cricketer. He submitted his resignation in protest.

Bihar ke Bacche

Normally, the incident may have ended there. However, it took an unusual twist when a small-town 'crusader', miffed at many injustices done to his home state by the top cricket body, took the fight on.

Aditya Verma was fifty years old in 2013, and had spent almost a decade trying to get justice for '*Bihar ke bacche* (children of Bihar)' from the courts. His fight against the BCCI had started when the state of Bihar was kicked out of the Board and the Ranji Trophy on political grounds. Since 2003, no Bihar team had been allowed to play in the competition. Verma's frustrations with the BCCI were spilling over and when he heard about Srinivasan's manipulations, he refused to take it lying down.

Verma petitioned the Mumbai High Court to stop Srinivasan's 'illegal' pardoning of his son-in-law without a proper probe. The high court stayed Srinivasan's action, saying the committee which gave Meiyappan a clean chit had not been formed in compliance with the BCCI rules. It directed the Board to form a fresh committee that would follow the proper procedure for dealing with such cases.

An arrogant Srinivasan convinced the Board to approach the Supreme Court to get the Mumbai High Court order quashed, bringing the whole issue into greater focus and wider media debate. Little did the Board and Srinivasan realize then how big a mistake that was. It would take almost three years of Supreme Court hearings—with the country's best-known and highest-paid lawyers representing each side, followed by the formation of two high-powered committees of eminent judges, including a former chief justice—to finally lead to a verdict that would dismantle the BCCI's administrative structure in 2016.

The Aditya Verma story is an absorbing account of all that is inspiring as well as disgusting in the world of Indian cricket. I had met Verma fleetingly during my coverage of domestic matches and had heard his grievances, but had never taken his self-righteous tales too seriously. I admit this was a mistake, and I was guilty of judging a person by how he spoke and dressed. Verma's typical Bihari accent and his attempts to speak in faltering English somehow, in many eyes, took away from the cause he professed to be fighting for.

Verma had introduced himself to me as a servant of Bihar cricket who wanted to help the children of Bihar to get justice from the BCCI. With a thick file of papers that included records of his state's cricketing woes, he said he sought nothing but recognition from the Board so that one of the largest states in India could once again participate in India's domestic tournaments.

The last time Bihar had played in the Ranji Trophy was in 2003–04, a team that included a young M.S. Dhoni. In the undivided Bihar, Jamshedpur was the centre of its cricket. Tata Steel was a big patron of cricket in the area, and employed a number of talented players who played in its corporate team. Many of these players would go on to play for Bihar in First-Class cricket. However, in

2000, Bihar was split into two, and Ranchi, the capital of the new state of Jharkhand, overshadowed Jamshedpur and its cricketing tradition.

In 2002, the president of the Bihar cricket body was the state's chief minister, Lalu Prasad Yadav. He did not support Dalmiya, and in that dramatic 2001 Board election in Chennai, Lalu's association had voted against Dalmiya. With his political standing and clout, Lalu could have emerged as a strong contender in the BCCI power games, thus Dalmiya saw him as an 'enemy' who had to be either bought out or marginalized.

The opportunity to neutralize Lalu arrived when BJP leader Kirti Azad formed his own rival cricket association in Bihar. The BCCI disenfranchised the Lalu-led association and bestowed official recognition on the rival body, making it an associate member. Azad was even appointed senior national selector.

Bihar, which had been a member of the BCCI since 1935 and even made the Ranji Trophy final once in 1975, had all of a sudden no representative team playing in Indian cricket. However, with the creation of Jharkhand, a new association and team was formed and received recognition from the Board in 2003. Dhoni moved to the new side and was appointed captain.

In 2007, Lalu became railways minister in the central government. When the Board refused permission to the rebel ICL to play in their stadiums, Lalu opened the Railways' grounds to them. This antagonized the Board further and reduced Bihar's slim chances to win back official recognition.

The same year, another rebel body appeared in Bihar. Named the Cricket Association of Bihar, the association's president was Bihar's prominent political leader Subodh Kant Sahay.

Joining this new cricket faction was a person well-versed with Bihar's grassroots cricket: the little-known Aditya Verma. Growing up in Chapra, Bihar, Verma would watch his father, Mahavir Prasad, listen to Test commentaries on the radio in the seventies and became interested in cricket. He was a cricketer himself, playing for his university team and later for a Tata Steel team that included Bihar's cricketing stalwarts such as Ramesh Saxena, Daljit Singh and Hari Gidwani.

Soon, Verma got involved in Bihari cricket politics, becoming a member of the Saran district cricket association. When the Board derecognized the Bihar association and approved the Jharkhand unit in 2003–04, Verma moved the courts. He claimed that majority of the Bihar districts were not with Jharkhand and the BCCI action was illegal.

Once the anti-Lalu faction headed by Dalmiya was removed from power, the BCCI, now led by Pawar, formed a committee comprising bigwigs Arun Jaitley, Shashank Manohar and N. Srinivasan to look into the Bihar affair. The committee concluded that the Jharkhand cricket association was 'fraudulently' formed and the Lalu-headed Bihar association was the real representative body from the region. The Jharkhand association head, Amitabh Choudhary, challenged this order in the high court and got a stay against it. Verma, not to be cowed down, petitioned the Supreme Court.

In the fast-moving world of cricket politics, all affiliations are subject to the immediate interests of its members. Keeping with this truism, the Board was now having a rethink. They sought time from the Supreme Court to respond and formed another committee to decide the fate of Bihar. According to Verma, Choudhary had by then ingratiated himself with the Board, and it was no surprise when the second committee found the Jharkhand body to be the rightful heir to the faction-ridden Bihar body.

Verma challenged this verdict in the Supreme Court. More than a decade has passed, and this case is still pending with the court. During this excruciatingly slow process of justice, Verma battled it out in the courts and in the Board's corridors of power. He had met all those who mattered in the BCCI, from Dalmiya and Pawar to Manohar and Srinivasan, but had faced only rejection. He was an angry man, but declares, 'I was being humiliated but what mattered to me was justice for Bihari children and I was willing to fight till the end.'

When the spot-fixing scandal surfaced in 2013 but Srinivasan absolved his son-in-law of any wrongdoing, Verma sensed an opportunity for revenge and decided to challenge this 'dishonest' decision in the Mumbai High Court. Instead of retreating once the high court ruled against them, the BCCI—despite opposition from many of its members—took the fight to the Supreme Court.

Verma was thrust into the national limelight as a petitioner fighting for the commendable cause of cleansing the Indian cricket administration of all its maleficence. The story of his fight for the rights of Bihar cricket was now of little relevance in the larger battle that was being fought in the highest court of the land. He began appearing on news channels as the face of public anger against the corrupt BCCI.

Bihar finally got recognition in 2016 after the Lodha panel decreed that every state in India, small or big, has to be represented on the Board and participate in First-Class cricket. Verma today finds himself on the wrong side of Bihar cricket politics, as his own association failed to find favour with the Board. But according to him this is not a problem. 'The problem is corruption in Bihar cricket, especially in team selection, where non-deserving players find a place using influence and money,' he says, promising to expose this corruption to the world.

Interestingly, Verma's views on Dalmiya and Srinivasan today are very different from the time when he was fighting against them. 'I am not afraid or ashamed of saying that, after having watched the Board so closely, Dalmiya was the best man to run the Board,' he states. 'Despite his flaws, I can say that Srinivasan too is genuinely interested in the welfare of cricket in India.' The Lodha reforms have also been good for Verma's twenty-three-year-old son, Lakhan. He has found a place in one of the India Cements teams, whose owner ironically is Srinivasan.

Many have wondered how Verma could afford his legal fight against the BCCI. The Board, by a rough estimate, spent Rs 300 crores on the battery of high-profile lawyers like Kapil Sibal, K.K. Venugopal and many others. Verma's association was represented by equally formidable lawyers, including Harish Salve and Nalini Chidambaram (wife of former Union Cabinet minister P. Chidambaram).

Verma, never one to shy away from a question, is forthcoming here as well. 'In the initial phase, neither Salve nor Chidambaram charged any money, as they both felt this was a fight for justice,' he reveals. When the arguments in court continued for a couple of years, the bills were footed by Subodh Kant Sahay, the president of the Bihar association on whose behalf the battle was fought. Verma is aware of the allegations that his fight in court was being funded by those who were opposed to the Srinivasan faction in the Board, but he says, 'I don't care about that, as I know the truth and I never compromised.' I have no reason to doubt his claims, though the allegations remain believable, given that the likes of Pawar and the absconding Lalit Modi were all against Srinivasan and not too unhappy that someone had taken the fight against him to the Supreme Court.

The BCCI somehow resisted even a Supreme Court ruling for more than two years, before finally being forced to implement the Lodha panel reforms. Even as of June 2021, the Board has not fully complied with the court order, has made many changes to the original recommendations and has sought more dilutions from the court.

While Verma's zeal, whoever it was supported by, eventually led to structural changes in the BCCI's constitution, most of those who became ineligible to remain in office due to age or tenure restrictions have still found a way to manipulate the system. They are ruling by proxy, having pushed their relatives into the important posts they can't hold themselves.

Anurag Thakur, the powerful BJP leader and sports and I&B minister in the central government, was forced to quit as the Board's secretary after submitting a wrong affidavit in the Supreme Court. He was lucky to escape being hauled up for contempt. However, in the new Board his brother Arun Dumal is the treasurer. Similarly, Jay Shah, son of the all-powerful Amit Shah, who was the president of the Gujarat Cricket Association, is the new Board secretary.

A positive development after the reforms is that Sourav Ganguly became president of the BCCI, though by all accounts the levers of power are still controlled by the Shah–Thakur duo.

The Probes

My contact with the cricket world during this period was very limited, though I did manage to collect some interesting information and some damning facts because both the court-appointed panels, one led by Justice Mukul Mudgal and the other by Justice R.M. Lodha, invited me to present my views before them. I also became privy to certain disturbing incidents due to my interactions with a serving police officer by the name of Bibhuti Bhusan Mishra. He had been appointed by the court to assist the Mudgal panel in sifting facts from fiction when investigating the betting allegations against officials and players.

After the two panels finished their investigations, their verdicts led to the two-year suspension from the IPL for CSK and Rajasthan

Royals (RR) teams, the removal of Srinivasan as Board president and the sweeping reforms to domestic representation already discussed. But before all this came to pass there were some very interesting incidents while the inquiries were still going on, some of which I was involved in or witness to.

The panel findings were that Meiyappan was one of the team owners of CSK and not just a 'cricket enthusiast', and was involved in betting. Along with its findings, the panel had also submitted a sealed envelope to the court that contained the names of certain officials and players whom it had either indicted for wrongdoings, or felt there was no conclusive evidence to prove that they were involved. The court, on the basis of the doubts raised in the sealed envelope, had directed Justice Mudgal to investigate further, giving them a few more months to dig deeper.

For this purpose the panel was provided the services of Mishra, who at that time was serving as the head of the Narcotics Control Bureau (NCB) based in New Delhi. At the conclusion of this second probe, another sealed envelope was handed over to the court, whose contents became a matter of much speculation and sensational reportage. The sealed reports have not yet been made public by the courts, and those who wrote the reports can't reveal the contents without the court's permission.

Though I have not seen these reports myself, I take full responsibility for what I write here, as it is based on my own interactions with the architects of these reports and other corroborative evidence. In any case, much of it appeared in different newspapers in bits and pieces. *The Indian Express* published two reports, one by the head of its investigative reporting team, Ritu Sareen and the other by its senior editor, Nihal Koshie, who extensively quoted Mishra in a story that appeared on 24 August 2018.

Sareen's report revealed, without quoting any source, that twelve people could be guilty of wrongdoing, including some players. Both her and Koshie's report contained some sensational details, and even hinted that a prominent Indian cricketer's integrity was under doubt. The committee had left their findings against that cricketer inconclusive, saying that to prove the player's innocence or complicity a further probe would be needed, for which they didn't have the time as they had to meet the court deadline to submit their report.

The Mudgal panel's first report had come to the conclusion about Meiyappan's official association with CSK on the basis of his accreditation with the IPL tournament committee, where he was officially listed as one of the CSK team owners. It had also the oral evidence of players and other officials that they did interact with him before and after the matches and that he had represented CSK when the owners were bidding in the player auction. He would also be present in the team dugout during the matches and whenever the team practised.

In the main report—which was in the public domain—no other names except for Srinivasan, Meiyappan, Sundar Raman and Raj Kundra were mentioned, as the panel may have felt there was no evidence to name any others without a further probe to establish their guilt or innocence. According to reports, the number of other names involved was twelve or thirteen, and the media started asking for these to be made public.

I wrote a column for *HT* that hinted at, among various suspected serious misdemeanours, the issue of conflict of interest which I feel is the bane of Indian cricket and needs to be rooted out. I reproduce the relevant portions of that column below:

> It was reported last year that Rhiti Sports, which represents various business interests of Dhoni, may, in fact, be owned

by the captain himself. Doubts were raised about where Arun Pandey, an Indian Airlines employee, when he founded the company and signed Dhoni for a Rs 200 crore three-year deal, got the funds from.

Later it was reported that Dhoni had bought 30,000 shares in the company and sold them back a month later. It would be extremely disappointing if the probe led by BB Mishra, a very honest and competent police officer, has not gone into this.

There is also speculation that one key player of India's World Cup-winning team has been named for being involved with bookies.

Rhiti Sports Management had signed up many Indian cricketers besides Dhoni, and the question of the company's ownership raised serious issues of conflict of interest. Mishra had tried to find out the facts of Rhiti Sports' ownership and the exchange of shares between the two. There were also allegations that Dhoni's wife Sakshi had been given shares in the real estate firm called Amrapali Builders.

The Amrapali real estate dealings found sparse mention in the media in 2014, but became a full-blown controversy five years later when, in 2019, the Supreme Court cancelled the Real Estate Regulatory Authority (RERA) registration of the Amrapali group. A report in *India Today* on 25 July 2019 stated that, 'in the forensic audit report, which was accepted by the Supreme Court on Tuesday, the auditors stated that Amrapali diverted money to Amrapali Mahi Developers Private Limited and Rhiti Sports Management Private Limited, the director of which is Sakshi. Dhoni reportedly holds a major stake in Rhiti Sports, which is also the same company which promotes the cricketer.' The article goes on to state, 'The Supreme Court gave a landmark judgment ... cracking its whip on errant builders for breaching the trust reposed by home buyers, the top court cancelled registration of Amrapali under the real estate law RERA, and ousted it from its prime properties in NCR by nixing the land leases.'

Among other facts that the forensic audit report highlighted was that in the period from 2009 to 2015, Rhiti Sports received a total of Rs 42.22 crore from the Amrapali group. The report gave details of the 'sham' agreements entered into between Rhiti and Amrapali, which also mentioned Dhoni. Further, it also dealt with an agreement for a sponsorship dated 20 March 2015, under which the Amrapali Group of Companies got the right to advertise in the IPL 2015 by having the CSK team wear their logo. The auditors wrote: 'It is observed that this agreement is on plain paper and executed only between Amrapali and Rhiti Sports Management Private Limited and there are no signatories on behalf of Chennai Super Kings to this agreement.'

Rhiti Sports later denied any wrongdoing and issued a statement that said: 'With utmost respect to the orders of Supreme Court, we would only like to clarify that the observation mentioned in a forensic report are bereft of proper information or relevant documents. The company has been in possession of all information and relevant documents that can establish the clean image and that the observations made in the said report are incorrect.' This case is still being heard in the court and final verdict has not been passed.

For me, the conflict of interest issue is one of the biggest ills plaguing the game. Ever since players became brands themselves, these allegations have surfaced from time to time over the past three decades.

I have seen agents being in more than mere 'friendly' relationships with important Board officials, selectors and journalists, while at the same time managing the careers of key cricketers, including the captain of the team. This phenomenon is very common in Indian cricket. No wonder Justice Mukul Mudgal found this conflict of interest one of the main causes of corruption in cricket. His report inferred that (a) the BCCI's measures to combat sport fraud are 'ineffective and insufficient'; (b) there is a need for 'stringent and effective control on Players' Agents'; and (c) the issue of 'conflict of interest and amendment of Clause 6.4.2 of the Regulation for Players, Team Officials, Managers, Umpires, and Administrators and BCCI Code' was a serious and widespread concern, flagged by many persons who appeared before the judge. They also added that the scope of the investigation needed to be much wider. Mudgal received several recommendations that the agents of the players needed to be investigated in order to get to the root of this problem of match-fixing and spot-fixing, 'as they have easy access to players and most of their credentials are suspect'.

The report made a mention of what I had to say on this matter, recording that 'Mr. Pradeep Magazine told us that even the agents had a number of conflicts of interest as these agents besides dealing with the players also dealt with the BCCI for their stadia advertisements, sponsorships amongst other things. This conflict of interest made BCCI's stance with regard to these agents soft and BCCI tended to ignore a lot of discrepancies in its conduct with agents. There is thus a need to institutionalize a mechanism of selecting agents and set regulations to govern them.'

I come now to another engaging aspect of the probe, which was handled by Mishra. Apart from whether the CSK–RR IPL match had been fixed and whether Meiyappan and Vindu Dara Singh were just betting or fixing as well, there were other serious allegations to get to the bottom of—including a star cricketer who had played a pivotal role in India's 2011 World Cup win being involved in fixing.

The Catch that Spilled

When Mishra started his probe, he was given just three months by the court to complete it. He began contacting people who could provide him with useful information or clues, and I was among the many journalists he summoned. I was a bit nervous and to calm my nerves I had taken my colleague and friend Jasvinder Sidhu along with me. Sidhu was a committed 'investigative' sports reporter and I thought he could be of use too.

Far from the intimidating, stern figure I was expecting to meet, Mishra was all courtesy, polite and well-mannered. He immediately put us at ease and we spent about thirty minutes just discussing mundane subjects like pressures of work and its impact on our daily lives. I could sense that he was a seasoned investigator and knew how to interact with different people while seeking information. Professional and meticulous, he appeared to be a man of high integrity.

That first meeting lasted a couple of hours. Sidhu and I spoke to him at length, passing on a lot of unverified allegations that he could pursue. I met him many times later in the course of his investigation, and soon, the curious journalist in me was seeking a news story if one was to be found. However, Mishra was shrewd and tactful and did not reveal much.

His findings were given to the Supreme Court in a sealed envelope, the contents of which was not disclosed to the public. This resulted in a lot of speculation that the report mentions big names among Indian cricketers to be involved in match-fixing, and that was why the Supreme Court thought it best to keep the names under wraps.

As an 'informant' who provided some of the leads and was aware of the progress of the probe, I can say with some degree of certainty that the report absolved most players against whom there were unsubstantiated allegations. Only one player was not totally absolved, but the findings were inconclusive and a further probe was recommended to determine whether the player was guilty. The investigations into this player has an interesting narrative.

The Justice Mudgal panel had three members: Mukul Mudgal himself; L. Nageshwar Rao, who was the additional solicitor general at that time and is now a Supreme Court judge; and Nilay Dutta, a prominent lawyer from Assam and also a member of the BCCI. Dutta, who passed away in September 2021, had been a Grade 1 umpire, standing in Ranji Trophy matches.

When the committee submitted its report indicting Gurunath Meiyappan, Dutta gave a dissenting note which did not find enough proof against Meiyappan. He digressed from the court brief and made many generalized observations about how match-fixing is widespread in Indian cricket, from the roots to the top, and more so in the IPL. He also introduced the fear of national security being threatened because of the links between underworld kingpins like Dawood Ibrahim and the bookies. He underlined the need for a Special Investigating Team to be set up to investigate all pending cases.

This was not the first time these fears had been articulated and suggestions made for a comprehensive probe to unearth what is widely believed to be an operation with an international network. Somehow Dutta's dissent did not get much attention from the media, despite its more sensational observations. Maybe that was because he was seen as simply wanting to divert attention from the culpability of Srinivasan and Meiyappan.

However, it made one very significant, pointed reference, which the Mudgal panel possibly included in its sealed report to the Supreme Court. It was not made public as it pointed a finger at one of India's top cricketers. Dutta referred to an undercover investigation carried out by *Sports Illustrated* in which 'a prominent Indian capped player was recorded interacting with the bookies'.

When I met Mishra for the first time, the *Sports Illustrated* story became central to our discussion. The cover story was done by an intrepid reporter by the name of Hina Zooni Pandit, who had worked with me at *HT* as a trainee for a brief period. A lot of First-Class cricketers and bookies were captured on tape in a sting operation, where they had revealed, according to the report, many prominent names on the bookies' payroll.

The cover of the magazine had the headline 'Cricket in a Fix'. In an undercover operation over six months, they had secured some sensational tape-recorded evidence. Some headlines from the article: 'Bookies claim $40 billion was shuffled from India to Pakistan during the World Cup; Everyone knows everyone: links between bookies, property dealers, politicians, cricket officials, police, players and players agents; Bookies claim Shahid Afridi rejects their approaches outright but allege many others are approachable.' The cover also carried Pandit's name prominently to highlight that it was she who had undertaken this risky undercover operation.

The *Sports Illustrated* story had appeared immediately after India won the 2011 World Cup. Kadambari Murali, who was by then the editor of *Sports Illustrated*, had got in touch with me at that time, revealing the names of the cricketers who bookies had claimed were on the take. They had not published the names as these were mere allegations and not proven facts.

Kadambari was particularly disturbed by one name that had figured in one of the taped sting operations. On the tape, a bookie was talking to a cricketer whose voice she said was clearly recognizable. Perhaps that was the only tape that established a direct link between a bookie and a cricketer, the rest being mere accusations or revelations that needed to be probed further.

Kadambari also told me that they had handed over unedited copies of all the tapes to the BCCI.

For Mishra, the challenge was to find those tapes and establish their veracity. I believe that he did manage to get hold of most of them, but the tape where the cricketer and the bookie were reported to have talked to each other was missing. However, with Pandit's help, Mishra managed to track the bookie who was alleged to have had the conversation with the cricketer. The bookie was unwilling to cooperate.

This issue dragged on and the probe was approaching its deadline when Mishra finally managed to convince the bookie to confront the player face-to-face to clear all doubts. A meeting was planned and the player was asked to come to the venue without being told who he was going to meet. Alas, the meeting never took place as at the last moment the bookie conveyed his inability to show up. After a long wait, the player, who according to eyewitnesses was in tears, was told to leave. Mishra's doubts about the player's integrity remained but there was no time left to pursue the lead.

After listening to calls between Meiyappan and Vindu Dara Singh recorded by Mumbai Police, Mishra absolved Meiyappan of fixing charges. The match in question was between Rajasthan Royals and CSK on 12 May 2013. The recordings revealed that Meiyappan kept changing his bets as the upper hand moved from one team to the other, and finally put his money on his own team, CSK, who lost the match. Meiyappan lost around Rs 69 lakh for betting on the wrong horse; Mishra believed that had he been involved in fixing he would have known CSK would lose the match.

However, Mishra became curious about why Mumbai Police had sought permission to tap the phones of Meiyappan and Singh. If they were given tip-offs, from who and where did these come? According to the law, permission to tap phones is asked for and granted only on grounds of threat to national security. The probe panel did seek answers from Mumbai Police and its then commissioner Himanshu Rai, but curiously, they did not respond.

Mishra was perhaps trying to find out if there were other vested interests within the Board who used their influence to settle scores with Srinivasan by 'persuading' the police to tap Meiyappan's phones, perhaps aware of his ventures into the betting world. He was surprised at the lack of response from Mumbai Police but could do nothing about it.

Mishra tried to join the dots and understand the modus operandi of the players, officials and agents that led to huge conflicts of interest and made them all vulnerable to corruption. He found the dealings between Rhiti Sports and the Amrapali Group suspicious, and almost established that at some point of time Dhoni had indeed held shares of Rhiti Sports. In an interview with Nihal Koshie of *The Indian Express* in August 2018, he explained at length how the agent–player nexus is potentially dangerous for the integrity of the game.

To quote from that article:

'Dealings can be in the form of agreement with the players or players endorsing products. A senior player or somebody who is an official who can select the junior player ... can arm-twist them (junior player) easily. I can arm-twist a junior player (by saying) "you select this particular manager or person for managing your clients or (business) affairs" ... The player is a little scared that unless he obliges, he could face some difficulty in the team. Maybe he will not be selected. So these things do happen. I got this information from my sources. I investigated. There is something the BCCI should investigate. A lot more will come out about deals between players and managers,' Mishra added. When asked if this nexus could affect team selection, Mishra said: 'It can. People will try to influence team selection.'

During his probe, Mishra met Arun Pandey of Rhiti Sports to unravel the truth of the report published on 3 June 2013 in the leading business newspaper *The Economic Times*. I quote from the report written by John Samuel, Ratna Bhushan and Ravi Teja Sharma:

> ET Investigations reveal that a 15 per cent stake bought by Dhoni earlier this year in the sports marketing firm that manages him has spawned a tangled web of business associations, raising issues of propriety and conflict of interest in at least two situations.
>
> The first situation is in his position as the captain of the Indian team in all three formats of the game. This sports marketing firm—Rhiti Sports Management set up by Arun Pandey, a close friend and business associate of Dhoni—also manages four other current cricketers, Suresh Raina, Ravindra Jadeja, Pragyan Ojha and R.P. Singh.
>
> This puts Dhoni in a conflicting position where he has 15 per cent share of profits earned by Rhiti Sports from managing these four players even as he opines or votes for them (Indian captain has no vote in team selection) in team selection meetings.
>
> The second situation is in Dhoni's position as the captain of the Chennai Super Kings (CSK), the Indian Premier League franchise for which he, Raina and Jadeja play and whose principal Gurunath Meiyappan is currently on charges of illegal betting and sharing information with bookies. So far Dhoni has maintained a conspicuous silence on the spot fixing and betting scandal raising whispers that his position is perhaps compromised by the ties that bind Rhiti and him to CSK and its ownership.

The report goes on to add:

Back in January 2012, after eight consecutive losses suffered by India, Srinivasan reportedly used his veto powers as president to stop a 3–2 vote in the selection committee to remove Dhoni as captain of the Test team.

Srinivasan is also the owner of India Cements, the company that owns CSK and in which Dhoni is a vice-president. And Rhiti, riding on its prized client Dhoni, markets CSK.

According to many media reports, the Indian Board under the presidentship of Dalmiya was keen to investigate Rhiti Sports Management's ownership as recorded in its 20 July 2013 working group meeting minutes.

In the interview with *The Indian Express*, Mishra expressed what the Mudgal probe report had written on its findings without getting into specifics and naming any player or an agent. Koshie had been painstakingly pointing out the player–agent nexus for a while, and back in July 2015 he had written an article that illustrated how even the captain of the Indian team was not immune to getting involved in these conflict of interest situations.

I quote extensively from his article:

On July 21, BCCI secretary Anurag Thakur wrote a letter to his colleagues, asking them to address the conflict of interest issue in Indian cricket by signing a declaration promising ethical integrity. Next week, India's cricketers will be asked to sign a similar undertaking. This, for many, will be easier said than done.

For, at least five of those players are associated with an agency that not only manages Virat Kohli but also has business links with the Indian Test captain, who has a big say in deciding the playing XI.

After Kohli replaced M S Dhoni as skipper last year, Ishant Sharma and Umesh Yadav have signed up with Cornerstone, an agency that already had Rohit Sharma, Murali Vijay and Shikhar Dhawan in its stable, apart from the captain.

The company is also in 'advanced talks' with Mohammad Shami. According to Cornerstone CEO, Bunty Sajdeh, there were many others who have expressed interest in associating with his firm.

At the same time, Kohli has launched a chain of fitness centres under the brand name Chisel and a clothing line, Wrogn, in collaboration with CSE Consulting, which is a sister concern of Cornerstone.

Asked to comment on the possible 'conflict of interest' involving the Indian captain, BCCI president Jagmohan Dalmiya said he needed to go into the details of the deal.

'If there's any conflict of interest on the player's part—financial or otherwise—we will look into it. But rest assured, guidelines for the players will be out soon,' he told The Indian Express.

Sajdeh, however, said he did not see anything wrong with partnering his star client in a business venture. 'We have invested in Chisel ... we have put in time, effort and manpower and structured the deal. We are also looking at four or five other similar business models, along the lines of Chisel and Wrogn, where the athlete has ownership and does not promote it like a model but like an owner. Tomorrow after he retires he has royalty coming to him,' Sajdeh told The Indian Express.

He stressed that there was no conflict of interest in the link that connects Cornerstone, CSE and Kohli. 'If Virat had ownership in the agency it would have amounted to a conflict of interest. In this case, he has no ownership in the agency. Virat is a client of Cornerstone and if CSE has any business interests with Virat or Rohit or Shikhar, I don't see a conflict of interest. CSE is a licensing company and we are doing licensing business with him. It is a legitimate business, plus I am not getting into any cricket business with him or any BCCI-related business with Virat,' Sajdeh said.

Mishra's interview, and Koshie's article that precedes it by three years, clearly spell out the dangers of letting these deals exist, as they make the captain of the team vulnerable to accusations of favouritism, which in turn could harm team spirit even if no wrongdoing has been proven or actually committed.

Throughout my career as a cricket journalist, I have been made aware of the pitfalls of this player–agent nexus. I pointed this out at length during my appearances before the Justice Mudgal panel, and again later when I was asked to appear before the Justice Lodha panel. In fact, during the latter hearing, my statement was almost entirely devoted to the theme of conflict of interest.

I found Justice Lodha seeking answers to all the right questions while his two co-panellists, Justice Ashok Bhan and Justice R.V. Raveendran, listened without intervening. The judge—a very polite, erudite man, whom I got to know well when I interviewed him after his report was out—seemed personally concerned about the lack of any ethical compass in the functioning of the Board. It appeared to me that he was surprised that most of the players, especially the ones recently active, did not think their wearing multiple hats put them in a potentially compromising position.

I remember Justice Lodha telling me that most of the players, including the 'greats of the game' wondered how could they be questioned on their integrity 'when they have done so much for the country'. Justice Lodha said he tried to make them understand that no one was accusing them of wrongdoing, but a system had to be put in place where a player, a captain, a selector or a coach could not have a business interest where he or his agent would be in a position to gain financially from it. Rules are formed not to test the honesty of people but to create a situation that does not leave them vulnerable to doing something wrong. Justice Lodha said, 'I told them, I am sure you won't do it, but someone else may do it. Why put him in that situation at all?'

No wonder that in his final report, where wide and sweeping reforms were recommended in the Board's constitution, the conflict of interest issue found prominent place. What constitutes conflict of interest and a proper mechanism to punish those who were guilty of it has been detailed in the recommendations.

For us journalists, in an era where getting direct access to players, especially the captain, is almost impossible, their agents can play a role in arranging an interview. It is no secret that nowadays if a journalist has to get an interview with a player he has to go through his agent. I have myself done some of my best interviews with a few legends of the game only after the agent has agreed to my request. Sometimes interviews are arranged only with the ulterior motive of promoting a product that the player may be endorsing. This is a well-laid out business strategy, as most papers and journalists would find it difficult to refuse an interview with someone like Tendulkar, Dravid or Kohli!

Since the IPL betting probe of 2013 resulted in the BCCI being forced to implement the Lodha panel reforms, we have seen Ganguly become the Board president and fellow former cricketers Anshuman Gaekwad and Shanta Rangaswami join the Apex Council, which is the supreme decision-making body of the cricket administration. There is now a players' representative body as well, with Ashok Malhotra being voted to the post of president by the players themselves.

However, the Board was soon trying to amend the new constitution, and took away the powers of the nine-member Apex Council—which is supposed to take all major decisions—and placed them back with the office-bearers (themselves). They also want a dilution of the three-year cooling-off period between terms of office, and many other such changes that, if permitted, would make the Lodha reforms almost meaningless. The Board has sought permission from the Supreme Court to implement the amendments they have made in the constitution, and no one is sure what the court's ruling will be.

In this continuing saga of power games, where does the conflict of interest issue stand? The Lodha panel has given a detailed brief on dos and don'ts, which at the moment no one seems to care for. Disappointingly, even Ganguly, instead of leading by example, finds nothing wrong in promoting a fantasy league that is a direct rival of the main IPL sponsor.

Indian cricket may be getting stronger by the day, but its administration, despite all the changes, continues to resist becoming transparent and accountable—as the Supreme Court verdict that mandated the implementation of the Lodha reforms attempted to make it.

The king is dead, long live the king.

14

Pakistan Visits and the Kashmir Issue

While the rest of my narrative has followed a roughly chronological path, I have clubbed together here my three visits to Pakistan due to their personal significance for me. As a Kashmiri Pandit born in a place with a contested history, I experienced first-hand the strife-torn love–hate relationship between my community and the majority Muslim population of the Valley.

By the logic of drawing a line cutting across the northwest region based on religion, after Partition, Kashmir—which was ruled by a Dogra Hindu, Maharaja Hari Singh—would have gone to Pakistan as the overwhelming majority of its subjects were Muslim. In fact, the majority of the population may have wished for an independent state, neither within India nor Pakistan. This is still a dream for many. Most Kashmiri Muslims do not consider themselves to be Indians and refer to the massive Indian Army presence in the state as an 'occupation force'.

Having spent my early years living on cordial terms with Kashmiri Muslims, and as a child receiving a lot of love from individuals of the Muslim faith, I was keen to visit Pakistan someday. Cricket writing provided me with that opportunity. My first visit to Pakistan was in 1997, when I was the sports editor of *The Pioneer*.

Even in the best of times, India's cricketing relationship with Pakistan has been frosty. By the time I started covering the sport more regularly, India had stopped touring Pakistan. India's tour to Pakistan in 1984 had been abandoned midway due to Indira Gandhi's assassination. After one more series in 1989, it took eight years for the relationship between the two countries to again be cordial enough for India to agree to play a three-match One-Day series in Pakistan.

From the early eighties, India was blighted by terrorism, riots and social unrest; we witnessed the beasts of prejudice, xenophobia, hatred and bigotry on the rise, which threatened the very survival of India as a democratic nation. By 1997, despite an unstable coalition government in power, relative peace had returned. After a period of economic reforms under the minority government led by Congress's P.V. Narasimha Rao, which lasted its full term of five years from 1991, the 1996 general elections again saw no single party winning a majority.

The BJP formed a government under Atal Bihari Vajpayee, but they lasted no more than a fortnight, failing to find sufficient allies to reach the majority figure in Parliament. V.P. Singh was offered the post of PM but he refused. Eventually, H.D. Deve Gowda—a former Karnataka chief minister from V.P. Singh's Janata Dal—became Prime Minister, leading a United Front government. He remained in the hot seat for 324 days before another leader from the same party by the name of Inder Kumar Gujral took charge.

Gujral was a migrant from Pakistan, and he worked towards a peaceful relationship with the neighbours during his 332-day tenure as Prime Minister. In May 1997, the Pakistani team visited India to play in a One-Day series celebrating fifty years of Independence. The Pakistani Board wanted India to reciprocate and participate in their celebratory matches in the autumn of that year. The Indian government approved the tour.

I was among the half-a-dozen journalists who were assigned to cover the tour by their respective media organizations. Apprehension and excitement were the two contrasting emotions that gripped me as I applied for a visa at the Pakistani Embassy at Delhi's Chanakyapuri. During the process, I came to understand that 'Kashmiris' were categorized as being different from Indians in the eyes of the Pakistani government. After effusively welcoming me into his room with a warm smile, the visa officer's face changed to a frown as he flipped through the pages of my passport. 'Sorry, you can't get a visa,' he said, pointing at the page that mentioned my place of birth as Srinagar.

He said that they were not authorized to issue visas to Kashmiris; special permission would need to be sought from Islamabad to issue a visa to me. However, they could not complete that process in time for me to depart on schedule for the tour. I pleaded with him, and though he expressed helplessness, he said he would try. Fortune smiled on me and I was finally granted a visa.

I was to realize later that my place of birth was a problem even with the Indian authorities. Renewal of my passport became a tedious process each time its validity expired. Apparently, there was a strict protocol in place for the passports of all Kashmiris born in the Valley, Hindu or Muslim, even those like me who had been living outside the state for decades. Before clearance, their residential address and antecedents in the state had to be verified by the local police, and this led to delays each time.

Made in India on Pakistani Soil

I remember the unease a few of us journalists felt as we landed at Karachi airport, not sure of the reception we would get. However, we got a shock of the pleasant kind when the cab driver who drove us from the airport to our hotel started to play the song *Made in India* by Alisha Chinai, an Indian pop star. The cab driver, on finding I spoke his mother tongue of Punjabi, became even more friendly. My fears and doubts disappeared and I felt like I was at home, among my own people.

Officially, alcohol is banned in Pakistan for the Muslim population. Only non-Muslims with a permit could buy liquor. However, liquor shops in Karachi were owned by a powerful politician, so that was not strictly applied. The first thing I focused on after reaching our hotel was to figure out how I could sustain my drinking habit on the tour. However, getting a drink proved elusive on that first night.

The next morning, I was joined by Ajay Shankar of *The Indian Express* in my search for a liquor store. We found one quite easily, and we were not even asked our religion or for a permit. Having ensured a supply of our life-blood, it was time to think about the cricket: the three-match One-Day series we were there to cover.

The first match was to be held at Hyderabad, Sindh, a five-hour drive from Karachi. I needed to provide a photograph to make the entry pass, but unlike my other colleagues, I hadn't brought any with me. Thus, I was forced to search for a shop that could provide instant photo prints. What I didn't know was that this quest would lead me to a moving experience of the traumatic history of Partition and the intense longing for 'home'.

Winding stairs took me to the first floor of a building where a photographer's shop was located. When the woman behind the counter understood that I was from India, she immediately shouted, '*Abu, neeche aa jao, India se aye hain* (Father, come down, someone has come from India).' The girl's excitement and the sparkle in her eyes suggested that she was thrilled by this fact.

An old man descended from the second floor. When I confirmed that I had indeed come from India, he hugged me, tears streaming down his cheeks. He had a poignant story to tell: of being uprooted from his moorings in a false hope that had ended in despair.

Originally from Uttar Pradesh, he was working as a tailor in Bombay in 1947. Like many Muslims in India, insecurity and the continuous threat of violence had instilled fear in him. When Partition came about, he was also lured by the dream of living in a country that was being created for those of his own religion, a 'pure land': Pakistan. He joined the Muslims migrating to the new country. It took him just a few months to realize that he had made a terrible mistake.

'This was not my country, not my home, not my people,' he lamented. He wanted to go back but could not, as the Indian government refused visas to all those who had migrated to Pakistan from India. 'Like a bird in a cage I yearned to return home, but all doors were closed.' Even after having accepted his new Pakistani citizenship, he still felt like an outsider in his land of adoption. He is part of an Urdu-speaking Indian community of migrants to Sindh called 'Muhajirs' by the natives. Simmering tension between the migrants and the locals has often spilled into violence.

This chance encounter remains one of the most enduring images of all my travels, during which I have been witness to the yearning for roots, with all its tragic and positive dimensions, among the Indian diaspora in different cricket-playing nations. During my visits to Pakistan in 1997, 2004 and 2006, I had many similar interactions that showed how deep the bonds go between the people of the two countries. They are ties that can transcend the hate brewed by the divisive politics of their governments. The cricketing rivalry between the two nations is bitter, intense, competitive and engaging, but it is just a subtext to the larger human need for peace and bonding that can override the divisive baggage of history.

Another surprise awaited us when we travelled to Hyderabad before the first match. The hotel that had been recommended to us had no rooms available. There was no vacancy anywhere as an India–Pakistan match had come to town. Seeing us stranded in the hotel lobby, a few locals approached us and offered to let us stay with them.

Among them was an old man who had been to India. He left with a promise to check for rooms in his company's guest house, but returned with disappointing news. However, he did bring back a large bowl of kheer (rice pudding) from his home. While the kheer was delicious, I found pieces of chicken in it. I did not have the heart to tell my vegetarian colleague Ashish Shukla, who was gobbling up his share with relish.

Finally, the hotel owner allowed us to sleep in the storeroom for that night.

The match at the dusty, breezy Niaz stadium was a disappointing outing for India, a low-scoring affair in which Pakistan overtook India's total of 170 in the 45th over. I can hardly recall an interesting moment from the actual cricket, but I vividly remember the Indian team being loudly cheered by local fans waving at the team bus. Contrary to what we had expected, there was a lot of warmth for the Indian team, and a complete absence of hostility.

The next encounter at Karachi's National Stadium made up for the lifeless first match. The stadium was overflowing with thousands of spectators and the contest had everything one would expect from an India–Pakistan match. It had a thrilling finish, with India needing eight runs from the last over to overhaul Pakistan's score of 265. Off-spinner Rajesh Chauhan sealed the chase with a six, and India won by four wickets with three balls to spare. Chauhan became an overnight star in India for his unexpected batting exploits.

In my memory though, the match is associated more with crowd trouble and the Indian team's lack of trust in the Pakistani officials and spectators. When India was fielding, the match was marred by incidents of stone-throwing from one section of the crowd. This resulted in four disruptions, the last of which—Pakistan had scored 265 for 4 in 47.2 overs at that point—was declared as the end of the innings by match referee Ranjan Madugalle when the Indian team walked off the field. The tourists refused to field further, stating they did not want to risk injury to a player.

The Indian media contingent, which included Ravi Shastri as a television commentator, was furious. Some even felt that it was part of a larger conspiracy and that it confirmed their belief that Pakistan was no place for an Indian cricket team to visit. Shastri, while talking to us, even said that he would tell Bal Thackeray (then leader of the extreme right-wing group Shiv Sena) never to allow an Indian team to visit Pakistan.

From the press box it was hard to figure out what exactly was going on, so I took a walk around the boundary line. All I could see were crowds desperate for the match to restart, with no sign of any hostility among them. Whosoever the miscreants were, they had done their disruptive job slyly and were now sitting quietly among the vast mass of peaceful cricket lovers.

I went to meet the Indian team manager, Madan Lal, who was understandably tense and jittery. 'They are throwing big stones at us,' he fumed. 'Someone could get seriously injured.' I realized he was contemplating not resuming play at all, which not only meant conceding the match but more significantly would have been a diplomatic disaster. I advised caution and reported what I sensed from my walk around the ground.

After much deliberation, the Indians agreed to continue the match. As Madugalle had terminated the Pakistan innings, no Indian fielder had to stand close to the boundary. The Indians agreed that the Pakistani total would have to be chased within 47 overs instead of the regular 50. After that, the match continued without disruption, and even though the crowd did not enjoy the nail-biting loss for the home team, there was no further violent or hostile reactions.

While making my way back to the hotel among thousands of disappointed people leaving the stadium, I spotted a young boy of about ten wailing loudly. I put an arm around him and asked him why he was crying. The sobbing child replied, '*Log kehte hain hume inse haarna nahi chahiye* (People say we should not lose to them).' His reaction was astonishingly similar to that of my relatives' and friends' children when India loses to Pakistan.

That night, members of the Indian media were invited to dinner at the home of legendary Pakistan batsman Zaheer Abbas. In his playing days, Abbas was known for his elegant batting and in fact had been a scourge of Indian bowlers in the seventies and early eighties. He had married an Indian Hindu woman from Kanpur by the name of Rita Luthra, who had adopted the Islamic name of Samina. Ashish Shukla and I were the first to turn up, and she welcomed us with touching warmth.

We thought we were early and that the rest of our media friends would show up eventually. However, no one else came. Our hosts were clearly upset by their invitation being roundly spurned. As our conversation progressed that night, Abbas and Samina eventually spilled their true feelings about the happenings on that tour. They cited the non-appearance of the other Indian journalists as another instance of Indians trying to slight and shun Pakistani people, and even felt that the stone-throwing incident at the ground was nothing but an Indian ploy to defame Pakistan.

According to them, there was no visible proof of any member of the crowd having been involved in that act. They said that no camera had captured a single instance of a stone being thrown at the Indian players. Where had the stones come from, then? In an outrageous claim, the couple said that the stones had possibly come from the pockets of the Indian players, who wanted to 'defame' Pakistan. Because there had been strict security checks on anyone entering the stadium, they felt that it was impossible for people to smuggle such missiles into the ground. I politely agreed with them and said that the majority at the ground were peaceful and welcoming, but also added that, as in India, there are always a few bad apples who create mischief and that does not mean they represent the general sentiment.

However, our hosts' grievance against the Indian team was not just shaped by what had taken place at the ground. They said that the Pakistani people and media had found the Indian team aloof, uncommunicative and even disdainful of the locals. Tendulkar, who was leading the side, had refused to speak to the press and had distanced himself from his Pakistani fans, refusing to even wave or smile at them. Pakistani cricket fans were angry and hurt, and Samina said that as an Indian she felt embarrassed by the behaviour of the Indian team, especially when people in Pakistan had nothing but love for them.

This conversation continued deep into the night and revealed to me that fractured relationships, if not handled maturely and with sensitivity, can lead to greater mutual suspicion. I tried to explain that the cricketers were young, possibly immature; that the stifling security and many strict instructions often resulted in paranoia, which may have forced them to keep to themselves and not interact with the public and even the press. I knew from my conversations with the Indian team that they were indeed apprehensive and suspicious of Pakistanis, and their remaining aloof may have been a defence mechanism to insulate themselves from the perceived threat they had been programmed to believe in.

The Abbas couple's hurt was genuine, though their version of the 'truth' may have been coloured by circumstances not of their own making. From my interaction with them that night, it became clear to me that this short tour, whatever the quality of the actual cricket played, had been a public relations disaster. The mistrust between the two nations was too large to be bridged by just a cricket tour.

The third and final match was played at Lahore. India was shot out for 216 after batting first, and Pakistan overhauled the target in only the 26th over courtesy a belligerent innings by Ijaz Ahmed, who scored 139 off just 84 balls, hitting ten fours and nine sixes. It was among the most brutal One-Day knocks I have ever seen. The series loss added one more to the list of Tendulkar's failures as captain.

On the eve of our departure, a couple of waiters at the hotel approached me. They had seen my passport, which was kept with the hotel manager, and knew my place of birth was Srinagar. That made them interested to interact with me as they were from the Pakistan side of divided Kashmir, which is called Azad Kashmir in Pakistan.

They seemed to be more comfortable speaking Urdu, and spoke in a dialect that was similar to the way the Dogras of Jammu region speak. Later, I found out that 'Azad Kashmir' had a mix of many communities: Punjabis, Gujjars, Jats and Mughals, among others. Fewer than two lakh people spoke Kashmiri, and that community was mostly concentrated in Neelum Valley in the northern part of 'Azad Kashmir', what we in India call the Pakistan occupied Kashmir.

The waiters wanted to know more about the Indian side of Kashmir, the issues we faced and if a political solution to the problem was possible. I welcomed them into my room and a lengthy conversation followed. The waiters were not happy about the lack of education, development and jobs in their home region that had forced them to seek work in Lahore. They said that many of their kind were spread across Pakistan, doing jobs where they had to work hard for limited rewards.

The waiters were speaking naively about equality and fraternity, and wanted both sides of Kashmir to come together to defeat the forces of exploitation. I was not only touched by their sentiment but also very surprised at their scathing criticism of the Pakistani government. I have met many friendly Muslims from 'Azad Kashmir' in England, many of them taxi drivers who spoke to me at length once they understood I too was from Kashmir, albeit from the Indian side. But no previous interaction could compare with that night in that cramped Lahore hotel room. It all ended in hugs and best wishes for one another, aware that we were unlikely to meet ever again.

In Pakistan, while Indian journalists who were Hindu were treated with tremendous love and warmth, I found there was an underlying tension, never overtly stated but simmering below the surface, whenever Indian Muslim journalists talked politics with their Pakistan counterparts. A senior journalist by the name of Javed Ansari—who was covering that tour for *India Today*—had throughout the tour flouted his Indian-ness with pride. I had to stop him once from getting into a lengthy, combative argument with a Pakistani journalist who was seeking a larger Muslim affinity with him. In strong words, Javed declared that he did not wish to be treated as anything other than an Indian, as he strongly believed the very idea of a nation based on religion was a flawed one.

I could sense a degree of discomfort and resentment among Pakistanis to see him so obviously proud of his Indian nationality. As happy Muslim citizens of a country where the majority of the population was Hindu, he was, in Pakistani eyes, a negation of the very idea of Pakistan—a country created on the basis of religious majoritarianism.

When Citizens Become Hosts: 2004, Lahore

In February 1999, the Indian Prime Minister Atal Bihari Vajpayee rode his peace bus to Lahore for a summit meeting with his Pakistani counterpart, Nawaz Sharif. On the bus were iconic Bollywood film personalities such as Dev Anand and Javed Akhtar, and Kapil Dev also found a seat. But this peace mission was followed within a few months by the Kargil skirmish, underlying the extremely fickle nature of the India–Pakistan relationship.

Five years later, the Vajpayee government was about to compete in the national elections hoping to be re-elected to another term. The Prime Minister, despite opposition from his deputy Advani, wished to reach out again to Pakistan. He was very keen that the Indian cricket team should visit the neighbours again for a full-fledged cricket tour. A series dubbed the 'Friendship Tour' was hastily arranged with government backing. There was a lot of pre-tour hype that this was not just about cricket, but also about 'peace and love'.

Pakistan had made unprecedented security arrangements and, in what many considered a risky step, it was decided not to have separate enclosures for the thousands of spectators coming from India. The tickets could be bought on a website, and one could choose one's own seats. This was in contrast to previous India–Pakistan matches, where the respective supporter groups were made to sit in separate enclosures for reasons of security and crowd control. It was only later that I realized that this non-segregation policy helped in building people-to-people relationships between the two nations.

I was not covering the tour as a journalist. Rather, I was keen to visit Lahore and watch cricket without the burden of writing reports and meeting deadlines. I bought tickets for myself, my wife, our eighteen-year-old daughter and a friend T.R. Ramakrishnan, who was a fellow former *The Indian Express* reporter. This time around my place of birth was a non-issue with the Pakistani embassy and getting the visa was a breeze.

So it was in April 2004 that the four of us boarded the bus to Lahore for a week-long trip that held exciting prospects away from cricket, which was just a ruse to visit Pakistan. We found that most of our fellow passengers were on their first visit to Pakistan, and like us, cricket was not the priority or the main reason for their visit. In a journey that lasted almost twelve hours, we became acquainted with several of our fellow passengers, most of whom had roots in Pakistan. Many of them had addresses of their ancestral houses in and around Lahore, from their parents or grandparents who had fled in the bloodbath of Partition. Some of them had only a vague idea of the place they would have to search for, based on the description they remembered their parents giving them.

My father had been posted as a customs official at Attari near the Pakistan border, and thus I was familiar with the region. When we passed the border, it did not seem like we had entered a different country, as everything appeared just the same: the land, the trees, the smells and the landscape, typical countryside in Punjab. Yet something had changed.

All of a sudden, a vociferous, passionate cry went up from the majority of the passengers: '*Jai kara Sherawali da*' (victory to the one who is mistress of the lion she sits on) that was followed by: '*Bol Sanchi darbar ki jai* (victory to the one who provides justice to all in her court)'. This is a very popular chant recited at temples in north India in praise of the goddess Durga, who is mostly portrayed as a female figure astride a lion. Other slogans such as *'Bharat Mata ki jai* (Victory to mother India)' too filled the bus, and to me they seemed like war cries. The descendants of refugees of the tragic Partition were announcing their return to their homeland, which they were now visiting as outsiders.

My xenophobic friend from Chandigarh, Jatinder, had also come to Lahore to try and find his ancestral home in Laxmi Nagar. He had memorized the location of the place from what his father had told him, and was surprised that the names of the streets and the locality remained unchanged despite most of them being Hindu in origin. At the house, he was moved when the present occupants welcomed him in and fed him a nice meal. As he described these touching moments to me later, I could sense that his ingrained animosity towards the 'other' had perhaps disappeared.

Our hotel was next to a bustling shopping complex, and after checking in, we stepped out to see the sights of the busy market. Our curious eyes and the bindi on my wife's forehead gave us away as Indian tourists visiting for the Test match. Reassuring smiles from strangers greeted us. Then something unexpected happened: two young women walked up to us and introduced themselves as medical students. They expressed warm words of welcome: 'Please feel at home. Pakistan is as much your country as it is ours, we are students and if you need anything do let us know. Enjoy your stay here and all the best.'

This spontaneous gesture of warmth from total strangers in a marketplace overwhelmed us. It set the tone of a visit that saw Pakistanis at every step going out of their way to make visiting Indians feel comfortable and welcome. It was as if the Pakistani public had taken upon themselves the responsibility of bridging the divide between them and their neighbours.

Though we had visas for only Lahore, we were keen to visit the archaeological site of the Indus Valley civilization near Harappa village, a four-hour drive from Lahore. Locals assured us that there would be no problem if we travelled out of Lahore, a risk we happily took without inviting any trouble. After moving around the ruins in Harappa, which was deserted, we walked towards the village. A young boy, barely in his teens, met us on the way and was thrilled to know we were from India. He was a fan of the Indian actor Shahrukh Khan and had written a letter to his idol. He had a request for us: could we post that letter for him once we were back in India? He asked us to wait while he fetched the letter from his home. Not having the heart to say no, we waited until he came back with the letter, written in Urdu.

The youngster also pointed out a particular row of houses and said that they had belonged to Indians, and no one lives in them anymore. We were told by other people later that it is true that in many villages in Pakistan, there are still untouched Hindu and Sikh houses, mostly in ruins now. Many of these houses are believed to be inhabited by the ghosts of those who fled or were killed during Partition, and no one dares to go anywhere near them.

We decided to watch a bit of cricket as well, and sitting among the crowds at the Gaddafi stadium, we saw that there were more Indian flags than Pakistani ones that fluttered in the Lahore breeze. However, the Indian flags were not just held by Indians—even Pakistanis were holding and waving them! There was a carnival-like atmosphere in the stadium. These were unbelievable scenes, very different from what I had witnessed in 1997, when the crowds, though not hostile, had been distinctly partisan and even aggressive in their support for their own team.

Though India eventually lost the match, the crowds were still cheering and waving Indian flags, as if India had won. We were sitting next to a young Pakistani IT professional from Lahore, and he was curious to know more about India and Indians. He expressed his happiness at finally having met Indians and understanding that, contrary to what he had believed, people from the other side of the border are just like his own people and not, as he laughingly put it, 'people with horns'.

It is hard to put on paper the exhilarating emotions we experienced that day. As we sat in the stands after the match had finished, we saw scores of people led by a local with an Indian flag in hand, dancing to the beat of a dholak. Even outside the ground, people kept walking up to us and greeting us with smiles. For those of us who were in Pakistan in 2004, the images of that nation are quite different from what we in the media portray today.

2006: A Country in Turmoil

One and a half years later, I was back in Pakistan to cover another Test and One-Day series. During the tour, I travelled the length and breadth of Pakistan: from Peshawar and Lahore to Rawalpindi and Faisalabad, seeing the country for all its diversity and divisions. Despite the uniformity of religion, the problem of terrorism was serious and one could sense that people were despondent and anxious. This was true not just for the urban middle classes with whom we mostly interacted, but also for the poor.

I remember a conversation I had with a taxi driver in Karachi who was worried about his child starting to lean towards jihadi thinking. He was worried about the influence the mullahs had on the children of the uneducated, and was envious of us Indians as he felt that we were able to educate our children with scientific, progressive methods. Pakistan, he felt, had taken the ruinous path of '*kattarpanthi*' (radicalization). This longing for modern education was a refrain I heard everywhere among the lower-middle classes, nearly all of whom felt that India had become prosperous because of better education.

There were also the urban, English-speaking Pakistanis who had started to feel threatened by the increasing spread of fundamentalism, especially among the lower classes, and many of them wanted to move out of the country.

The Pakistan cricket team indulged in public display of religiosity that many Pakistanis found troublesome. Inzamam-ul-Haq, the captain at the time, was a devout Muslim who prayed five times a day as prescribed in the Quran. Most of the team began following this practice. This spread of religion in the Pakistani team was said to have been initiated by Inzamam's predecessor, Saeed Anwar. Anwar had turned to Islam for solace after he lost his young daughter and even became a preacher during the latter part of his career.

Bob Woolmer, their South African coach, did not seem too worried about this overt display of religion. In fact, he said that it kept the team motivated and together. 'In any case, nothing is being forced on anyone,' he said, perhaps referring to the two non-Muslims in the team: Danish Kaneria, who was Hindu, and Yousuf Youhana, a Christian.

However, Youhana had by then converted to Islam and changed his name to Mohammed Yousuf, stunning the Christian community in Pakistan, which included his own mother. The conversion was often a topic of uncomfortable debate among his fans and even those Pakistanis who weren't followers of cricket. Youhana himself had refused to join the debate, saying that it was a personal matter. However, his mother had been quoted in the newspapers expressing her shock at her son's conversion. Had Youhana, one of the most outstanding Pakistani batsmen ever, converted to Islam in the belief that a non-Muslim could never become captain of the team, an ambition he must surely have nursed?

Whatever the reasons, his change of religion had come as a shock and a disappointment to his own minority Christian community, mostly Dalit converts and living on the margins of society. I remember taxi drivers outside my hotel in Lahore, most of them Christians, expressing their dismay and a sense of loss at what their idol had done. *'Dhokha'* (betrayal) was the word used for Youhana's act, and he was accused of having sold his soul to improve his prospects in the Pakistani team as well as in a society dominated by Islam.

It was only while travelling in Pakistan in 2006 that I became aware of the fault-lines in a nation dominated by one religion and the dangerous spread of fundamentalism that was causing deep unrest in society. These were not evident to me on my previous visits.

The most interesting part of my travel was the stay in Peshawar, the capital of Khyber Pakhtunkhwa, where the first thing that struck me was the diction and the accent of the Urdu language which people spoke there. While I sat in the taxi with my wife Mukta and daughter Aakshi who had joined me in Pakistan for part of the tour, I recognized the sing-song way and the emphasis on certain syllables as exactly the way a Kashmiri speaks in Urdu. The wizened faces, the general features of the population and their manner of speaking too were replicas of those in the place I was born in. I wrote a piece in the *Hindustan Times* on how I had been gripped by a sense of nostalgia and almost felt as if I had traced a lineage of the majority that now lived in Kashmir.

In the high-scoring, thrilling One-Day match played in the city, Tendulkar scored a scorching century to help India reach 328. But that was not enough as Pakistan won by three wickets in front of an aggressive and restless crowd that, for security reasons, had been forced to walk for more than a mile to the stadium.

Our next stop was Islamabad, the national capital, a contemporary and modern city when compared to the quaint Peshawar. Islamabad had been built on barren land in the sixties, and therefore—in stark contrast to the ancient city of Rawalpindi adjacent to it—has wide roads, marketplaces and houses functionally laid out in a geometrical pattern that reminded me of Chandigarh.

The match in Rawalpindi, where India cruised to a seven-wicket win, is not much more than a blur in my mind. What I remember instead is that the manager of the Islamabad hotel we were staying in had a dislike for Indians. He claimed that he had been ill-treated in India because he was a Pakistani. This struck a rare note of discord, the only time I sensed resentment towards Indians on my three visits to Pakistan.

India went on to win the rest of the One-Day matches, played at Lahore, Multan and Karachi, to sweep the five-match series 4–1.

One of the many lasting connections I made in Pakistan was with Osman Samiuddin, among the best Pakistani cricket writers. He understands his country's cricket, history and politics well. Samiuddin invited us to his brother's home in Karachi for dinner. One of the dishes he made was shab deg, a dish made with turnips and mutton. It is very popular in Kashmir among both Muslims and Hindus, and is one of my favourites.

This was a period when I was reading Sadaat Hasan Manto, who is among the most celebrated Urdu writers. Manto, who had migrated to Pakistan during the Partition, wrote searing short stories that exposed the underbelly of a society and also highlighted the human cost of Partition. Later, when I read one of his letters written to Jawaharlal Nehru, I had discovered that Manto was a Kashmiri, much to my parochial delight.

In the letter dated 27 August 1954, Manto referred to their common roots while criticizing Nehru for his anti-Kashmiri policies. More relevantly, the letter mentions shab deg twice. He writes:[7] 'Between us Pandit brothers, do this: call me back to India. First I will help myself to Shaljam Shabdeg at your place and then I will take over the responsibility for Kashmiri affairs.' And then, near the end of the letter: 'Every morning you will have to treat me to salty tea (Kashmiris call it noon chai) along with a kulcha. By some means Shaljam Shabdeg will have to be available every week.'

In Kashmiri, we call the dish gogji syun, and it is one more example of common cultural heritage between the two divided nations. In a food court in Islamabad, I had had another familiar dish, mounji gaad (fish cooked with a green vegetable called knol khol), which the stall had described as a 'special Kashmiri dish'.

Though I never met a Kashmiri-speaking person on my three visits to Pakistan, it was obvious in my interactions with the locals that the Kashmir issue remained a sore point that troubled them no end. The Pakistani educated middle class felt 'betrayed and cheated' at the Indian government's 'repression' of the Muslims in Kashmir, and expressed their anger in no uncertain terms. The common opinion among many elderly people was that because India is so big and powerful, it behaves like a bully. Their wish was that it should instead be like an 'elder brother' and take care of its weak, estranged 'younger brother'.

Kashmir, at Home without a Home

It was around that period I started visiting Srinagar more often, finding any pretext, sporting or otherwise, to get my office to send me there for reporting. I was trying to renew my connection with my homeland to make sense of the tragic loss of my roots. My holiday visits to Kashmir had stopped after 1989 and our family home was abandoned soon after.

In this attempt to reconnect with the land of my birth, I was neither bitter nor thirsting for revenge. The same could not be said for many of my relatives, some of whom had left the Valley in the dead of night, fearing for their lives. They had seen several among their community, even their own relatives, killed; when a call for

Azadi was made from the loudspeakers of the mosques, a wave of terror would sweep over the Hindus.

I heard many stories of Muslim neighbours urging Hindu residents to not leave, though the terror of the militants was such that they could not assure their safety either. In many cases, fleeing Hindus had left their house keys with their neighbours, who had assured them that they would watch over anything left behind. For every story of a hostile neighbourhood there were multiple accounts of friendship and support. It was the killings by the terrorists that forced the Hindu Kashmiris to flee their homes.

What I find interesting is that younger people seem to have more hatred against the Muslims. There is a strong belief among them that Kashmiri Pandits were butchered on the streets of Srinagar and the locals had joined in these attacks. It is not that older people have a lot of sympathy for Kashmiri Muslims or that they do not blame them for forcing them out, but their level of hatred is far lower. Given a chance they would still want to return to Kashmir and try to recreate the old world where they lived happily side-by-side with Muslims even if they were the 'other'.

My own early childhood impressions from the late fifties and early sixties are more of friendly individual interactions with an underlying tension between the two communities. During peaceful times, Pandits too saw India as an alien land where the more adventurous would aspire to go for better economic opportunities. Only at the time of crisis did India become a protector that could save us from annihilation.

In 1989, Mufti Mohammad Sayeed of Kashmir had been just sworn in as the country's first Muslim home minister when his daughter Rubaiya was kidnapped by militants. The Indian government released arrested terrorists in return for her release. Kashmir erupted and thousands poured onto the streets shouting Azadi slogans.

M. Ishaq Khan, a professor at Kashmir University, had written a book called *Kashmir's Transition to Islam*,[8] published in 2002. In the book, he concludes that the majority of Hindus who converted to Islam did so under the influence of Sufism, which had taken root in the eighth century and spread throughout Kashmir by the fourteenth century. Khan argues that the lure of equality for all, regardless of caste or religion, is what attracted the majority of lower-caste Hindus in Kashmir to Islam. He also acknowledges the coercive and even brutal role played by Sultan Sikandar Shah Miri, known as Butshikan (idol-breaker), in the late fourteenth to early fifteenth century in converting Hindus to Islam, but not to the extent that is widely believed and documented.

Khan's book presents a more benign face of Muslim influence in Kashmir, represented through the Sufi saints whose call for justice, equality and love attracted many Kashmiris. Though no one denies the role these saints played in spreading Islam in Kashmir (and also in the rest of India), many contest the claims that they played a greater role than the sword and brute force in mass Hindu conversions.

I am not a historian, but what had always fascinated me was the fact that Kashmiri Hindus in the Valley comprised only Brahmin Pandits. I remember being told at home and outside that we are the only community in India which does not believe in the caste system and that is the reason why there are no lower castes in our small community, an assertion that glossed over the fact that all the lower castes had converted to Islam.

I was to become aware much later in life that during Ashoka's time, Kashmir was almost entirely a Buddhist land. How Hinduism and later Islam literally purged the Valley of Buddhism was not the subject of popular folklore in our homes in Kashmir. Instead, we heard the tales of the reign of terror unleashed by Miri as he forcibly converted Hindus to Islam. We were often told that during those terrible days only a few Brahmin families had refused to convert, and all the surviving Hindus in Kashmir were their progeny. In the oral narration of our history, the lower castes did not exist.

Among the historical examples given by Khan is a revered Sufi saint of Kashmir called Nund Rishi, also known as Sheikh Nur-ud-din Wali. Nund Rishi was a follower of another revered Sufi saint of Kashmir by the name of Lal Ded, a Shaivite mystic saint whose *vakhs* (verses) were part of everyday life discourse at our homes when I was a child.

Poet Ranjit Hoskote, in the introduction to his translation of Lal Ded's poems in exquisite simple English prose, *I, Lalla*, writes:[9] 'Vitally, given that Kashmir is now almost completely Muslim region, it is instructive to recall that Lalla is regarded as a foundational figure by the Rishi order of Kashmiri Sufism, which was initiated by Nund Rishi or Sheikh Nur-ud-din Wali (1379–1442), seen by many as her spiritual son and heir.'

Lal Ded was also revered by Muslims, while Hindus claim Nund Rishi as one of their own. Nund Rishi's tomb is at the famous shrine of Charar-e-Sharif. In 1989, when Kashmiris realized that Azadi could be a reality, they came out on the streets in thousands and planned a march to the Charar-e-Sharif Dargah to thank their patron saint for granting 'deliverance' from Indian rule. The shrine was razed to the ground in 1995 during a gun battle between Indian security forces and terrorists who had taken shelter there. It was rebuilt later and I visited the shrine on my trip to Srinagar in 2004.

On that trip I also made an appointment with the professor and met him at his home. I still remember I was nervous as this was only my second visit to a Kashmiri Muslim family. The first had been with my brother and mother to a well-known Muslim business family of Srinagar in the seventies. In the typical Kashmiri tradition of hospitality, they had served us kebabs, which my mother was reluctant to eat, fearing they would be made of beef. After much persuasion and assurance that it was not beef, she did eat them, though I am not sure that she was convinced. It was not that she thought her hosts were lying, but her mind had been conditioned to believe that any meat that Muslims cooked had to be beef.

Khan's welcoming smile, and the Kashmiri kahwa and takhtech (tea and sweet bread) he served, put me at ease. In his narration of events, it became clear that the brutal phase of terrorism of the early nineties had been terrible for all Kashmiris. He said that the militants started killing anyone who did not cave in to their demands, which was not the Azadi people had hoped for. 'Most of them came from the lower strata, Wattals and Zamadars (scavengers) and they [the militants] would demand money, even women, from the locals,' said the professor, 'and that turned people against them.'

Khan also felt that the exodus of the Pandit community—which was the backbone of bureaucracy, banking and education in the state—led to a collapse of administration and created a lot of problems for the people. According to him, these were some of the factors that made terrorism and the gun culture unacceptable to the common Kashmiri. They were the sufferers now and hankered for respite, which was a reason for the relative peace prevailing at that time in the Valley. Khan told me that there had been a time in the nineties when hardly any shop would open, the streets would be deserted and no one would dare venture out after 4 p.m. Fear, whether of security forces or militants, had turned Srinagar into a ghost town.

A cousin of mine, Vijay Bakaya, had served as the principal secretary to the chief minister of Kashmir and later became the chief secretary of the state. He was the divisional commissioner at the time of the mass migration of Kashmiri Pandits from the Valley, and responsible for all the arrangements made in Jammu for the fleeing migrants.

Being a Kashmiri Pandit himself, Bakaya was the link between the Pandits and the controversial J&K governor Jagmohan at the time when Pandits were being targeted by militants. As I was seeking answers to what had actually transpired during that period and whether Jagmohan, as his detractors said, had facilitated Pandit migration instead of stopping them, I asked Bakaya for his version of the events during that harrowing period.

'I had hundreds of Pandits who trusted me coming over seeking guarantees for their security and threatening to otherwise move out of the Valley,' recalls Bakaya, saying that some of the Pandits described a sense of fear caused by chants from mosques asking Pandits to leave. There were anonymous threats and intimidatory posters that made them want to leave.

According to Bakaya, he did convey his apprehensions to Jagmohan and requested him not to allow the Pandits to move out of the Valley but instead 'create temporary camps for them outside Srinagar, guarded by the security forces till they felt safe to return home'. He says Jagmohan was not in a position to spare army men to safeguard those camps and there was a worry that the Pandits could have become sitting targets for the militants.

In 2009, I had another opportunity to visit Kashmir, to do my first-ever report on a political event. That year, Sajjad Lone announced that he would contest the Lok Sabha elections as an independent candidate.

Sajjad's father was the well-known separatist leader Abdul Ghani Lone, who was killed by a terrorist in 2002 during a public rally. Sajjad was articulate and spoke in fluent English, never mincing his words in advocating for Kashmir's independence from India on TV debates. He had inherited his political outfit, the People's Conference, from his father. Until then, the party had boycotted elections, much like all the other separatist leaders and parties since 1987. But in 2009 he had decided to abandon that policy.

From Kashmir's point of view, it was a stunning development for a mainstream separatist to swear by the Indian Constitution and participate in its democratic processes. Being a Kashmiri Pandit, I found this an exciting scenario and I wanted to go to Kashmir to meet Lone and write an eyewitness account of his first rally. My employers agreed and I went on a short visit that had a lot of hectic travel and emotional churning.

I travelled from Srinagar to Handwara town, home to the Lones and one of the hotbeds of militancy in the nineties. I had to take the Baramulla–Kupwara highway, a road not many would dare to take during the peak of militancy. I had two people accompanying me: a taxi driver called Ali Mohammed, who had driven many visiting journalists on their Kashmir assignments, and Waseem Andrabi, a photographer. Ali Mohammed was old enough to vividly remember those peaceful days when Pandits were an integral part of life in Kashmir, and he was of immense help in finding old connections and forgotten names for me. Andrabi, much younger and full of energy, represented a generation that had only lived under the shadow of guns, curfews, protests, terror killings and repression.

During the three-hour drive from Srinagar, we regularly passed military convoys and many makeshift camps housing security forces. Soon, we reached the house where Sajjad's secretary had asked me to come. It was the day when Sajjad was launching his campaign, one that many felt could be a turning point in Kashmir's political history. I introduced myself as a Kashmiri Pandit on a journey of rediscovery with no malice or hatred in my heart. Busy, distracted and on a tight schedule, Sajjad briefly said that he was happy to let me be part of his entourage for the day, which included few scheduled meetings in villages surrounding the town.

That day, I saw first-hand how difficult it was for Sajjad to make people understand his turnaround from being a hardcore supporter of Azadi to now agreeing to swear by the Indian Constitution. Over the course of my interactions with him on that day and some other occasions since, I found him to be a pragmatic person. He said that after the 9/11 terror attacks in the USA, the world had changed forever. 'Let us be realistic, we can now never get Azadi and have to look for options that allow us to live with dignity and respect,' he stated.

He carried his late father's walking stick everywhere to serve as a reminder to his people that he was carrying forward Ghani Lone's legacy. Sajjad would emphasize in his speeches that he had not sold out to India but would now air their grievances in the Parliament. On the way to one of the villages, we had lunch at a local's home, and later had tea at someone else's home; in each place he did not forget to remind his assistants to take care of me. In one of the public meetings, he even forced me to sit on the makeshift stage with him, and told people that a Kashmiri Pandit from Delhi was among them and it was their duty to rebuild the old, broken bridges.

Sajjad had married Asma, the daughter of Amanullah Khan, who is the founder of the Jammu and Kashmir Liberation Front, a militant outfit that advocated a Kashmir independent of both India and Pakistan. He was now walking a dangerous tightrope as his wife, a Pakistani citizen, was being denied a visa to come to India. The couple could not live together, and I could sense that a part of him wanted to live in a liberal world free of religious dogmatism. However, the more ambitious part of him wanted political power.

In 2018, Sajjad would become part of the ruling Peoples Democratic Party and BJP alliance. He was even projected as a BJP-supported candidate for the post of chief minister at one point. However, along with all mainstream Kashmiri political leaders, he was put under house arrest in August 2019 when the Modi government abrogated Article 370 that had given special powers to the state. Kashmir's status was changed from a state to a Union Territory.

Back in 2009, before my flight back to Delhi from Srinagar, I went on a tour with Ali Mohammed to those areas of Srinagar that I had known well. They were the places where our relatives had lived and I had often visited. I had heard that Rattan Rani, the doctor who had delivered me, had never left Srinagar. Despite her old age, she was still practising in the interior of the town near Habba Kadal, an area once largely inhibited by Pandits. I was keen to visit her, and thanks to Ali Mohammed's efforts we traced her house in Tankipora.

The Muslim caretaker of the house took me inside to a room where an old lady sat behind a desk. An almirah full of medicines stood behind her. According to the caretaker, her memory was fading and she was now no longer treating patients, something which she had not stopped doing even at the height of militancy. She had refused to move out of Srinagar, not heeding the requests of her children who were living outside the state to come live with them. Muslim neighbours and friends had taken care of the doctor who had tended to the medical needs of the larger Kashmiri community.

I tried my best to help her recall a memory from over five decades ago: the Magazine family, a patient of hers called Raj Dulari and the birth of a child, who was now standing in front of her. She asked me to write down the names, which I did on a piece of paper. She smiled, though I doubt she could recall a past that I was trying to connect with.

I came out of the house overwhelmed by many emotions. The frail old woman had withstood the onslaught of time and the traumatic upheavals of her homeland. She had had the courage not to flee and abandon her roots. I felt, somehow, we had betrayed her.

15
Cricket as a 'Unifier'?

In 2009, Sajjad Lone's joining the mainstream gave hope that the separatist political narrative in Kashmir could be moulded in favour of India. Four years later, it was cricket that provided a golden opportunity to soften the anti-India sentiment in the hearts and minds of the people in the Valley, when India selected a Kashmiri Muslim for the Indian cricket team.

It was 2013, and the cricketer was twenty-four-year-old Parvez Rasool. He was included in the fifteen-member senior Indian squad to tour Zimbabwe. For most of India it may have mattered little that Parvez would be the first Kashmiri Muslim to play for India, but in the context of Kashmir's alienation from the Indian mainstream, it was a significant development and its impact in the Valley needed to be assessed.

For decades, the Jammu and Kashmir team had been a participant in the Ranji Trophy championship without producing any positive results. They were the whipping boys in the league, and an odd good performance or two was an exception among the regular defeats. I remember watching a Ranji game during my childhood in Srinagar, and the memory of the backdrop of chinar trees and the Zabarwan hills is still embedded in my mind. Abdul Rouf, a fast-bowling all-rounder, was the Kashmiri cricketing hero of the sixties, and his occasional flashes of brilliance would cheer our spirits.

The severe Kashmir winter means no cricket can be played for half the year, which affected the sport's popularity in the region. Nepotism, administrative politics and the constant tussle with the Jammu region over selection matters had stymied the state's cricketing growth. Club cricket was popular but suffered from a lack of proper infrastructure and coaching facilities. All these factors were behind the pathetic performances of the senior state team.

It is only in 2011 that the Jammu and Kashmir cricket association tried to inject some professionalism into the team, by trying to emulate other cash-rich cricket associations in the country in hiring a big name as a professional coach. Farooq Abdullah, the state association president, appointed Bishan Singh Bedi as the team coach for three years. However, within a couple of years the relationship turned sour. Bedi, a stickler for discipline and loath to deviate from his methods of training and selection, decided to part ways with the association. Yet, Bedi had made a positive impact during his tenure, much like he had with the Punjab Ranji team in the early nineties. The J&K team had become competitive and had started winning matches.

Among the many talented players in the team was Parvez Rasool, an off-spinner whose bowling had been modelled in the classical traditions of loop and flight. Parvez acknowledged that Bedi's inspirational presence and guidance had helped him to believe in himself and raise the quality of his game. 'Bedi sir has a huge role in my success,' he told the media after he was selected to play India A in January 2013. 'Initially, I was a batsman who could bowl off-breaks, but it was at his (Bedi) insistence that I began to concentrate more on developing my bowling skills.'

Six months later, Parvez was selected for the senior Indian team, led by Virat Kohli, that was to play five One-Day matches against Zimbabwe. He was not the first Kashmiri player to be selected to play for India. That distinction goes to the player who would be Rasool's roommate on that Zimbabwe tour: Suresh Raina. A dynamic left-handed batsman who was chosen to play for India while still in his teens, Raina came from a family of Kashmiri Pandits—his father had migrated from Kashmir before 1986. However, as Raina was born and raised in Ghaziabad in Uttar Pradesh and played First-Class cricket for his state of birth, he couldn't be considered a true home-bred Kashmiri cricketer.

Yet, for Kashmiri Pandits, Raina's entry into the Indian team in 2005 remains a moment to cherish. And in the Kashmir Valley, where Muslims now formed almost 99 per cent of the population, Parvez's selection was a matter of great pride. An Azadi-chanting public now had one of their own wearing Indian colours on a cricket field.

Wounded Town Plays Straight

I felt it would be interesting to delve into the reactions of the Kashmiri people on Parvez's selection, especially in the backdrop of the mass anti-India sentiment prevalent in the state and their alienation from the rest of India. I travelled to Srinagar even as the Indian team was on their way to Zimbabwe in July 2013.

After talking to a few people on the streets of Srinagar about Parvez, I headed for his hometown of Bijbehara. It is a tehsil in Kashmir's Anantnag district, situated about forty kilometres from Srinagar on the National Highway that connects the Valley to

Jammu. Among the many things it is known for is the willow tree, whose wood is used to make cricket bats.

The hub of bat-manufacturing is Sangam village, which is just a few kilometres from Bijbehara. There one can see rows and rows of willow wood put out to dry under the sun by the side of the road. For cricket bats, Kashmir willow is considered second only to genuine English willow. Bat-manufacturing used to be a roaring industry in the state—worth Rs 60 crore in annual turnover according to one estimate—and provided jobs to hundreds of people, before unrest, militancy and protests brought it to its knees.

Bijbehara is politically significant, as it is the hometown of the late Mufti Mohammad Sayeed. It was also the place where, on 22 October 1993, security forces fired on a mob of thousands who were protesting on the streets, killing many of them. The protests were over the Hazratbal Mosque siege in Srinagar. The mosque had been stormed by the army after around forty militants had taken refuge there.

A report in *India Today*, written by journalist Harinder Baweja in November 1993, stated: 'It was a case of snatching defeat from the jaws of victory. In terms of religious status, Srinagar's Hazratbal Mosque, which houses what is believed to be a hair of the Prophet Mohammed, is to the Kashmiri Muslims what the Golden Temple represents to the Sikhs. But last week, as the army siege completed a fortnight of high-tension drama, its symbolism extended beyond religious boundaries. For one, a mere 40-odd second-rung militants had held the government to ransom for 15 days and succeeded in turning the Hazratbal siege into a contentious international issue.'

There were widespread protests across the Kashmir Valley, with many people fearing that the mosque may have been damaged. Bijbehara was no different, and thousands marched in the streets and on the National Highway, shouting slogans against the Indian government. The Border Security Force fired at the crowd, claiming they did so in self-defence. It resulted in the tragic death of at least thirty-one protestors (non-official figures had the count at fifty-one) while around 200 were injured. For a town with a population of only around 20,000, this toll left almost every household affected, even if the dead or the injured did not belong to their family.

Parvez was four at the time. I discovered while interacting with the people of Bijbehara—including Parvez's friends and his elder brother Asif—that the massacre, as they called it, had left a deep scar that Parvez's selection to the Indian team could not erase.

I was accompanied on my visit to Bijbehara by *HT* photographer Waseem Andrabi and taxi driver Ali Mohammed, the same duo who had taken me around Handwara in 2009 when I was following the election campaign of Sajjad Lone. There is a comfort in the familiarity of your 'own', a feeling of oneness, even if there may be a huge disagreement in the way you view the world around. While travelling with them in the car, eating together and even talking politics and the excesses of the state and the plight of Pandits in our mother tongue Kashmiri, there was this fellow feeling of togetherness which was reassuring.

Andrabi was a cricket buff and saw hope in Parvez's emergence as a national cricketer of repute, feeling that it could help heal the past wounds between Kashmir and India; while the much older Ali Mohammed would at every opportunity remind me that Andrabi's generation did not know what it was like in the 'good old days', when Pandits were an integral part of the Valley. For Ali Mohammed, I represented a past he had interacted with and had fond memories of. For Andrabi, I belonged to a community he had only heard of and probably had never seen until he met me. We reached Bijbehara before noon and drove straight to the green, picturesque cricket ground that is a part of the town's government school. That year, the local state cricket association had launched a twelve-team T20 cricket tournament modelled on the IPL. On that day, one of the matches of the new league was being played at Bijbehara. While Andrabi searched for Parvez's home, I started interacting with the players and spectators. There must have been at least a couple of hundred people watching.

When I talked with the locals, I did not hide my Kashmiri Pandit identity. Sometimes the discussions would even move to the topic of the fiercely nationalistic community of Pandits. Had they not been forced out of the state, what would be their place in a region seeking to break away from India? I quoted many of the people I spoke with that day in a report I wrote for *HT* that was published on 28 July 2013. I'll reproduce some of those conversations here.

I initially asked if Parvez's selection for India—referred to as an 'occupying force' by many of them—had changed their allegiance and softened their anger against the Indian government? I was not surprised at the surety and finality of their answer, which was a unanimous 'No'. Had I asked this question to the older generation, maybe the reaction would have been different, possibly more reconciliatory. But the majority of the crowd at the cricket ground that day was young and passionate.

Once the question of loyalties cropped up in the context of Parvez and India, the shadow of the 1993 shooting made its dark presence felt. There were many at the ground who had either been told of what transpired that day, or had their own memories of the horror. One of them was Bilal Ahmed, who remembers having counted forty-two bodies, among them his cousin's. As the ground was within the school premises, there were many teachers from the school watching the match. One of them was Imtiaz Ahmed, who reiterated the stance that even if one Parvez played for India, their allegiance did not change. It did not heal old wounds. 'In this very cricket ground the security forces would ask the residents to assemble after those brutal killings, humiliating and insulting us,' he said. 'Do you think any one of us has forgotten that incident?

Just because Parvez is going to play for India, you think we are going to support India?'

However, they all wanted Parvez to do well. The same good wishes did not extend to the Indian team. I posed what I thought was a challenging question. There is no hiding from the fact that in the Kashmir Valley there is strong support for the Pakistani cricket team, especially when they play against India. Would they want Parvez to do well even against Pakistan? There was a pause in their answers, which until then had been one-sided and decisive in tone. I could see a bit of confusion, though eventually the answer was again 'No'. 'If he comes in the way of a Pakistan victory, we would not support even him,' was the general sentiment.

I probed further, asking them if they didn't think it was unfair to take advantages and benefits from a country that one willingly represented and yet, in one's heart, opposed? When Parvez played for India, surely he would put India's interests first and not want the team he was playing for to lose? Bilal responded: 'We don't label as traitors the Kashmiris who work for the government of India. Even my passport states that I am an Indian national, and I can't say I am not if I want to travel abroad. This is called pragmatism.'

By then the people around me were all aware that they were talking to a Kashmiri Pandit, one who was provoking them with all sorts of questions. Yet I could sense no animosity towards me. When the interaction shifted to the targeting of Pandits, the locals were defensive, blaming the terrorists and Jagmohan who they believed helped them move out of the Valley. I asked them how Pakistan could be their role model when there was more sectarian strife, killings and unrest there than in most parts of the world. They justified their beliefs by saying that Pakistan had fallen into the wrong hands, because Islam does not discriminate and there is justice for all in it. 'Will there be justice for someone like me, who belongs to a different religion and does not subscribe to many of your practices?' I asked. There answers was: 'In our rule, we will make exceptions for the minorities.'

There was no point going deeper; their worldview was shaped by their religion and circumstances. Protests and oppression were their reality, the seeds of which were sown in a blood-soaked history of mistrust. I moved on. Andrabi had found Parvez's parents, and they were waiting for me at their home.

The house was a typical Kashmiri wooden structure, and the drawing room had the standard *kaleen* (carpet) on which we were seated. When Ghulam Rasool talked about his son, he measured his words carefully, well aware of the political ramifications of his son's selection for India. He had been a cricketer himself, having represented his district, Anantnag, in the domestic league. He had to face all sorts of hardships to support his son's cricketing ambitions. I realized that the father was very much aware of the danger of his son playing for India becoming a political tool in the hands of various vested interests. As a result, he was wary of the media glare, worried that it might adversely affect his son and even the family in Kashmir. That is why he did not want his son's selection to be seen through a political prism. 'Why mix the two? He is a cricketer and it is the dream of any sportsman to play for the national team, an honour to play with and against the best in his field. And to excel with the best will be his next goal,' he said.

Parvez Rasool's story is not just one of a Kashmir-bred youth making it to the Indian team, but also of a village boy making it in the Srinagar-centric cricket structure of the Valley. As one of his former teammates put it, 'Parvez has opened a door that had seemed shut for us. Now we feel it is possible to play for the national team.'

On our way back from Bijbehara, I had a long conversation with Andrabi. He had more objective observations to make, not letting his personal allegiance influence his judgement. He agreed that there was a widespread anti-India feeling, especially among the youth, but he believed that Parvez's playing for India could soften their sentiments, especially if he became a star player for the team. However, I was more inclined to believe in what one of the spectators I had spoken to at the cricket ground had said: 'This is not a trade-off where India selects a Kashmiri Muslim and we in turn support India and forget our aspirations and forgive the brutalities committed by their security forces against us.'

In an anti-climax, Parvez was not picked in the playing XI for the entire series. Among the fifteen-member squad, which had a few other newcomers, he was the only player who did not get to play a match, despite the opposition being a weak team that failed to win even one match in the five-match series.

Rajeev Shukla, a Congress politician who was an important BCCI functionary of the time, was even quoted in a newspaper report during the series as saying that Parvez's playing for India would send positive signals to Kashmir. Yet, Virat Kohli, who was still establishing his credentials as captain, chose not to select him. Parvez, who continues to perform well in domestic cricket, finally made his debut in a One-Day match against Bangladesh a year later. However, after getting another chance in a T20 match against England in 2017, he was never selected for India again.

I have never met Parvez as I had retired from active reporting by the time he made his debut. From what I have heard, he is a shy, reserved young man who continues to concentrate on his cricket while trying to avoid the pitfalls of being caught in the politics surrounding him. I still wonder what would have been the reaction of his young admirers in Bijbehara if he had become an Indian cricket star. What if he demolished Pakistan with his all-round skills? I am sure that despite their anger against the Indian government, they would have found it hard to keep up the contradiction of wishing Parvez well but not the Indian team.

On the evening of the day I had visited Bijbehara, I had a long chat in my hotel room in Srinagar with Shabir Hussain, who at the time was the executive editor of a local English daily called *Kashmir Observer*. I had met him in Delhi earlier and we were on friendly terms. Shabir agreed that aversion to India was very deep-rooted among the younger generation. 'It will be very sad if the Indian media or the politicians sell this as some kind of normalcy indicator,' he said about Parvez's selection. 'Let sport remain sport and let's not politicize it. A Kashmiri playing for India does not change the nature of the Kashmir issue.' About the contradictions faced by Parvez's well-wishers in his hometown, he said, 'Duleepsinhji and Ranjitsinhji played for England when India was ruled by them. Yet, we remember them as Indians.'

Shabir is a keen observer of the Kashmir problem having personally experienced the events of the traumatic nineties. He recalls the 'daily atrocities on the hapless Kashmiri population by the security forces. Terrorism was taking root, killings were common and the army was torturing and humiliating people on the roads.' He was in his teens then and anger started to brew in him. He decided to cross the border and get trained as a militant. Shabir's father was a police officer and during one of his postings, Shabir's family had stayed in Kupwara, an area close to the border from where many young men would cross over to the other side. With a friend called Adil, he ran away from home in Srinagar with the aim of getting arms training across the border.

Once they reached Lolab, they became part of a group of around forty young men ready to take the plunge and cross over. However, his plans were foiled because it started to snow, making it impossible to cross the border. They decided to bide their time and stay in the area. Soon, they had run out of money and were forced to leave the hotel they were staying in, spending the night freezing in a nearby forest, tired, exhausted and worried that they might be spotted by the security forces.

In the morning, they heard azan blaring from a mosque, and they rushed to take shelter there. The mosque turned out to be Sopore town's famous Jama Masjid. The maulana of the mosque was suspicious and wanted to know why they were there. They told him the truth. The maulana said he understood their feelings but picking up a gun was not the only way to fight the enemy: 'You can serve your people in various other ways. It is best you go back to your homes and study.' The duo's misadventure ended there and they returned home.

Shabir recounted this chapter from his past without any trace of emotion that would have indicated what value he attaches to that experience. He had grown up now, had written for various publications, including the magazine *Tehelka*, and when he narrated this story to me, he had become an editor of a local English daily. Pragmatic, forward-looking and fluent in both Urdu and English, Shabir is one of thousands of Kashmiri Muslims who feel completely alienated from the Indian state. He is aware that his teenage bravado was a foolhardy exercise and had he succeeded in crossing over, he would have been dead by now. Like the vast majority of those who, after training in Pakistan returned as 'militants', he would one day have been gunned down by Indian security forces in one of the encounters that were routine occurrences in the blood-tainted landscape of Kashmir in the '90s and still are.

I had come to Kashmir to spin a story of hope, a local lad playing for the Indian cricket team had brought feelings of solidarity with India into the minds and hearts of the Kashmiri people. Instead, all I could gather were threads that when woven together created a picture of a disgruntled, wounded populace living in anger and pain, with no room or space for forgiveness or reconciliation in their minds.

The Displaced

In my many visits to Kashmir, I never found my identity as a Kashmiri Pandit any hindrance in interacting with the Muslims. However, if the discourse turned to the topic of the Pandit 'exodus' of 1990, they would become defensive. Some would even express regret at not having done enough to ensure that the Pandits could continue to live in the Valley. This had also been experienced by Vivek Raina, a fellow Kashmiri Pandit who had settled in Delhi. 'There is not a single Kashmiri Muslim who is not guilt-ridden at what happened to our community during that traumatic period between 1988 and 1990,' he states.

Vivek grew up in surroundings where he had more Muslim friends than Hindu. He lived in the mixed Chattabal neighbourhood of Srinagar, and his family had deep-rooted ties with Muslim families. In 1989, he was an eighth-grade student at Kashmir's famous National School, situated in the same Karan Nagar locality where I had spent my early childhood. Oblivious to a world that was changing for the worse around him, the schoolchildren were busy rehearsing for grand celebrations to mark the school's fiftieth anniversary. Those celebrations were cancelled, and within a year his family would have to leave their house and belongings in the dead of the night and flee for their lives.

He recalls that he could sense a troubling disquiet around him. The 1987 assembly elections had led to bitterness when the Muslim United Front (MUF) claimed that the results had been manipulated by the Congress—who were in alliance with the National Front led by Farooq Abdullah. Large sections of people felt disgruntled and there were reports that some unsuccessful MUF candidates had crossed the border to get military training in Pakistan.

Then a bomb exploded in Lalchowk and a Pandit was killed in crossfire between militants and the security forces. These incidents left the community worried, but there was no panic. Vivek remembers a slogan being chanted by the protestors that was reassuring: '*Pandit–Muslim Bhai Bhai, Bhartiya Fauj Kahan Se Aye* (Pandits and Muslims are brothers, where did the Indian Army come from?).' However, soon the mosques started to blare taped slogans of Azadi, which were stridently anti India.

This was followed by a wave of killings targeting prominent people from both communities. High court judge Neelkanth Ganjoo, BJP leader Tika Lal Taploo and Kashmir Doordarshan director Lassa Kaul were among the Pandits killed, while in the Muslim community the vice chancellor of Kashmir University, Mushir-ul-Haq, was brutally murdered.

The Rainas in Chattabal were worried now, but still not thinking of leaving the Valley. Vivek's father, Omkar Nath, was in the health services, working at the government medical college, and his family felt reassured by the support of the Muslim neighbourhood, who would tell them not to panic.

During the same period the Indian government released a few dreaded Kashmiri militants in exchange for Home Minister Mufti Sayeed's daughter Rubaiya, who had been kidnapped by the terrorists. Frenzied crowds poured onto the street in celebration, and the sloganeering now became stridently anti India and even Islamic in nature. Soon, most mosques began to play tapes with Islamic slogans that reverberated across the city.

Then Jagmohan took over as the governor of the state for the second time. One day, from the balcony of his three-storeyed house, Vivek saw thousands of people marching on the Gaw Kadal, a bridge in Srinagar. Soon they were running in panic. To deal with the uncontrollable crowd, the security forces resorted to firing, resulting in at least twenty-eight deaths (once again figures vary, going up to even three hundred), and the incident became known as the 'Gaw Kadal massacre'. Shortly after, Vivek's uncle Ramji, who stayed on the ground floor of their house, was accosted by CRPF personnel when he was out to buy milk. When he told them that he was a Pandit, he was beaten up and told: '*Kashmir ka kutta bhi Pakistani hai* (even a dog in Kashmir is a Pakistani).'

The frequency of killings increased and Vivek remembers the worst of these: a nurse at Sher-i-Kashmir Hospital, who was raped and then horrifically dismembered. It had become a free-for-all: the Pandits were trapped between the increasingly brutal state repression and the aspirations of the Muslim masses who now believed that they would get Azadi soon. All the while, the militants carried out brutal killings and bomb attacks, anyone seen as pro India was on their hit list, be it a Hindu or a Muslim. No one could guarantee the safety of the Pandit community.

One night a rumour spread that a mob had planned to raid Pandit houses and indulge in loot and plunder. The Rainas, whose house had a steel front door, wired it with electricity so that anyone forcing their way in would get electrocuted. Vivek, all of fourteen, sat armed with a cricket bat to protect himself and his four-year-old sister Priyanka from any attack. After a few hours passed, he got bored with the lack of action and asked his parents why no one came, only to be roundly scolded.

Later, Vivek discovered that his Muslim neighbours too had made preparations for their safety and had spent that night in as much panic and fear as his own family. They had heard a rumour that the Indian Army would attack Muslim houses that night, rape their women and kill them.

The final straw for the Rainas was the letter threatening harsh reprisals if they didn't leave that was delivered to their house. They made stealthy arrangements with four other Pandit families of the area and fled their homes around 2 a.m. hiding in the back of a truck.

Vivek's story is similar to that of most Pandit families who were living in Kashmir in that period. In a rough estimate released by Kashmiri Sangrash Samiti based in Srinagar, around 400 Pandits were killed in the Valley from 1990 to 2011; of these, around 250 died in 1990 alone. The figure is much larger in the case of Muslims: anywhere between 50,000 and 100,000, depending upon the source. Official estimates were lower while human rights activists claimed higher numbers.

I first met Vivek in 2010, two decades after his traumatic experience. He was then thirty-four, had an MBA degree and seemed to be doing well in life. He was remarkably free of any bitterness or rancour about his Kashmir days, and had just started a Facebook group called *Sare Samiv, Aakh Raz Lamev* (All together, pull the rope in one direction)'. This is a famous vakh from the revered mystical poet Lal Ded, which exhorts inclusiveness.

The aim of the group was to mend the broken bridges of the past and get Pandits and Muslims on one platform to share their sorrows so that they could understand each other better and realize they have much in common despite what had happened in the nineties. Vivek views that period as an aberration and says, 'We need reconciliation and rehabilitation, not revenge—this is the sentiment of the majority.'

He recalls the story of how their Muslim neighbours saved his grandfather and his family during the Kabali raid (Pakistan Army attack) of 1947. They were living in Wadwan village, around ten kilometres from Srinagar, when news came that the Kabalis would reach the village soon. The neighbours made sure that Dina Nath Raina and his family moved to Srinagar, and when the Kabalis did raid the village, they pretended to be the owners of their house so that the Kabalis wouldn't loot it.

Vivek says that when they were in a camp in Jammu, many Kashmiri Muslims would come searching for their Pandit friends and neighbours and request them to return home. He recalls one such close friend who had spent almost a month to trace his father in Jammu. The man broke down when he finally found them.

Though the Rainas sold their Chattabal house in 1994, the pull of their roots led them to build a new house in Srinagar's Shivpura locality in 2013. They were not the only Pandit family to do so. He recalls that they found it difficult to get a priest to perform the *grih pravesh* (house warming) ceremony as three or four other Pandit families were also moving into their newly built houses that same day.

The vocal support from the right-wing Pandits for the abrogation of Article 370 by the Modi government in 2019 could have an impact on the wishes of many Pandits who want to return to Kashmir, or have already done so. According to one estimate, around 2000 to 3000 Pandit families are already living in the Valley. Vivek is not sure what that impact would be, but fears that the government's step may well purge the Muslims of the guilt they feel at the tragic manner in which the Pandit community had to flee the Valley. That could mean another wedge being driven between the communities, one worse than what the events of the nineties had done.

My own experience is a mix of nostalgia and pragmatism. Even if I'm drawn back to my roots and want to return, the lack of jobs more than any lack of security make the move impractical. Also, our Karan Nagar house was destroyed and flattened during the 2011 floods. In 2015, I made a visit to negotiate the sale of the property. Everyone, as usual, was very welcoming.

I visited Ahdoos, the famous hotel on Residency Road, where my father and his Pandit friends would have their evening tea and kebabs in the fifties almost every day before returning home from work. I imagined a return to a past of freezing winters, lovely sunny summers, a house buzzing with life where stern elders disciplined restless youngsters, the many siblings of a joint family dreaming of a future full of hope. I remembered the child who felt snug and secure in the lap of a Muslim elder, who gave in to each of the little boy's fancies and showered him with selfless affection.

Acknowledgements

My attempt in this book to combine cricket and the socio-political life that existed around it while I was growing up, and later as a journalist, would have been impossible to achieve without the help and kindness of people I know well and, more importantly, those I may not have known well or at all.

Many thanks to Amit Agarwal, who was with HarperCollins and whose persuasion pushed me into this project. My gratitude to New India Foundation and Ramachandra Guha for embracing it and giving me the confidence that I was on the right track.

Before I began writing, I spent a few months in Chandigarh's Panjab University library, researching on the past, poring over files of *The Indian Express* and *The Tribune* so that my memory would not play tricks on me. For facilitating its use and making me comfortable for the many hours I spent there daily, I thank the staff of the library and its head, Dr Raj Kumar, and also my colleague Saurabh Duggal.

Acknowledgements

I am grateful to Arun Lal, Bharat Reddy, Maninder Singh, Chetan Sharma, Ashok Malhotra, Chinmoy Roy, Ratnakar Shetty and Aditya Verma for sharing useful information. Many thanks to Anirudh Chaudhry for clarifying many doubts regarding the financial structure of the BCCI and to Amrit Mathur for helping me in understanding better the nature of its politics.

Heartfelt thanks to my earnest friend Clayton Murzello for responding to my many queries, and to poet and author Ranjit Hoskote for deepening my understanding of Kashmir's Sufi past.

My attempt to recreate the Tiger Pataudi era through his eyes was made easier by Sangeeta Bharali Das, who diligently transcribed his many taped conversations with me, running into over twenty-four hours.

Thanks to my brother Lalit, aunt Sheela Dhar, Deepa Bakaya, Shabir Hussain and Vivek Raina for clearing many doubts of a past I was trying to make sense of.

Thank you to Sharda Ugra, whose courageous writings have illuminated my own understanding of the rights and wrongs of Indian cricket.

In its final shape this book was made possible through the efforts of Siddharth Saxena and Rohit Mahajan, who scanned its pages to correct many errors with the care one usually reserves for one's own work. I have no words to thank them both.

Thanks also to Rivka Israel for vetting the first draft, to Tapojoy Mondal for dusting the book of the fluff and to Udayan Mitra for putting it together.

Also to Akshaya Mukul, Ajaz Ashraf, Kunal Pradhan, Jasvinder Sidhu, Rahul Bhattacharya, Sandeep Dwivedi and Shruti Debi for their support.

A big shout out to two longstanding friends who have been part of my journey and this book: Randhir Dhindsa and Jatinder Chadha. Randhir is today a senior member of Alcoholics Anonymous, and banker–cricketer Jatinder Chadha is happily spending his time and earnings on playing golf.

I am beholden to Tushita Centre and Kabirji for their life-changing meditation sessions that enabled me to deconstruct the past without the prism of my prejudice.

To my wife Mukta for her many valuable interventions. And to both Mukta and my daughter Aakshi for always being there.

Notes

1. A.L. Basham, *The Wonder That Was India*, Picador India, 1954, 1963, 1967, p. 345.
2. Sunil Gavaskar, *Runs 'n Ruins*, Rupa, 1984, pp. 139–141.
3. *Ibid.*
4. Sunil Gavaskar, *One Day Wonders*, Rupa, 1985, pp. 13–14.
5. Dilip Doshi, *Spin Punch*, Rupa, 1991, p. 131.
6. Sachin Tendulkar, *Playing It My Way*, Hachette India, 2014, p. 243.
7. Sa'adat Hasan Manto, *For Freedom's Sake: Selected Stories and Sketches*, Oxford University Press, 2001, pp. 192–193.
8. Mohammad Ishaq Khan, *Kashmir's Transition to Islam: The Role of Muslim Rishis (15th to 18th Centuries)*, Manohar Publishers, 2002.
9. Ranjit Hoskote (tr.), *I, Lalla: The Poems of Lal Ded*, Penguin Classics, 2011.

Index

Aakshi, 3, 84, 320
Abbas, Zaheer, 46, 310, 312
Abdullah, Farooq, 332, 342
Abdullah, Sheikh Mohammad, 9
Advani, L.K., 85
Afridi, Shahid, 294
Agenda, 154
agent–player relationship, 166
Ahmed, Bilal, 336
Ahmed, Ghulam, 26
Ahmed, Ijaz, 312
Ahmed, Imtiaz, 336
Ahuja, Harvinder, 114
Akhtar, Javed, 314
Akhtar, Shoaib, 206
Akram, Wasim, 125–126, 129, 207
Ali, Iftikhar, 24

Ali, Muhammad, 20
Ali, Syed Abid, 22
All India Radio, 74
Amarnath, Lala, 134
Amarnath, Mohinder, 18–19, 209
Amarnath, Surinder, 18
Amrapali Mahi Developers Private Limited, 289
Amrapali real estate dealings, 289–290
Amre, Praveen, 90–91
Amritsar, 14
Anand, Dev, 314
Andrabi, Waseem, 328, 335–336, 338
Anjali, 165
Ansari, Javed, 313
anti-corruption unit, 148

355

anti-Mandal agitation, 84–86
anti-Sikh riots, 1984, 81
Anwar, Saeed, 126, 141, 319
apartheid, 200
Aradhana (film), 11
Arlott, John, 17–18
Article 370 abrogation, 346
Ashraf, Ajaz, 149, 154
Assam Cricket Association, 269
Ata-ur-Rehman, 125
Atwal, A.S., 75
Azad, Desh Prem, 52
Azad, Kirti, 186, 282
Azad Kashmir, 312–313
Azharuddin, Mohammad, 93, 97, 105–106, 116, 127, 130, 133–135, 137–139, 143, 146–147, 149, 158, 161, 169–170, 180

Babri Masjid demolition, 36, 75, 79, 85, 91
Bailey, Trevor, 18
Bakaya, Vijay, 326–327
Bala, Rajan, 116–117
Banerjee, Mamata, 156
ban from cricket, 93, 95, 97, 105, 125, 143, 190, 197, 202, 225
Bangar, Sanjay, 178
Bannerjee, Sambaran, 180
Basham, A.L., 38
basketball league, Delhi University, 118
bat-manufacturing, 334
Baweja, Harinder, 334

BBC's *Test Match Special*, 17
Bedi, Bishan Singh, 13, 15, 19–20, 23, 27, 41, 56, 102, 106–111, 183, 332
    fair play and respect for umpire's decision, 109
    love-hate relationship with Sunil Gavaskar, 108
    as manager of Punjab team, 107
    problematic relationship with captain, 106
    vs Mehra, 106–107
    vs Punjab Cricket Association, 110
Bengal, 172, 237–238
bhadralok, 172
Bhan, Justice Ashok, 300
Bharatiya Janata Party (BJP), 239, 266–267, 277–278, 304, 329
Bhartia, Shobhana, 247, 249, 260
Bhattacharjee, Buddhadeb, 239
Bhindranwale, Jarnail Singh, 75, 79
Bhogle, Harsha, 184
Bhushan, Ratna, 297
'The Big Picture' column, 260
Bihar cricket politics, 282–284
Bihar politics, 89
Bijlani, Sangeeta, 132
Bindra, Inderjit Singh, 71, 77, 121, 146, 157, 170, 270
Blacks and Indians, tension between, 199–200

Blofeld, Henry, 18, 105
Board of Control for Cricket in
    India (BCCI), 31, 56, 71, 93,
    100, 113, 118, 137, 141–142,
    145–146, 162–163, 179, 190,
    192–193, 202, 210, 213, 246,
    261–264, 267, 270, 275–276,
    280, 284, 286, 291
    BCCI–ICC standoff in 2001,
        203
    conduct with agents, 291
    election and administrative
        procedures, 266–270
    games and politics, 264–271
Boje, Nicky, 170
Bond, Shane, 263
Borde, Chandu, 12, 26
Bradman, Donald, 148, 167
Brahmins, 8, 14
broadcasting rights, 112–113,
    166, 262
    sale of, 113–114
Brunch, 239
Bukhatir, Sheikh Abdul Rehman,
    98
Burlton Park, 15
Burn Hall School, 5

Cairns, Chris, 263
captaincy contentions, 56–57, 59,
    64, 66–68, 138, 168–169, 178–
    179, 218–220, 223, 227–236
Chadha, Dr Ravinder, 52, 54–55
Chadha, Jatinder, 70, 78, 316

Chandigarh, 39, 74
Chandigarh Press Club, 83
Chandigarh's Sector 16 stadium,
    52
Chandila, Ajith, 278
Chandra, Subhash, 262
Chandrachud, Y. Y., 162–163
Chandrasekhar, B.S., 12–13, 17
Channel Nine, 262
Chappell, Greg, 173, 182, 184–
    185, 187, 205–206, 208–209,
    213, 223–236, 239–240,
    242–243, 246–247, 249–250,
    253, 257–258, 261–262, 264
Chappell, Ian, 167, 209
Charar-e-Sharif Dargah, 325
Chaturvedi, Ravi, 17
Chauhan, Rajesh, 308
Chavan, Ankeet, 278
Chawla, Prabhu, 112, 120
Chawla, Sanjeev, 170
Chennai Super Kings (CSK), 279,
    286–288, 295, 297
Chidambaram, Nalini, 285
childhood years, 5–7
Chopra, Aakash, 208, 213
Choudhary, Amitabh, 227, 229,
    283
Clarke, Michael, 213, 221
Club cricket, 332
coach–player rift, 197–198
    Chappell–Ganguly rift, 68,
        227–236, 240, 251
communal riots, 9

Congress Party, 266–267
Contractor, Nari, 24–25
Cornerstone, 299
Cozier, Tony, 16
Cricinfo website, 215, 224, 243–244
Cricket Association of Bengal (CAB), 29, 112, 180
Cricket Association of Bihar, 282
Cricket Board *vs* players, 93–97, 192
cricket fans, 20, 127–128, 132, 172, 237, 239, 251, 309, 311
cricket matches, 6, 11. *see also* Indian Premier League (IPL)
   Adelaide Test, 2004, 187
   Australasia Cup, 101
   Australian tour India Test series, 213–216
   Bangalore Test of 1987, 64
   Barbados Test, 139
   Benefit Series matches, 98–99
   Bombay Test, 13
   Champions Trophy, 252
   commercial value, 94–95
   conspiracy theory, 16–17, 20–22
   Delhi Test, 13
   Deodhar Trophy, 92–93
   Duleep Trophy, 86, 90, 175
   fielding, 16
   Hamilton Test, 115–116
   Headingley Test at Leeds, 2002, 178
   Hero Cup, 112, 114
   home series against New Zealand, 160
   India–Australia series of 2001, 173–174
   India–Pakistan match, 99, 101, 103–105, 304–305, 308–312, 314, 318, 320–321
   1979–80 India–Pakistan series, 35
   India–Sri Lanka semi-final, 126–129
   India's tour of New Zealand, 1994, 114–115
   India's tour to Sri Lanka, 2001, 179
   India *vs* England 1979 Test series, 95
   India *vs* Pakistan match, Sharjah, 98
   inter-college cricket tournaments, 18–19
   Irani Trophy match, 41
   masala matches, 94–96, 100
   moment of India's win in Trinidad, 17
   as money-spinning exercise, 97–106
   One-Day matches, 67, 119, 166, 252, 304, 333
   Packer's World Series Cricket, 57
   1997 Pakistani tour of India, 305

Index

Ranji Trophy matches, 18,
  20, 40, 51, 69–70, 73, 86,
  90–91, 107, 148, 186, 214,
  237, 280–282, 293, 332
star status of top cricketers,
  93–94, 96–97
1966 test against West Indies,
  28
Test of England's tour of
  India, 202
in times of social unrest,
  86–91
1999 tour of Australia,
  160–161
tour of Australia, 2003,
  205–206
1967 tour of England, 29
1974 tour of England, 19, 23
1996 tour of England,
  131–139, 152
2002 tour of England, 190
1994 tour of New Zealand, 91
1979 tour of Pakistan, 58
2004 tour of Pakistan,
  210–213
1962 tour of West Indies, 25
1971 tour of West Indies,
  16–17, 20–22
1997 tour of West Indies,
  139–145, 156, 162, 168, 245
tour to Pakistan, 2004, 191
tour to Pakistan, 2006, 250
victory against New Zealand,
  1968, 24

West Indies–North Zone
  match, Jalandhar, 15
white players, 13
World Cup, 1983, 55, 59, 63,
  76, 93, 95
World Cup, 1992, 87, 89
World Cup, 1996, 87, 113,
  121–129, 166
World Cup, 1999, 144–145,
  157–158
World Cup, 2003, 193,
  195–216
World Cup, 2007, 213, 215,
  243, 250, 256–259
World Cup, 2011, 291
Cronje, Hansie, 106, 142,
  144–145, 205
Crowe, Martin, 148

Daali Bhatta. *see* Brahmins
'Daali Bhatta,' 8
Dalmiya, Jagmohan, 88–89, 121,
  131, 146, 177–179, 190–193,
  202, 210, 226, 262, 266,
  270–271, 274, 283–284, 298
Deccan Herald, 101
Ded, Lal, 325
Delhi Doordarshan, 112
Delhi's Press Club, 120
Denness, Mike, 202–203
Deonarine, Narsingh, 165
de Silva, Aravinda, 127, 148
Dev, Kapil, 41–42, 46, 52, 54–55,
  57–68, 90, 93–94, 99–100, 105,

115–116, 119–120, 123–124,
138, 146–148, 157, 159–160,
162–163, 169–170, 219, 314
controversial statements,
60–63
Dev, Sunil, 268–270
Dhaliwal, Kamal, 80, 83
Dhindsa, Randhir Singh, 39–40,
43
Dhindsa, Sukhdev Singh, 145
Dhoni, M.S., 163, 207, 263–264,
281–282, 289, 297–298
Dona, 189
Doordarshan, 20, 98
Doshi, Dilip, 98
Dowling, Graham, 13
Dravid, Rahul, 68, 131, 135,
160–161, 178, 182, 185, 187,
190, 193, 197–198, 211–221,
226, 229, 233, 235, 240–241,
244–247, 251–253, 256, 258,
301
Dravidian movement, 155
Duggal, Ajay, 119
Dumal, Arun, 286
Dungarpur, Raj Singh, 31–32, 90,
93, 241–243
Dunne, Steve, 128
Durani, Salim, 12, 26
Durgiana Temple, 14
Dutt, Biswanath, 266–267
Dutta, Nilay, 293

The Economic Times, 297

Emburey, John, 209
Emergency years, 43, 54
Engineer, Farokh, 34
ESPN Cricinfo, 125

Farrow, Father, 6
Fernandes, George, 267–268
Financial Express, 156
Friendship Tour, 314

Gaekwad, Anshuman, 183, 301
Gandhi, Indira, 30, 37, 43, 81, 304
assassination of, 79
Gandhi, Kasturba, 200
Gandhi, Mahatma, 9, 37–38,
198–200, 203
interpretation of Gita, 38
My Experiments with Truth, 38
Gandhi, Rajiv, 81, 91
Ganguly, Chandidas, 179, 254
Ganguly, Nirupama, 240
Ganguly, Snehasish, 180
Ganguly, Sourav, 54, 86, 88–89,
131, 135, 169, 172–173,
175–183, 188–189, 191–194,
196, 205–208, 210, 213–215,
217–222, 225, 228–236,
238–241, 250, 252–257, 264,
286, 302
Ganjoo, Neelkanth, 343
Gavasinder, 109
Gavaskar, Sunil, 13, 17–18, 33–35,
55, 57–68, 73, 100, 108–109,
116–117, 138, 163, 221–222, 231

Index

One-Day Wonders, 66
Runs 'n Ruins, 61
Gaw Kadal massacre, 343
Ghosh, Amarendra Nath, 29
Gibbs, Herschelle, 170
Gidwani, Hari, 283
Gilchrist, Adam, 214
Giles, Ashley, 251
Gill, K.P.S., 52
Gloster, John, 232
Godse, Nathuram, 37
Goel, Rajinder, 15, 52, 54, 78
Gooch, Graham, 106
Gopinath, C.D., 22
Govindraj, D., 22
Gowda, H.D. Deve, 304
Greig, Tony, 19
Gujarat Cricket Association, 286
Gujarmal, Raj Bahadur, 264–265
Gujral, Inder Kumar, 304
Gupta, M.K., 147, 149–150, 170
Gupta, Shekhar, 10, 12, 42–43, 46–47, 72, 120–123, 152

Hadlee, Richard, 116
Harmandir Sahib (Golden Temple), 14
Haryana Cricket Association, 53–54, 89
Haynes, Desmond, 209
Hazratbal Mosque, 334
Hazratbal Mosque siege, 334
Headley, George, 148
Hendricks, Ron, 72

Hindi journalism, 46
The Hindu, 133, 224
Hinduism, 5
Hindu–Muslim differences
  food, 8
  level of literacy, 7
  tensions, 8, 36, 79
Hindus, 2
Hindu–Sikh relationship, 14, 74, 79
Hindustan Times (HT), 2, 153, 164, 167, 174, 191, 227, 260, 268, 272, 288, 320, 336
Hoskote, Ranjit, 325
Hum Saath-Saath Hain, 103
Hussain, Shabir, 340–341

Ibrahim, Dawood, 100, 105, 277, 293
ICC Test Rankings, 207
India Cements, 271
Indian Cricket League (ICL), 262
Indian diaspora–player relationship, 117–118
The Indian Express, 46–47, 60, 69, 72, 74, 80, 86, 100, 111–112, 114, 120, 131, 133, 136, 152–153, 157–158, 162, 174, 238, 271, 287, 306
Indian Muslim journalists, 313
Indian Parliament attack, 2001, 210
Indian Premier League (IPL), 151, 265, 335

allegations, 275–277
bookies and betting, 279, 293–302
Lodha reforms, 300–302
Modi vs Srinivasan, 275, 277
player auction, 272–273, 275
Indian Telegraph Act 1885, 112
India Today, 67, 120, 150, 157, 334
India Today Group, 174
Indo–Pak war, 1965, 10
inter-college cricket tournaments
DAV College vs Hindu College, 18–19
St Stephen's College vs Hindu College, 18
International Cricket Council (ICC), 148, 202–203, 263
BCCI–ICC standoff in 2001, 203
Inzamam-ul-Haq, 263, 319
Iqbal, Asif, 35, 99, 335
Iqbal, Tamim, 257
Irani, Dr Ali, 136–138, 147
Irani Cup match, 73

Jadeja, Ajay, 147, 151, 159
Jadeja, Ravindra, 297
Jagdale, Sanjay, 280
Jaisimha, M.L., 22
Jaitley, Arun, 268–269, 277, 283
Jammu and Kashmir cricket association, 332
Jats, 39
Jat Sikhs, 39, 41

Jayantilal, Kenia, 22
Jayasuriya, 126
Jenkins, Chris Martin, 18
Jharkhand cricket association, 283
Johnston, Brian, 18, 23
John Wright's Indian Summers, 184
Jones, Dean, 148
Jones, Simon, 250
Joshi, Prabhash, 46–47
Joshi, Vineet, 92
journalism, 248
deskmen, 49
editing, 48
evening's entertainment, 50
page-making, 48
professional life, 50
proofreading, 48
reporter, 49, 79
sports, 43–46, 247–248

Kabali raid, 345
Kabalis (tribals), 9
Kadal, Habba, 330
Kaif, Mohammed, 194, 196, 223, 227, 233
Kalbag, Chaitanya, 259
Kaluwitharana, 126
Kamath, Ashok, 114
Kambli, Vinod, 74, 86–87, 92, 124, 128, 130
Kaneria, Danish, 319
Kanitkar, Hrishikesh, 143
Kargil conflict, 1999, 210

Kashmir, 1–2, 82, 84, 87, 238, 323–330
   Ahdoos, 346
   Anantnag, 338
   Bijbehara, 334, 336, 339–340
   cultural heritage of, 322
   Hindu–Sikh–Muslim unity, 9
   Karan Nagar, 3, 6, 342
   Muslim figures of, 2–3
   Pandit 'exodus' of 1990, 342–347
   politics, 327–329
   Srinagar, 12, 312, 322, 327–330, 333–334
Kashmiri Hindus, 7–8, 82, 323–324
Kashmiri Muslims, 2, 303–304, 323, 325–326, 331, 334, 339, 341–342, 346
Kashmiri Pandits, 3, 303, 305, 323, 326–329, 333, 336–337, 342, 346
Kashmir Observer, 340
Kashyap, Krishan, 47, 50
   practice of drinking rum, 50
Kaul, Lassa, 343
Khalistan, 75
Khalistani movement, 52, 79, 154
Khan, Amanullah, 329
Khan, Imran, 46, 57
Khan, M. Ishaq, 324–326
   Kashmir's Transition to Islam, 324
Khan, Shah Rukh, 277, 317

Khan, Zaheer, 181–182, 188, 226, 230, 232
Khanna, Rajesh, 11
Kohli, Virat, 163, 299, 301, 333, 339
Kolkata Knight Riders, 277
Koshie, Nihal, 287–288, 296
Krishnamurthy, Pochiah, 22
Krishnan, Ramanathan, 44
Krishnan, Ramesh, 44
Kumar, Dilip, 36, 114
Kumar, Krishan, 264
Kumble, Anil, 102, 178–179, 182, 185, 190, 198, 207, 247
Kundra, Raj, 288

Lahore–Delhi–Lahore bus service, 210, 315
Lal, Arun, 93, 186
Lal, Bansi, 54
Lal, Kishen, 9
Lal, Madan, 15, 18–19, 137–138, 142, 144, 183, 309
Lal, P., 37
Lall, Premjit, 44
Lamba, Raman, 186
Lara, Brian, 33, 118–119, 148
Latif, Rashid, 143
Lawry, Bill, 13
Laxman, V.V.S., 161, 182, 196, 223, 243
Le Corbusier, 39
Lee, Brett, 160, 212
Lele, Jaywant, 160

Lewis, Tony, 201
linotype machine, 48
live feeds of matches, 98, 133
Lloyd, Clive, 15, 33, 118, 128
India Today, 184
Lodha, R.M., 53, 286
Lodha reforms, 300–302
Lone, Ghani, 327–329
Lone, Sajjad, 2, 327–329, 331, 335
Luthra, Rita, 310

Made in India (Alisha Chinai), 306
Madugalle, Ranjan, 309
Magazine House, Srinagar, 4–5
Mahanta, Prafulla Kumar, 269–270
Mahendra, Ranbir Singh, 54, 57, 66, 89, 177, 226, 273–274
Malhotra, Ashok, 52, 54–55, 58, 76, 88, 186, 302
Malhotra, Jagmohan, 327, 337, 343
Malik, Salim, 105, 141
Mamus, 117
Mandal Commission, 74, 82
Mandela, Nelson, 200
Mandir–Masjid politics, 82
Mangeshkar, Lata, 103
Manjrekar, Sanjay, 90, 127, 135
Manjrekar, Vijay, 25–26
Mankad, Vinoo, 173
Manohar, Shashank, 213, 283
Manto, Sadaat Hasan, 321
Mantri, Madhav, 63, 99

manual scavengers and sweepers, 85
Mascarenhas, Mark, 166
match-fixing scandal, 35, 97–98, 100, 104–106, 138–151, 192, 291
   IPL fixing scandal, 271
   Justice Qayyum report, 105
   spot-fixing scandal, 278, 284
Mathur, Amrit, 212, 266–267
Mayawati, 154
McGill, Stuart, 187
McGrath, Glenn, 125, 160, 198
Media–captain–coach relationships, 137–138
Mehra, R.P., 106–107
Mehta, Annabel, 165
Meiyappan, Gurunath, 279–281, 288, 291, 295–296
Menon, Suresh, 112
Merchant, Vijay, 14, 16, 20, 22, 148
metal typesetting, 48
Miandad, Javed, 99, 143
Minna, Ashwani, 40–41
minorities, 7
Mishra, Bibhuti Bhusan, 286–287, 289, 292, 294–297, 300
Mitchley, Cyril, 128
Mitra, Chandan, 152, 154–156
Modi, Lalit, 264–265, 270, 273–274, 276–277, 285
Modi, Narendra, 86, 329

Modi Entertainment Network, 265
Mohammed, Ali, 328–330, 335
Mohan, R., 133
Mongia, Dinesh, 198
Mongia, Nayan, 116, 147
Moody, Tom, 209
More, Kiran, 93, 226, 235
Mudgal, Justice Mukul, 286–288, 291, 293
Mugabe, President, 195
Muhajirs, 307
Mukerjea, Jaidip, 44
Mukherjea, Indrani, 261
Mukherjea, Peter, 261
Mukherjee, Abhishek, 99
Mukta, 3, 320
Murali, Kadambari, 250, 294
Musharraf, General Pervez, 210
Mushir-ul-Haq, 343
Muslim United Front (MUF), 342
Muthiah, A.C., 268–269

Namboodiri, A.V.S., 86
Narcotics Control Bureau (NCB), 287
Nath, Omkar, 343
national sports editor, 114
Nawaz, Sarfaraz, 57
Nehra, Ashish, 181–182, 188, 199, 226, 230
Nehru, Jawaharlal, 9, 21, 39, 321
Newspaper Today, 173
NewspaperToday.com, 158

NewsX channel, 261
Not Quite Cricket, 143, 145, 148
Ntini, Makhaya, 201

'objective' reporting, 49
Oey Brahmina. *see* Brahmins
Ojha, Pragyan, 297
Operation Blue Star, 1984, 79–80
Orwell, George, 98
Outlook, 143, 146, 162

Packer, Kerry, 56, 262
Pakistani cricket writers, 321
Pakistani television, 19
Pandey, Arun, 289, 297
Pandit, Hina Zooni, 294
Pandit families, 2
Pandits, 3
Panipat, 10
Panjab University, 39
part-time reporters, 50
Pascoe, Len, 132
Pataudi, Tiger, 12, 16, 20–25, 27–36, 108, 172
Patel, Jasu, 12
Patel, Parthiv, 213
Pathan, Irfan, 241, 252, 255–257
Patiala District Cricket Association, 51
Patil, Sandip, 65, 73, 132, 136, 138, 183, 197
Paul, K.K., 144
Pawar, Sharad, 226, 239, 253, 262, 270–271, 274, 284–285

People's Conference, 327
The Pioneer, 140, 152–156, 304
Player, Gary, 109
Player–administrator
  confrontations, 100–101
Player–bookie nexus, 140–144,
  147, 149–151, 162, 170–171
players' rivalries, experiences of,
  55–68, 133–134
  Dravid–Tendulkar
    differences, 211–213
  Tendulkar–Azharuddin clash,
    162
Playing It My Way, 211
Pokhran nuclear test, 37
Ponting, Ricky, 214
Prabhakar, Manoj, 139, 143,
  146–147, 162–163, 186
Pradhan, Kunal, 153
Prasad, Mahavir, 282
Prasad, Venkatesh, 116, 135
Prasanna, Erapalli, 13, 20–21, 23,
  33, 41
privy purse abolition, 30
public relations officers (PRO),
  51
Punjab Cricket Association, 18,
  71, 77, 110, 265
Punjab First-Class (Ranji Trophy)
  team, 16
Punjabis, 14–15
Punjab Ranji Trophy team, 81
Purie, Aroon, 174
Pushkar, Sunanda, 276

Qayyum, Justice Malik
  Mohammad, 125
Qadir, Abdul, 57

Rabada, Kagiso, 201
radio commentary, 12, 16–17, 21,
  283
  live ball-by-ball commentary,
    73
  popularity of radio
    commentators, 13–14, 18
Rai, Himanshu, 296
Railways Sports Board, 267
Raina, Suresh, 252, 297, 333
Raina, Vivek, 342–346
Rajasthan Cricket Association,
  273
Rajasthan Royals, 295
Rajasthan Royals team, 287
Rajasthan Sports Act, 274
Ram, N., 224
Ramakrishnan, T.R., 315
Raman, Anand P., 158, 173–174
Raman, Sundar, 288
Ramesh, Sadagoppan, 207
Ram Temple agitation, 82
Ram Temple movement, 75
Rangaswami, Shanta, 301
Rani, Rattan, 330
Ranatunga, Arjuna, 148
Rao, L. Nageshwar, 293
Rao, P.V. Narasimha, 113, 304
Rao, Raghunath, 67
Rashtriya Rifles, 3–4

Rasool, Ghulam, 338
Rasool, Parvez, 2, 331–334, 336–339
Rathour, Vikram, 109
Raveendran, Justice R., 300
Ray, Satyajit, 172
Real Estate Regulatory Authority (RERA), 289
Reddy, Bharat, 95, 98–99
Redpath, Ian, 13
religiosity of Pakistanis, 319–320
Rendezvous Sports World (RSW), 275
reporting, 49, 79, 133
    cricket, 69–72, 133
'reservations' problem in cricket, 201–202
Rhiti Sports, 288–290, 298
Richards, Vivian, 18, 33, 36, 76–77, 118
Rishi order of Kashmiri Sufism, 325
Roberts, Andy, 33
Rouf, Abdul, 332
Roy, Chinmoy, 225, 254–255
Roy, Pankaj, 173
Roy, Pranab, 186
Roy, Raja Rammohan, 172
Rubaiya, 343
Rungta, Purushottam, 273

'*Sabse bada khiladi* (the greatest player)' campaign, 123
Sahay, Subodh Kant, 282, 285

Sajdeh, Bunty, 299
Sakshi, 289
Salve, Harish, 285
Salve, N.K.P., 61–62, 266
Samiuddin, Osman, 321
Sammy, Darren, 165
Samuel, John, 297
Sanatan Dharam School, Panipat, 10–11
Sanghvi, Vir, 247, 249, 261
Sara, 165
Saraswat Kashmiri Brahmins, 5
Sareen, Ritu, 287–288
satellite TV, 121
Saxena, Ramesh, 283
Saxena, Siddharth, 153
Sayeed, Mufti Mohammad, 323
Scindia, Jyotiraditya, 277
Scindia, Madhavrao, 266, 268, 270, 274
Scindia, Vasundhara Raje, 273–274, 276
Sehwag, Virender, 181, 187–188, 202–203, 205–208, 223, 241, 243, 256–257
selection committee and team selections, 107, 180, 196–198, 207
    controversial selections, 16–17, 20–22, 31
    team selections for Haryana, 52–53
    vice-captain selection, 33–34
Setalvad, Anant, 13

Shah, Amit, 286
Shah, Jay, 286
Shakeel, Chhota, 277
Shaljam Shabdeg, 321–322
Shami, Mohammad, 299
Shankar, Ajay, 306
Sharif, Nawaz, 314
Sharjah crowd, 102–103
Sharjah press box, 101
Sharma, A.N., 206
Sharma, Ajay, 147–151
Sharma, Bindu, 154
Sharma, Chetan, 52, 76
Sharma, Narendra, 69
Sharma, Ramu, 86
Sharma, Ravi Teja, 297
Sharma, Yashpal, 76
Shastri, Ravi, 66–67, 73, 93, 191, 309
Shastriji (teacher), 10
Sheahan, Paul, 13
Shekhar, Chandra, 89
Shukla, Ashish, 308, 310
Shukla, Rajeev, 339
Sibal, Kapil, 285
Sidhu, Jasvinder, 292
Sidhu, Navjot Singh, 76, 115, 133
Sikhs, 14, 84
Singh, Amar, 22
Singh, Balbir, 49
Singh, Daljit, 283
Singh, Gursharan, 76
Singh, Hanumant, 65
Singh, Harbhajan, 181, 187–188, 207, 226, 241

Singh, Khushwant, 80
Singh, Maharaja Hari, 303
Singh, Maninder, 186
Singh, R.P., 241, 297
Singh, Rahul, 80
Singh, V.P., 82–83, 86, 89–90, 267, 304
Singh, Vindu Dara, 279, 291, 295
Singh, Yograj, 41–42, 52
Singh, Yuvraj, 181, 194, 212, 222–223, 227, 233
'sleeping beauty,' 241
Smith, M.J.K., 13
Sobers, Gary, 29, 76
social justice, 83
social justice and equality, 9
Sohail, Aamer, 105, 126
Solkar, Eknath, 17
Somnath Temple, 85
South Africa, 201, 204
  Black-dominated areas, 200, 204
  Durban, 199
  Kwazulu-Natal area, 199
  Phoenix Ashram, 200
  Phoenix settlement, 198
South African Board, 202
South African cricket, 201–204
sponsors, 95, 190
Sport and Pastime, 12
Sports Illustrated, 294
sports journalism, 43–46, 247–248
Sportsweek, 12
Sreesanth, S., 278

Srikkanth, Kris, 94, 97
Sriman, R., 45
Srinagar violence and killing, 1–2
Srinath, Javagal, 135
Srinivasan, N., 270–271, 273, 275, 279–281, 283, 285, 296, 298
Star Sports channel, 112–113
Stewart, Alec, 148
Strydom, Pieter, 170
Super Eight, 256
Suraj, 11, 84
Surana, Mahendra Singh, 274
Swanton, Jim, 18

Tagore, Rabindranath, 172
Tagore, Sharmila, 30
Taploo, Tika Lal, 343
T20 cricket tournament, 262–264, 335
team selections, 107
television commentator, 105, 184, 309
Tendulkar, Ajit, 165
Tendulkar, Sachin, 33, 86–87, 92–93, 101, 115–116, 125, 127, 130, 134–135, 137, 139–140, 142, 144, 158–160, 163–170, 178, 182, 190, 196, 202–203, 205, 211–213, 243–244, 247, 254, 256–257, 261, 301, 311, 320
tennis tournament, father–son, 44–45
9/11 terror attacks, 329

terrorism, 75
Test Match Special, 18
Thackeray, Bal, 309
Thakur, Anurag, 286, 298
Thapar, Karan, 147
Thapar, Lalit Mohan, 152
Tharoor, Shashi, 275–276
The Times of India, 42, 44, 179, 191
Trescothick, Marcus, 251
Trevor, 208

Udal, Shaun, 251
Ugra, Sharda, 184
Umrigar, Polly, 12, 26
under-arm bowling, 208–209
United Progressive Alliance (UPA), 239
untouchable castes, 5

Vaidyanathan, Siddhartha (Sidvee), 243–245
Vajpayee, Atal Bihari, 154, 209, 267, 314
Vasu, Anand, 215, 217, 227
Vaughan, Michael, 250
Vengsarkar, Dilip, 40–41, 73, 93–94, 97, 99–100
Venkataraghavan, S. 33–34, 57
Venugopal, K.K., 285
Verma, Aditya, 280–282, 284–286
Vijay, Chander, 40
Virk, G.S., 277
Viswanath, Gundappa, 13, 35

Vivekananda, 172
V.K., Karthika, 143

Wadekar, Ajit, 13, 17, 20, 23, 87, 108, 115–117, 124, 132
Wadhwaney, K.R., 99–100
  Indian Cricket Controversies, 99
Wali, Sheikh Nur-ud-din (Nund Rishi), 325
Walters, Doug, 13
Warne, Shane, 141
Wassan, Atul, 186
Waugh, Mark, 124, 141
Waugh, Steve, 189
Whatmore, Dav, 209
Why I Killed Gandhi, 37
Williams, Henry, 170
Wilson, Paul, 224
Wisden cricket magazine, 174
The Wonder That Was India, 38
Woolmer, Bob, 144, 319
WorldTel, 166
worldview, 5, 9
Wright, John, 183–188, 193, 196, 208, 221, 223

Yadav, Lalu Prasad, 89, 154, 282–283
Yadav, Mulayam, 154
Yamunanagar, 10, 14
Youhana, Yousuf, 319
Younis, Waqar, 101
Yousuf, Mohammed, 319

Zee TV network, 262

About the Author

Pradeep Magazine is a cricket writer, columnist and former sports editor of *The Pioneer*, the *India Today* e-paper and *Hindustan Times*. He began his journalistic career in 1979 with the Chandigarh edition of *The Indian Express* and was its cricket editor in 1999–2000. Widely travelled, Magazine has covered international cricket in every Test-playing nation; he is the author of the book *Not Quite Cricket* that exposed the match-fixing scandal much before it surfaced in 2000.